Routledge Revivals

Studies in Profit, Business Saving and Investment in the United Kingdom 1920-1962

The results of the 1959 Glasgow University investigation into British industrial profit, business saving, and investment are the subject of this book, originally published in 1965. Part 1 presents original estimates of profits in British industries 1920-1938, which when linked with Government estimates of such profits since 1948, permit long runs studies of the fortunes of individual industries. In addition, the appropriation of profit between dividends and business saving is also estimated for manufacturing industry 1920-1938. Part 2 begins the analysis of the extensive financial data collected in the Glasgow enquiry and is concerned with the effects of the size of a firm on its financial performance. The financial performance of large companies quoted on the Stock Exchange with a sample of small unquoted private companies and unincorporated firms is compared.

T0382892

Economic Studies in Profit, Business Saving and Investment in the United Kingdom 1920-1962

Volume One

P.E. Hart

First published in 1965
by George Allen & Unwin Ltd

This edition first published in 2021 by Routledge
2 Park Square, Milton Park, Abingdon, Oxon, OX14 4RN
and by Routledge
605 Third Avenue, New York, NY 10158

Routledge is an imprint of the Taylor & Francis Group, an informa business

© 1965 George Allen & Unwin Ltd

Publisher's Note
The publisher has gone to great lengths to ensure the quality of this reprint but points out that some imperfections in the original copies may be apparent.

Disclaimer
The publisher has made every effort to trace copyright holders and welcomes correspondence from those they have been unable to contact.
A Library of Congress record exists at LCCN: 65002204

ISBN 13: 978-1-032-02374-8 (hbk)
ISBN 13: 978-1-003-18326-6 (ebk)
ISBN 13: 978-1-032-02412-7 (pbk)

DOI: 10.4324/9781003183266

STUDIES IN
PROFIT, BUSINESS SAVING
AND INVESTMENT
IN THE UNITED KINGDOM
1920–1962

VOLUME I

BY

P. E. HART

WITH TWO CHAPTERS BY
JAMES BATES

London
GEORGE ALLEN & UNWIN LTD
RUSKIN HOUSE   MUSEUM STREET

PRINTED IN GREAT BRITAIN
in 10 point Times Roman type
BY SIMSON SHAND LTD
LONDON, HERTFORD AND HARLOW

PREFACE

At the University of Glasgow, for various periods between 1959 and 1964, James Bates, G. R. Fisher, G. Garton, K. Maywald and I investigated some of the economic problems involving profits, savings and investment in British industries. A continuous stream of suggestions and questions flowed from our mentor, Dr A. K. Cairncross who was Professor of Applied Economics in the University of Glasgow, and we are deeply indebted to him for all his advice. It soon became apparent, however, that we could not begin to answer the most important questions with the limited data published for the United Kingdom. In particular, we needed longer time-series of key economic variables and further disaggregation of the figures, if possible to the level of the individual firm. The only way to obtain the required data was to compile the figures ourselves. Volume I of these studies summarizes the data collected, and though some preliminary analysis of the results is provided in Part II of the present Volume, a more detailed analysis is reserved for Volume II.

Collecting information is expensive and we are deeply grateful to the Carnegie Trust for the Universities of Scotland for its generous financial assistance to the Glasgow Profits Research Project. We were also very fortunate to receive the ready co-operation of many persons and institutions who provided basic data and we have pleasure in acknowledging such help from Mr J. R. Bellerby, Dr R. Hope, Sir Arthur Wheeler, the Department of Applied Economics (University of Cambridge), the London Stock Exchange, Moody's Economist Services Ltd, the National Institute of Social and Economic Research, Oxford University Institute of Statistics, and Steven Lindsay, Scott & Co. (Chartered Accountants).

The bulk of the processing of the data was carried out in the University of Bristol and I am very grateful to Mrs E. M. Smith for research assistance, to Miss C. Gibson and to Miss R. Cockram for their computational assistance, to Miss C. Bidmead and to Miss A. Kearn for typing the present volume, and to Mr S. J. Henderson for preparing the index. My colleagues in the University of Bristol, and my former colleagues in the University of Glasgow, have helped me considerably by their criticisms and encouragement. I should like to thank Professor D. J. Robertson of the University of Glasgow for acting as editor, and Dr K. Maywald, formerly Research Fellow in the University of Glasgow, for his efficient organization of the microfilming of company accounts and for his invaluable comments on Part I of the present volume.

University of Bristol   P. E. HART

CONTENTS

PREFACE   *page* 5

PART I: PROFITS AND THEIR APPROPRIATION
        IN INDUSTRIES IN THE
        UNITED KINGDOM 1920–38
1. Introduction and Summary of the Time-Series
   of Profit   11
2. Character of the Estimates   34
3. Extractive Industries   60
4. Manufacturing Industries   69
5. Construction and Public Utilities   93
6. Transport and Distribution   103
7. The Appropriation of Company Profits in
   Manufacturing Industry   116

PART II: THE EFFECTS OF THE SIZE OF FIRM
  8. Alternative Measures of the Size of Firms
     by JAMES BATES   133
  9. Growth and the Size of Firm   150
 10. The Profits of Small Manufacturing Firms
     by JAMES BATES   181

LIST OF WORKS CITED   213

LIST OF TABLES   219

LIST OF FIGURES   222

INDEX   223

Numbered references in the text are to the List of Works Cited

PART I

PROFITS AND THEIR APPROPRIATION
IN INDUSTRIES
IN THE UNITED KINGDOM 1920–38

CHAPTER 1

INTRODUCTION AND SUMMARY
OF THE TIME-SERIES OF PROFIT

1.1. PURPOSE OF THE PRESENT STUDY

PERHAPS the simplest way to introduce the present inquiry is to say that it attempts to investigate profit and its components in the same way that Chapman[36] studied employee compensation and Stone[90] studied consumers' expenditure in the United Kingdom 1920–38. Part I of Volume I presents estimates of the profit earned in each industry in the inter-war period and is thus a contribution to the comprehensive set of social accounts which is being prepared at the Department of Applied Economics in the University of Cambridge. Since official estimates of profit in each industry exist for the period since 1948,[9] the results in Part I permit any economist or economic historian interested in the long-term trends in the prosperity of an individual industry to undertake an analysis of the figures of its profit for over thirty-five years. Moreover, there is no reason why this period should not be extended. The Oxford Institute of Statistics[111] has estimated profit in each industry for 1909 and has also given useful information on the division of profit between industries in 1888 and 1892. These three years could serve as benchmarks. The *Economist*[100] has published samples of profit since 1909, and many of the company accounts in the archives of the London Stock Exchange are also available for this early period, so that a starting point for such a backward projection already exists.

In addition to the time-series of profit in each industry, Part I also contains estimates of the appropriation of gross profit of manufacturing companies. This appropriation cannot yet be extended to individual industries with manufacturing, because of the absence of sufficient information about depreciation in published accounts, but the proportion of gross trading profit and other income which was distributed as dividends in each manufacturing industry is estimated in Chapter 7 for the period 1920–38.

Part II of Volume I is concerned with the effects of the size of the

11   DOI: 10.4324/9781003183266-2

firm on its financial performance. The starting point for describing such effects is the measurement of the size of the firm. There has been considerable argument about the most appropriate measure of size, and Dr James A. Bates reviews this controversy in Chapter 8. He also presents a systematic comparison of the various measures of size for large samples of firms in the United Kingdom and in the United States.

The estimates in Part I rest in part on samples of company accounts drawn on the assumption that the observed changes in the profits of large companies were typical of the unobserved changes in the profits of small companies and unincorporated firms. This hypothesis is discussed and tested in Chapter 9 of Part II of the present volume. The data used in the tests relate to the United Kingdom and to the United States for various years before and after the Second World War. The requisite data are scarce and therefore each scrap of information is valuable and has to be used in an attempt to reveal the relationship between the size and the growth of a firm's profit.

In the United Kingdom information about the profits and finances of small firms is almost non-existent. One source of information is the survey of small business carried out by the Oxford Institute of Statistics in 1955–56. Dr Bates, who was then working on this survey at Oxford, has made a comparison of the financial performance of these small firms with that of large companies quoted on the Stock Exchange during the same period. The results are reported in Chapter 10. They are extremely interesting in their own right, but they also serve as an introduction to the analyses of the profitability, and of the savings and investment policies of large companies, which will be undertaken in Volume II of this study.

It will be seen that Volume I is primarily concerned with measurement and description. But just as the compilation of time-series of consumers' expenditure led Stone[90] into the econometrics of consumers' behaviour, so the time-series of profit and dividend distribution lead the present investigation to the econometric analysis of the financial behaviour of firms. Description and measurement of economic variables are necessary but insufficient parts of economics *proper*, to use the Marshallian term quoted by Stone,[90] page xxiv. It is essential to combine economic facts and economic theory, first for the purpose of testing theoretical relationships between economic variables, secondly for estimating the form and the parameters of such relationships, and thirdly for predicting the future behaviour of the dependent economic variables. Such a combination is also useful for a fourth purpose—the specification of new economic theories.

Though a close study of the facts is not essential in order to specify new hypotheses, it is fair to say that in practice a familiarity with the quantitative aspects of a particular economic problem is often a very useful aid to the formulation of a new hypothetical relationship, which may help economists to solve, or at lease simplify, the particular problem being considered. Familiarity with orders of magnitude enables the quantitative economist to select what are likely to be the most important variables in a theoretical relationship. Furthermore, the statistical techniques used in testing, estimation and prediction compel the quantitative economist to learn some mathematics, particularly calculus and linear algebra, and this knowledge of mathematics is an extremely valuable by-product, because it enables him to assess the internal validity of the models of the purely theoretical economists. In short, there are many reasons for combining economic theory, economic facts, statistical techniques and mathematical reasoning into one analysis, dubbed 'econometrics' for the sake of brevity, when studying the behaviour of profits, business savings and investment.

Volume II begins with Part III which will contain an analysis of the factor distribution of income. This is made possible by the data of Volume I, together with the time-series of employee compensation estimated by Chapman,[36] and by the official estimates of the distribution of the national income between profits and wages in individual industries since 1948. Part III will also contain a cross-section study of the variations of profit-margins between firms in the same industry. This will be followed in Part IV by an econometric analysis of the relationships between profits, dividends and business savings. Time-series regression analyses are made possible for the period 1920–62 by combining the data of Volume I and the official estimates of the appropriation of profit in manufacturing industry published in the Inland Revenue Reports[1] since 1948. These will be followed by cross-section regression analyses of the determinants of dividends, based on data compiled by the National Institute of Economic and Social Research and by the Board of Trade for the period 1949–62. Finally, in Part V, Mr G. Garton will analyse the investment behaviour of companies in the inter-war period, using the sets of company accounts sampled in connexion with the estimation of profits in Part I of Volume I.

The reliability of these econometric analyses partly depends on the accuracy of the basic data used. Economists are well aware of the limitations of most economic data: studies by Morgenstern[72] and by Roy,[83] to cite only two, illustrate the dangers involved in manipulating figures which are subject to error. In one example, Roy[83] measured the effects of error on the estimation of the proportion of the total expenditure of the middle-classes in 1938 which was devoted to 'motoring and travel', and to 'other services', and concluded that when errors were taken into account, the first proportion was between 7 per cent and 19 per cent, and the second proportion was between 4 per cent and 23 per cent. In Roy's own words, 'These are not helpful conclusions. Guesses made without all these extensive calculations would hardly give less reliable estimates. In fact, once these particular assumptions about the errors in the basic statistics are made, the past labours [of research and computation] are found to have borne no fruit at all. Common sense and rules of thumb would be less expensive in time and trouble.'

One may have every sympathy with these remarks. Nevertheless, it would be unwise to regard all economic data as unreliable as the estimate of middle-class expenditure on motoring in 1938. The accuracy of the estimate of profit in each industry in Volume I is assessed and it is fair to say that benchmarks of profit at least are very reliable, because they are based on Inland Revenue data. The interpolations between the benchmark years vary in accuracy between industries and Chapters 1 to 7 contain estimates of the percentage errors involved. Most of the data used for the econometric analyses in Volume II are based on company accounts and for the period since 1949 errors of measurement are negligible. For the period 1920–38 the measurement of dividends is free from error but the measurement of business saving is not. For both periods there are errors of sampling and the probable distribution of the population of changes in company profits is therefore discussed at length in Chapter 9. But sampling errors are common to measurements in many subjects other than economics and there is no reason to be despondent about the sampling errors in this study.

In short, the Inland Revenue totals from unpublished company accounts and samples of the published company accounts are among the most reliable of economic data. In spite of the shortcomings of published company accounts in 1920–38, they are undoubtedly more reliable than the family budgets in the Ministry of Labour's inquiry into consumers' expenditure 1937–38, on which the estimates criticized by Roy were based. Furthermore, there were no independent measurements of total consumers' expenditure on particular commodities to check the results estimated from the Ministry of Labour's samples, whereas the estimates of profit in each industry for 1927,

1932 and 1936–38 compiled by the Oxford Institute of Statistics from Inland Revenue[111] sources serve as an invaluable check on the index numbers of profit estimated from samples of company accounts.

Common sense is certainly less expensive in time and trouble than the laborious compilation of the data in this study. It may be true, for example, that common sense would tell us that profits in each industry fell in 1926, the year of the general strike, without the bother of estimating profits in 1925, 1926 and 1927. In fact, as a glance at Table 1.1 will show, profits did fall in 1926 and the common sense view is confirmed, up to a point. But common sense does not necessarily tell us anything about the extent of the fall or about the variation of the movement between individual industries. Indeed, on some occasions common sense may be very misleading. For example, in the coal-mining industry net profit increased between 1925 and 1926 as can be seen from Column (3) of Table 3.3. But there was a catastrophic fall between 1926 and 1927: total net profit in coal-mining was negative in 1927 and remained negative in 1928, so that profit in 1926 coal-mining was at a local maximum in spite of the fact that the coal-miners were in the van of the general strike which would lead us to expect a local minimum in 1926. This paradox cannot be attributed to inaccurate estimates: the figures, which were in fact compiled by the Mines Department of the Board of Trade from an *enumeration* of the accounts of all the coal mines, may be regarded as being subject to errors of less than 3 per cent.

The explanation is an interesting example of the danger of relying exclusively on common sense. The Board of Trade figures were published for each quarter and it is clear that all the profit in 1926 was made in the first four months of the year—for the remaining eight months there were no profits, but also no losses because the mines were not operating. In 1927 the mines made a positive profit in the first quarter but then incurred losses for the remainder of the year so that a negative profit emerged for the whole of the year's operations. From the point of view of the mine-owners, the months in 1926 when the mines were closed and made zero profit were more prosperous than the months in 1927 when the output of coal was high, as can be seen in Column (1) of Table 3.3, but when losses were being incurred.

This is one example where common sense and rules of thumb may be misleading, but it must be admitted that there are many other cases where they are entirely justified. The problem is that it is difficult to know when such cases arise until after an attempt at measurement has confirmed the common sense approach. After all, it frequently happens that the common sense opinions of one set of economists cannot be accepted by another set and in order to resolve the conflict of views an appeal to 'the facts' has to be made, even if the facts in question are subject to error. Indeed, important decisions on economic policy are made every day on the basis of figures which are subject to much greater error than the estimates of profit in this study. This does not imply that errors in the present estimates may be ignored. On the contrary, each chapter in Part I attempts to measure the errors of the estimates and goes to great lengths to reconcile them with all available alternative information. It must be emphasized that any person using these estimates should also study the sections on reliability and comparability and think whether the conclusions he has derived from the particular time-series could be seriously affected by the errors specified. Like other quantitative economists he may maintain a healthy scepticism towards the figures and methods he uses in reaching any economic decision, but surely he should not abstain from reaching a conclusion. Someone has to provide economic advice and if economists do not do this, on the grounds that the only available information is subject to error, then administrators, financial journalists, bankers and politicians will nevertheless use the available information, and though they may be less aware than the economists of the limitations of the data, they will still influence economic policies which affect us all. Indeed, it may be argued that because of his specialized training the quantitative economist is under a special obligation to contribute to the economic interpretation of the data available, even if they are very approximate. In addition, it may also be argued that he is obliged to improve and extend the statistics required to reach decisions on economic policy, even if the compilation of new sets of figures is a somewhat irksome chore. There is much truth in both arguments.

1.2. PREVIOUS STUDIES OF PROFITS, BUSINESS SAVING AND INVESTMENT IN UNITED KINGDOM, 1920–62

Previous studies in this field may be analysed by the basic source of information used. The primary source of any study of profits, dividends, business saving and investment is the set of accounts prepared by each firm to measure its own financial performance. Trading accounts, profit and loss accounts and balance sheets are generally inspected by the Inland Revenue authorities in the course of deciding a firm's tax liabilities and the aggregation of such results by the Inland Revenue has led to several studies of profits.

The classic study of Inland Revenue data was carried out by Stamp,[86] who had worked in the Inland Revenue and was familiar with all the intricacies of the figures. Though this work relates to the period before 1920, it is still a useful guide to all subsequent workers in this field of research. No less important is the evidence submitted by Coates to the Colwyn Committee on National Debt and Taxation.[19] Coates was the director of the Statistics and Intelligence Department of the Inland Revenue, and the data at the disposal of this department, from the 1920s to the present day, are so important and of such high quality that it is most unfortunate that the necessary permission and resources were not given to it to continue and extend his work. The tremendous scope for economic research provided by such material was seen by many economists, including Keynes,[59] who, in his review of the Colwyn Committee report, wrote in characteristic vein:

'These results have been made possible by the large number of detailed accounts now available in the hands of the Inland Revenue Department. "The number of accounts furnished voluntarily," Mr Coates tells us, "now approaches a quarter of a million." Of what incomparable value to economic study and to the science and practice of administration the continuous analysis of this material and publication of the results would be. With but a little development the Statistical Department of Somerset House could furnish us with a continuous census of production and a curve of profit for the whole of British industry. Hundreds of thousands of pounds spent on this embryo department would be well spent. As it is we have an occasional tit-bit of information thrown us in an appendix to a Report on another subject by a gentleman who is no longer an official. I suspect that the scandals of economy are far greater and far more permanently injurious to the public good than the scandals of extravagance ever were.'

But the required expenditure, which could have been much less than Keynes's hundreds of thousands of pounds, did not take place, partly no doubt because of the desire for economy but also because of the prevailing objections of many firms represented by the Federation of British Industries. To quote from the preface of Clark,[37] page vi:

'. . . The Federation of British Industries have successfully maintained their obscurantist attitude against the publication of true figures of industrial profits as shown by the income-tax assessments. Their object is to conceal the high profits which are being made in certain trades, but owing to the publication of the annual figures under the Import Duties Acts this will not be possible for much longer.

'It may be noted that in the United States the assessed profits of each industry, analysed in a number of ways, are published by the Federal Income-tax Authorities. . . . I would hold that figures relating to the profitability of different industries as a whole are a matter of public concern which no vested interests have any possible right to conceal. . . .'

Clearly, the Inland Revenue authorities could not be expected to publish or analyse figures of profits if the representatives of industry objected. The assessment and collection of taxes depends on the goodwill of the firms being taxed; if many of them decided not to provide the Inland Revenue with trading accounts, or to delay giving any information for as long as possible, it would be extremely difficult to collect the taxes. It was therefore imperative not to weaken the readiness of firms to co-operate with the Inland Revenue.

The Inland Revenue did not publish any industrial analysis of profits or of profitability after that made by Coates until the 92nd Inland Revenue Report,[1] Cmd 8052, which appeared in 1951 and related to the financial year ending in 1949. This contained an industrial analysis of profits for 1947 and for the three pre-war years 1936 to 1938. The 94th Inland Revenue Report,[1] Cmd 8436, published two years later, contained an analysis of the profitability on turnover of a large sample of companies subdivided into industries and relating to the three pre-war years 1936 to 1938 and to 1948. This summary of the breakdown of turnover is now published regularly, but it is worth noting that the current summaries contain less detail than the early analyses; they exclude the trading account items as proportions of turnover, though this information was published until the 96th Inland Revenue Report for 1953.

The final study based on Inland Revenue material which may be mentioned here is that undertaken by the Oxford Institute of Statistics.[111] Their enumeration of the gross true income, the wear and tear allowances, and the net true income for each industry for the years 1927, 1932 and 1936–38 is invaluable to Part I of the present study of profits.

In addition to the sets of accounts presented to the Inland Revenue authorities for tax purposes, there are the profit and loss accounts and balance sheets which are published and deposited with the Registrar of Companies. The two sets of accounts are not the same; unincorporated firms and private companies were not obliged to publish any accounts and public companies were not obliged to send copies of trading accounts to the Registrar of Companies. Since the various Companies Acts did not define all the items which could be deducted before arriving at a figure of profit, unlike the precise definitions under the Income Tax Acts, the calculations of profit in published company accounts varied from company to company and were therefore less reliable than the Inland Revenue totals.

Nevertheless, published company profits have been regarded as useful guides to true profits. The *Economist*[100] still publishes the total profits of samples of company accounts which it has received regularly since 1909. The figures for the period 1909–36 were summarized by Parkinson.[74] The results of the *Economist* samples of accounts have been used by Stamp[87] in his index of profit, and by Clark[37] and Radice[81] in connexion with their investigations into business saving. In his comparison between dividend distribution before and after the Second World War, Prais[79] also used the *Economist* samples for 1936–38. In addition, separate samples of company accounts have been drawn by Carruthers,[35] by Hope[56, 106] and by Coase, Edwards and Fowler[98] in connexion with their investigations into the profits and finances of industries during the interwar period. The present study is also partly based on separate samples of company accounts in the period 1920–38, but it has the advantage of being able to use the analysis of the Inland Revenue figures made by the Oxford Institute of Statistics.

One of the effects of the Companies Act 1948 was to improve the quality of the information in published company accounts so that for the period since 1949 it has been possible to make very reliable summaries of the finances of the company sector. The National Institute of Economic and Social Research[110] and the Board of Trade[6, 7, 8] have summarized the accounts of a large sample of companies quoted on the Stock Exchange. The study of the accounts of companies in the iron and steel industry in [98] has also been extended to the post-1949 period by Foldes and Wilson.[47] Tew and Henderson[92] have edited and contributed towards a series of studies of samples of company accounts for the period 1949–53. Barna[28] used samples drawn from the same data in his study of investment in British industry. Volume II of the present study will make much use of all this post-1949 data, but there is still much more research to be done before all the economic information is extracted from the available data.

Finally, the Censuses of Production[4] for 1924, 1930 and 1935 are useful sources of information on the total sales and value added in each industry in mining, manufacturing, construction and the public utilities. The primary source here is the individual Census return made by the establishment, but this in turn is based primarily on trading account information. This source may be supplemented by data for 1933 and 1934 obtained under the Import Duties Act for certain industries. The analysis of profits and profitability by Clark[37] was based on such material.

This review of previous studies in this branch of economics reveals three main sources which have determined the scope of previous research, namely, the Inland Revenue data, the published company accounts, and the Census of Production figures. But there has been no previous attempt to bring all these sources together to construct time-series of profit in each industry in the period 1920–38. This attempt is made in Part I of the present study. The details for each industry are given in Chapters 3 to 6, while Chapter 2 describes the techniques and definitions used in the estimation of profit. The remainder of the present chapter provides a summary of the time-series of profit, together with a commentary on their reliability and a comparison with other estimates.

1.3. SUMMARY OF THE TIME-SERIES OF GROSS PROFIT

A summary of the time-series of gross profits in the United Kingdom 1920–38, sub-divided into major industrial sectors, is given in Table 1.1. It will be noticed that this table omits the profits of the finance industry and of the professions. The insurance, banking and finance industry was excluded because of the inadequacy of the benchmarks described in [111], because of the misleading nature of banks' accounts, because of the large proportion of profit earned by unincorporated firms without any obligation to file company accounts with the Registrar of Companies, and because of the conjectural adjustment for net interest which has to be made in social accounting. An attempt was made to estimate profits in the finance and professions group 1920–38, using the time-series in the Inland Revenue category, 'Finance, Professions and other Profits', but the results were too unreliable to publish. However, further investigations of such profits are being made by Dr Feinstein at the Department of Applied

Economics, Cambridge, in connexion with his summary of the United Kingdom Social Accounts since 1900.

The category of miscellaneous services, Order XXIII in the 1958 Standard Industrial Classification, does not appear because some of its constituent items (catering, hotels, laundries, etc.) are in fact included in the distributive trades in Column (6) of Table 1.1 for reasons given in Chapter 6. Entertainment is omitted from this table though it is included in 'Other Profits' in the Inland Revenue finance

TABLE 1.1. *Summary of the Time-Series of Gross Profit by Industrial Sector, United Kingdom, 1920–38 (£m.)*

YEAR	EXTRACTIVE INDUSTRIES (1)	MANUFAC- TURING (2)	CONSTRUC- TION (3)	PUBLIC UTILITIES (4)	TRANSPORT (5)	DISTRIBU- TION (6)	TOTAL (7)
1920	233·6	326·9	11·0	14·4	47·6	291·7	925·2
1921	123·1	179·2	8·0	12·3	30·8	262·4	615·8
1922	132·8	242·3	6·0	17·3	79·8	295·7	773·9
1923	146·1	261·8	5·0	17·4	76·8	296·8	803·9
1924	124·6	269·9	6·0	16·6	77·5	320·2	814·8
1925	101·6	258·5	11·0	17·0	74·8	320·8	783·7
1926	96·0	229·1	15·0	15·9	59·6	313·7	729·3
1927	68·0	267·2	17·0	20·7	82·9	334·7	790·5
1928	73·9	277·2	6·0	22·0	84·6	345·4	809·1
1929	91·7	274·8	13·0	22·4	87·8	339·3	829·0
1930	99·9	252·1	9·0	25·6	82·0	312·8	781·4
1931	83·5	220·2	8·0	21·3	70·2	295·1	698·3
1932	82·7	185·2	9·0	23·2	54·5	265·1	619·7
1933	104·0	218·7	13·0	23·1	66·4	279·9	705·1
1934	121·8	255·3	15·0	23·4	74·9	300·7	791·1
1935	117·2	304·4	15·0	25·0	82·7	322·2	866·5
1936	135·5	351·1	19·0	26·6	88·9	342·2	963·3
1937	118·6	392·5	19·0	28·3	111·0	351·1	1020·5
1938	116·9	379·0	20·0	28·4	96·1	333·9	974·3
m	114·3	270·8	11·8	21·1	75·2	311·8	805·0

category and will have to be estimated jointly with profits in the finance and professions sector.

There is no item for the gross trading surpluses of the five public corporations operating before 1938, namely the Central Electricity Board, the British Broadcasting Corporation, the Electricity Board for Northern Ireland, the London Passenger Transport Board, and the Scottish Special Housing Association. But this deviation from the current National Income Blue Book[9] practice is less important than it appears; the profits of the first and third are included in electricity within public utilities in Table 1.1, the profits of the fourth public corporation are included in transport, and the profits of the second and fifth were too small to be given separate treatment.

Finally, the profits derived from undertakings abroad, which are given individual treatment in the Inland Revenue Reports[1] and by the Oxford Institute,[111] are also excluded from Table 1.1. Such profits should be studied together with the profits generated in the United Kingdom and remitted overseas as part of the estimation of the balance of payments of the United Kingdom, 1920–38. But to do this systematically would require a separate treatise.

The summary of gross profits in Table 1.1 relates to extractive industries, manufacturing, construction, public utilities, transport and distribution. The size of each sector of gross profit is shown by the *m* row, which measures the average gross profit earned in each sector over the whole period. The largest sector in terms of average gross profit in the period 1920–38 was distribution, so that in one sense Britain was still a nation of shopkeepers in the inter-war period. Manufacturing was second and the extractive industries of agriculture, fishing and mining formed a surprising third largest sector, in spite of the well-known depression of profits in these industries during the period. The explanation is given by Table 3.1 in Chapter 3, which shows that agricultural profit was by far the largest component of Column (1) in Table 1.1, and this type of profit obviously contained a very large labour component representing the services of the many farmers and their families, so that it differed from the kind of profit earned in manufacturing. The same reasoning applies to distribution, but to a lesser extent; non-corporate profits in the distributive trades were probably less than 60 per cent of total distributive profit whereas the corresponding figure for agriculture would be nearer 100 per cent. It should also be noted that assessed profits of such industries with a large non-corporate element are affected by changes in the taxation exemption limits. The adjustments to the benchmarks made necessary by such changes, which are being calculated by Dr Feinstein at Cambridge, are unlikely to be large for industry as a whole, but may well be important for individual industries such as retail distribution or construction.

The estimates in Table 1.1 are plotted on a semi-logarithmic scale in Figure 1.1. An inspection of Figure 1.1 reveals upward trends in the profits of public utilities and construction and a downward trend in the profit of the extractive industries. The other industrial sectors experienced fluctuations but no marked trend over the period. It can be seen that fluctuations in profit were highest in the construction industry and lowest in the distributive trades.

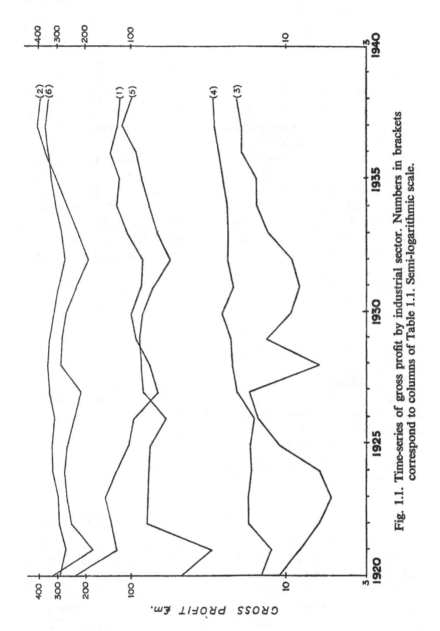

Fig. 1.1. Time-series of gross profit by industrial sector. Numbers in brackets correspond to columns of Table 1.1. Semi-logarithmic scale.

23

In spite of these differences between the sectors the general pattern of the movement of profit is very clear. The boom after the First World War was followed by a slump in 1921, accentuated by strikes in transport and in coal-mining. The recovery was slow and in fact profits never reached their 1920 level until 1935. The effects of the general strike in 1926 and the acute depression of trade 1929–33 are clearly seen in the time-series. The recovery after 1933 reached a peak in 1937 but in 1938 there were slight decreases in profits of each sector, except construction, where profit remained much the same between 1936 and 1938.

The total of gross profit in Column (7) of Table 1.1 cannot be used as a measure of total profit for the purpose of social accounting without further adjustment. First, it is necessary to include the profits of the finance and professions sector. Secondly, if it is desired to construct estimates of national income 1920–38 it is essential to have some measure of capital consumption. Thirdly, it is desirable to adjust the time-series of profit for stock appreciation. A fourth possible adjustment to the total in Table 1.1 concerns the effects of the excess profits duty. This extremely complicated tax is discussed in Section 2.4 where it is concluded that only the figure for 1920 need be adjusted, but that the necessary addition is probably about 4 per cent which is within the error band surrounding the estimate for 1920—the least accurate of all the figures—so there is little point in making it.

These adjustments to the figures in Table 1.1 may be necessary to estimate national income and may be important in a particular economic problem being investigated. However, for many purposes the unadjusted figures in Table 1.1 will be satisfactory and the increased comparability with current Blue Book[9] estimates of profit will not compensate for the increased error introduced by making the adjustments.

1.4. RELIABILITY AND COMPARABILITY OF THE ESTIMATES

The Central Statistical Office[10] regards its estimates of profit as being subject to an error of plus or minus 3 per cent: the relatively high accuracy is due to the fact that the basic data are obtained from the Inland Revenue's inspection of firms' accounts. However, estimates of profit cannot be completely accurate, even when all the resources of the Central Statistical Office and the Inland Revenue are employed to compile the figures. The errors involved in the present estimates may or may not be important, but it is essential to have some idea of their source and their probable magnitude.

It is convenient to distinguish four sources of error. First, there are the errors of measurement associated with mistakes in returns to the Census of Production,[4] with insufficient information in published company accounts, with errors in the results of Chapman,[36] Maywald[99] and others which have been used in compiling the present estimates of profit. Secondly, there are the estimation errors involved in interpolating, in differencing, in adjusting for income tax and the like. Thirdly, there are the coverage errors such as those associated with the assumption that the results for England and Wales were typical of the whole United Kingdom, or the assumption that the whole building industry was adequately represented by the part covered by the Census of Production. Fourthly, there are the errors involved in sampling from company accounts.

In Chapters 3 to 6 the reliability of the time-series of profit for each industry is allocated to the conventional categories of error, namely category A with 3 per cent error, category B with between 3 and 10 per cent error, and category C with more than 10 per cent error. The simplest method of estimating the error in the total figure of profit is to compute a weighted average of the errors for each industry. A glance at the weights of total profit in Table 1.1 shows that the most inaccurate estimates, those for construction have relatively little weight in total profit. But neither have the most accurate figures, such as those for the public utilities. The errors in the total clearly depend very heavily on those in manufacturing and distribution, and for both of these sectors samples of company accounts were used to interpolate between the benchmarks. The benchmarks themselves are probably accurate to within plus or minus 3 per cent, though the qualification has to be made that in 1932 losses were probably large and cannot be estimated within these limits of error. The estimates of year to year changes based on company accounts may well be accurate to within plus or minus 3 per cent of the absolute figure of profits for some years, but it is unlikely that this is true for all years. A measure of the variation in the changes in profits between different companies in the same industry in different years is given by the standard errors in Tables 4.2, 6.3 and 6.4. They also measure sampling errors, though it must be remembered that the other errors listed in the previous paragraph are probably more important. On the whole, it seems prudent to place the accuracy of the figures of total profits in category B in spite of the greater accuracy of the benchmarks for 1927, 1932 and 1936–38.

Another guide to the accuracy of the figures in Table 1.1 is provided by the estimates made in earlier works on the subject. Alternative estimates of profits for individual industries compiled by Carruthers,[35] by the *Economist*[100] and by Hope[106] are reviewed in the Chapters 3 to 6, particularly in Chapter 4 on manufacturing industries, and there is no need to make a further comparison between the totals derived from these sources and the total profits series in Table 1.1, because the differences between them are simply the sum of the differences between the estimates for individual industries. But there are additional sources of information on aggregate profits which are not broken down into industry groups which may be compared with the aggregate figures in the present study: first, the figures of gross income in the Inland Revenue Reports,[1] and secondly the index numbers of profits estimated by Stamp.[87]

The gross income assessed for income tax under Schedule D, defined in Section 2.2, was published annually by the Inland Revenue throughout the period. This figure was analysed by countries within the United Kingdom, so that it is possible to allow for the effects of the formation of the present-day Republic of Ireland by excluding it for the whole period and assuming that the fluctuations in the total gross income of Northern Ireland were proportionate to those in the total gross income of England and Scotland 1920–22. There was also an analysis by major industrial sector, such as 'mining, manufacturing and productive' or 'finance, professions and other profits', but the wear and tear allowances and the reduction and discharges were not analysed, so that it is impossible to make comparisons between the gross incomes of such groups and the gross true incomes of corresponding groups of industries in Table 1.1.

Before 1927 the income tax assessments on profit were in effect based on a three-year moving average of profit, so that any figure derived from Table 1.1 has to be averaged for the same period before making any direct comparison. Unscrambling the Inland Revenue time-series 1920–27 is possible, but a comparison between an unscrambled Inland Revenue time-series of profit and the present estimates would test not only the accuracy of the latter but also the accuracy of the unscrambling techniques. That is, the observed differences could be attributed to errors in *both* series. Consequently, it is better to average the estimates in Table 1.1 and then make the comparison. Further important differences must be borne in mind. First, agricultural profit included in Column (1) and co-operative surpluses included in Column (6) of Table 1.1 were not assessed under Schedule D during the inter-war period and are excluded from the Inland Revenue figures. Secondly, profits of local authorities and of the finance and professions group are excluded from Table 1.1 even though they were assessed for income tax under Schedule D.

The comparison between the Inland Revenue, the Oxford Institute of Statistics and the present estimates of total profits is carried out in two stages. First, a detailed comparison is made for the benchmark years of 1927, 1932 and 1936 which shows the relationship between the various definitions of profit. Secondly, the time-series of total gross true income compiled from Inland Revenue reports is compared with the corresponding time-series in Table 1.1.

In order to simplify the comparisons for the years 1937 and 1938, national defence contribution has been excluded from Tables 1.2 to 1.4, which explains the small discrepancies between profits for 1937 and 1938 in Table 1.1 and their counterparts in Tables 1.2 to 1.4.

Row (5) in Table 1.2 shows the total gross true income in the Inland Revenue categories of mining, manufacturing, productive, transport, distributive, finance, professions and other profits. The estimates of gross true income for the same trades 1936–38 were taken from the 92nd Inland Revenue Report and are given in Row (8) of Table 1.2. Part of the difference between Rows (5) and (8) is attributable to the different measures of income from overseas in Rows (4) and (7). If these figures are added back to the estimates of gross true domestic income in Rows (5) and (8), to get Rows (3) and (6) respectively, it can be seen that the differences between the two sets of estimates derived from Inland Revenue Reports are very small—about 3 per cent of Row (6) on the average over the three years 1936–38. These small differences may be attributed partly to the fact that the Inland Revenue analysis of profit by trade groups, on which Row (8) is based, relates to *trading profit* and excludes any non-trading income and other miscellaneous assessments under Schedule D which may be included in Row (3), as explained in the 92nd Inland Revenue Report,[1] page 55. In addition, the figures for 1936–38 in the 92nd Inland Revenue Report were based on a 20 per cent sample and the results were subsequently adjusted by interpolation techniques based on the 196·6 forms, described in Chapter 2. These provide further sources of discrepancy.

The total gross true income estimated by the Oxford Institute of Statistics is given in Row (9) which is slightly smaller than the Inland Revenue figures for 1936–38 in Row (6). This small discrepancy is mainly attributable to the fact that the Inland Revenue authorities interpolated between 1936 and 1938 on the basis of their collections of 196·6 forms whereas the Oxford Institute did not use these forms, as explained in [111].

The Oxford Institute estimates in Row (9) may also be compared with the Inland Revenue figures in Row (3) for each of the benchmark years 1927, 1932 and 1936–38. Once again the differences are very small, less than 3 per cent on the average. However, there is a 5 per cent discrepancy for 1927. When the different estimates of overseas income in Rows (4) and (10) are subtracted the average discrepancy between the two sets of estimates increases slightly. There is a 7 per cent difference between Rows (5) and (11) for 1927 but by a coincidence there is an almost exact agreement for 1932.

Total gross profit estimated in the present study is shown in Row (16). For purposes of comparison, agricultural profit and the surpluses of co-operative societies have been subtracted from, and the profits of the finance group have been added to, the total in Table 1.1. The difference between Row (16) and Row (11) is due partly to the fact that profits in the railway industry have been based on the published accounts for 1936–38 rather than on the Oxford benchmarks, as explained in Chapter 6, and partly to the fact that Row (16) excludes profits of local authorities.

Total gross profit in Row (16) may also be compared with the Inland Revenue figure in Row (5) for each year 1922–38. The differences between them for the benchmark years of 1927, 1932 and 1936–38 can be seen in Table 1.2 and comparisons in the previous two paragraphs between various estimates of profit explain the detailed differences between Rows (16) and (5). Column (3) in Table 1.3 gives the time-series of Row (5) for 1922–38 which may be compared with the corresponding time-series for Row (16) given in Column (4) of Table 1.3. To aid this comparison, time-series are plotted in Figure 1.2.

The second standard of comparison is set by the general profit index computed by Stamp.[87] This index is also summarized by Carruthers.[35] It is a combination of the Inland Revenue profits assessed for income tax under Schedule D and a chain index of the profits of companies reporting to the *Economist*, though Stamp corrected the *Economist* figures of profit to make them relate to calendar years. A comparison between Stamp's index and the corresponding index derived from Column (7) of Table 1.1 is made in Table 1.4 and in Figure 1.3. The coefficient of correlation between the two series is given by $r^2 = 0·81$ and the regression coefficients are given by $b_{12} = 0·65$, and $b_{21} = 1·23$ where the subscripts refer to the column numbers in Table 1.4. The *Economist*[100] index of total

TABLE 1.2. *Review of Estimates of Total Profit, United Kingdom, 1927, 1932, 1936–38 (£m.)*

	1927	1932	1936	1937	1938
Inland Revenue					
(1) Total Gross Income assessed under Schedule D (excluding item 'Interest on War Securities, etc.')	1290·3	973·5	1293·0	1385·2	1296·5
(2) *Less* item 'Other Reductions and Discharges'	221·0	187·4	217·4	225·0	195·4
(3) Row (1)—Row (2)	1069·3	786·1	1075·6	1160·2	1101·1
(4) *Less* item 'Dominion and Foreign Securities, etc.'	90·5	73·3	86·5	73·4	72·2
(5) Row (3)—Row (4)	978·8	712·8	989·1	1086·8	1028·9
(6) Total Trading Profits (92nd Report)	—	—	1117·0	1195·0	1118·4
(7) *Less* 'Undertakings abroad, Finance abroad'	—	—	91·8	114·8	94·7
(8) Row (6)—Row (7)	—	—	1025·2	1080·2	1023·7
Oxford Institute of Statistics					
(9) Total Gross True Income	1014·3	760·9	1095·7	1160·8	1065·2
(10) *Less* 'Adventures outside UK'	107·3	48·6	88·2	110·1	92·9
(11) Row (9)—Row (10)	907·0	712·3	1007·5	1050·7	972·3
Table 1.1					
(12) Column (7) *plus* finance profits	955·5	764·7	1114·3	1156·5	1099·3
(13) *Less* Agricultural profit (Table 3.1)	65·0	68·0	107·0	87·0	85·0
(14) Row (12)—Row (13)	890·5	696·7	1007·3	1069·5	1014·3
(15) *Less* Surplus of Co-operative Societies (Table 6.2)	25·8	28·4	32·9	35·1	36·9
(16) Row (14)—Row (15)	864·7	668·3	974·4	1034·4	977·4

TABLE 1.3. *Comparison of Inland Revenue Total Gross True Income with Estimates of Total Gross Profits, United Kingdom, 1920–38 (£m.)*

YEAR	TOTAL GROSS INCOME (1)	TOTAL REDUCTIONS AND DISCHARGES (2)	TOTAL GROSS TRUE INCOME (3)	TOTAL GROSS PROFIT (4)
1922	1159·1	257·7	901·4	771·6
1923	1158·6	221·4	937·2	841·5
1924	1191·1	227·2	963·9	869·9
1925	1198·1	209·7	988·4	820·5
1926	1153·8	216·2	937·6	775·9
1927	1199·8	221·0	978·8	767·8
1928	1222·1	224·3	997·8	776·3
1929	1206·5	246·2	960·3	809·5
1930	1085·6	229·3	856·3	806·5
1931	943·9	209·1	734·8	769·6
1932	900·2	187·4	712·8	668·3
1933	967·4	185·5	781·9	735·6
1934	1004·0	187·2	816·8	801·3
1935	1086·3	183·9	902·4	881·7
1936	1206·5	217·4	989·1	974·4
1937	1311·8	225·0	1086·6	1034·4
1938	1224·3	195·4	1028·9	977·4

TABLE 1.4. *Comparison of Estimates of Total Gross Profit with Index Numbers Compiled by Stamp and by the* Economist, *1936=100*

YEAR				TOTAL GROSS PROFIT INDEX (1)	STAMP'S GENERAL INDEX (2)	THE ECONOMIST INDEX (3)
1920	..	..	..	96	88·8	101·1
1921	..	..	..	64	57·0	57·9
1922	..	..	..	80	75·0	67·2
1923	..	..	..	83	78·1	75·1
1924	..	..	..	84	83·0	82·6
1925	..	..	..	81	86·4	88·9
1926	..	..	..	76	81·6	87·0
1927	..	..	..	82	88·4	92·0
1928	..	..	..	84	88·1	93·6
1929	..	..	..	86	88·6	97·2
1930	..	..	..	81	77·0	82·9
1931	..	..	..	72	64·2	60·9
1932	..	..	..	64	61·7	57·1
1933	..	..	..	73	68·6	64·3
1934	..	..	..	82	78·8	76·9
1935	..	..	..	90	87·4	86·4
1936	..	..	..	100	100	100

profit is given in Column (3) of Table 1.4, with 1936=100, and also plotted on Figure 1.3. The relevant coefficients are $r_{13}^2=0.64$, $b_{13}=0.45$ and $b_{31}=1.42$.

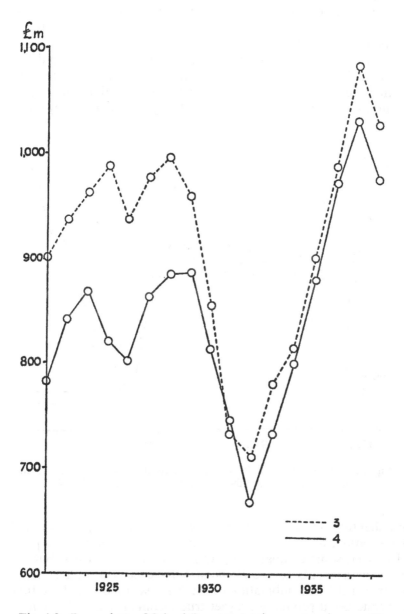

Fig. 1.2. Comparison of Inland Revenue total gross true income (3) ando ttal gross profit (4) in Table 1.3.

The relatively high coefficients of correlation reflect the closeness of the agreement between the comparable series. Figure 1.3 shows the importance of the differences between the index numbers for particular years. The reasons for preferring the estimates in Table 1.1 to the index compiled by the *Economist* are explained in detail in Chapter 4. Briefly, the latter index is based on profits after depreciation, after debenture interest and after taxation on corporate saving. It is therefore influenced by changes in tax rates, by changes

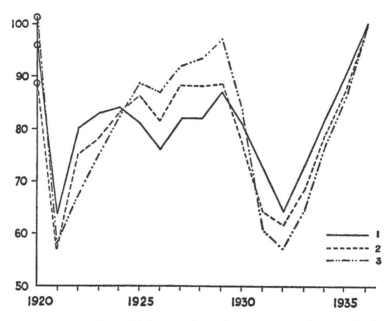

Fig. 1.3. Comparison of index numbers of total gross profit (1), with the Stamp index (2) and the *Economist* index (3) in Table 1.4.

in debenture interest and by the somewhat arbitrary provisions for depreciation, and none of these changes reflect changes in profits. Moreover, some companies operating primarily overseas, but sending their accounts to the *Economist*, have been included. Stamp's index, which is a combination of the *Economist* index and the Inland Revenue taxed profits series (net true income taxed under Schedule D), thereby suffers in part from the defects of the *Economist* index. In addition, its fluctuations before 1927 were reduced by the Inland Revenue practice of basing assessments on three-year moving averages of profits. For these reasons the time-series of Table 1.1 is also preferable to Stamp's index.

1.5. CONCLUSION

From the review of the reliability of the estimates summarized in Section 1.3, it may be concluded that the time-series of profit in Table 1.1 are preferable to previous estimates and are reliable enough for the economic analysis conducted in Volume II. A further assessment of the reliability of the data is given in Chapters 3 to 6 on individual industries, which are arranged in their order of appearance in the Standard Industrial Classification 1958, beginning with Chapter 3 on the extractive industries. Chapter 4 is on manufacturing industries, Chapter 5 on the construction and public utility trades, and Chapter 6 is on transport and the distributive trades. Chapter 7 presents estimates of the appropriation of profit in manufacturing for 1920–38, to complete the compilation of data in Part I of this study.

But before considering the estimates of profits for individual industries it is necessary to provide a detailed explanation of the sources, definitions, coverage, industrial classification, company accounts and sampling techniques used in Part I. All these details are explained in Chapter 2 which follows.

CHAPTER 2

CHARACTER OF THE ESTIMATES

2.1. INTRODUCTION

A BREAKDOWN of total company profits by industry has been published by the Central Statistical Office in the annual Blue Book on *National Income and Expenditure*[9] since 1947. The annual Inland Revenue Reports, on which the Central Statistical Office's estimates are based, contain a breakdown of profit for unincorporated firms in each industry. Indeed the Inland Revenue industrial analysis of corporate and non-corporate profit is available back to 1936. However, the figures for 1936–38 were based on a 20 per cent sample and have been superseded by the estimates prepared by the Oxford Institute of Statistics for 1927, 1932 and 1936–38.[111] In Part I of the present study, the profit of each industry is estimated for each year during the period 1920–38, using a variety of sources of information to interpolate between the Oxford Institute's benchmarks. A summary of the results has been given in section 1.3 and full details of the estimates are given in the Chapters 3 to 6. Each chapter includes an assessment of the reliability of the time-series and compares them with other estimates.

The Blue Book[9] estimates the appropriation of company profits between dividends and interest, taxation, and undistributed profit before providing for depreciation and stock appreciation, but this analysis is at the highest level of aggregation. There are no corresponding figures for companies within individual industries. Fortunately, the Inland Revenue Reports[1] provide appropriations of sales for large samples of company accounts, classified by industry, and these invaluable series provide appropriations of profit for each industry back to 1936. Chapter 7 of Volume I extends the appropriation of manufacturing profit back to 1920, using information collected from samples of company accounts and the Inland Revenue benchmarks for 1936–38.

The present chapter describes the character of the estimates in the following order. Section 2.2 explains the definitions of profit and section 2.3 describes the industrial classification used. After a critique of company accounts in section 2.4, section 2.5 explains the sampling

 DOI: 10.4324/9781003183266-3

scheme used to estimate the change in profits between the bench-mark years. The scheme is then tested in section 2.6 and the method of interpolation between the Oxford Institute benchmarks is explained in section 2.7.

TABLE 2.1. *Comparison of Inland Revenue Measurements of Profit, United Kingdom, 1951 (£m.)*

Gross Income		
(1) Individuals and partnerships	1,481	
(2) Companies, local authorities, etc.	3,206	
(3) **Total**		**4,687**
Adjustments		
(4) Overcharges, etc. ..	491	
(5) Losses	142	
(6) Interest and expenses	106	
(7) **Total**		**739**
Gross True Income		
(8) Individuals and partnerships	1,244	
(9) Companies and local authorities, etc. ..	2,704	
(10) **Total**		**3,948**
Depreciation Allowances		
(11) Individuals and partnerships	107	
(12) Companies, local authorities, etc.	772	
(13) **Total**		**879**
Net True Income		
(14) Individuals and partnerships	1,137	
(15) Companies, local authorities, etc.	1,932	
(16) **Total**		**3,069**
(17) Exemptions		33
(18) **Actual Income**		**3,036**
(19) Gross True Income of public corporations, etc.		262
(20) Assessments on interest, occasional profits, etc.		174
(21) **Gross Trading Profit**		**3,512**

2.2. DEFINITIONS AND SOURCES

It is generally agreed that the profit made by a firm is the difference between its sales and its costs, but formidable problems arise when attempting to define sales and costs. For example, what allowance, if any, should be made for stock appreciation or for the depreciation of capital? These two problems alone have generated much controversy: answers to them are to some extent arbitrary, and since such answers influence the measurement of profit, it follows that the latter figure also contains an arbitrary element. There are many other problems raised when trying to define profit, but enough has been said to show that any attempt to formulate an ideal definition of profit would require a separate treatise and would be out of place in the present work.

Fortunately, the precise definition of any economic variable is often less important than the fact that it is consistent with a definition used elsewhere. This is the case here. A primary aim of the present research is to construct time-series of profits 1920–38 which are comparable with the existing estimates of profits 1948–62 made by the Central Statistical Office, and it is therefore necessary to follow the official definitions and methods as far as is possible. These have been explained in detail in [10] and all that is needed here is a brief description, together with an indication of the extent to which the methods can be followed for the period 1920–38.

The current Blue Book on National Income[9] estimates three types of profit: incomes of companies, of self-employed persons and of public corporations. An analysis of profit by orders in the Standard Industrial Classification is given for non-manufacturing industries, though the distinction between the three different types of profit is generally not made within each order. For manufacturing industries, the Blue Book contains an industrial analysis of corporate profit, but there is no such analysis for other types of profit.

The Central Statistical Office compiles figures of profit from information supplied to it by the Inland Revenue authorities, who in turn obtain their information from the accounts submitted to them by companies and unincorporated enterprises in connexion with the assessment of their taxation liabilities. Some of this basic information is published by the Inland Revenue in its annual reports, though it must be remembered that the published Inland Revenue figures are before the various adjustments listed in [10], especially pages 152–63, and from the point of view of social accounting they are somewhat crude. Nevertheless, these raw figures are relevant to the extension of the existing profit series back to 1920, simply because the estimates made from the Inland Revenue data for 1927, 1932 and 1936–38 constitute the benchmarks from which all other estimates of profit in the period 1920–38 must be measured. Accordingly, it is necessary to describe the Inland Revenue definition of profit in more detail.

There are several Inland Revenue measurements of profit, but the figure with most economic interest is gross true trading income assessed under Schedule D. The relationships between the various Inland Revenue measurements of profit are set out very clearly in each annual report. For example, the 97th Inland Revenue Report[1] (Cmd 9351) gives sufficient information in its Tables 28, 29 and 31, pages 50–4, to illustrate these relationships in Table 2.1. Briefly, 'gross income assessed' is the profit which the Inland Revenue *thinks* a particular firm earns, and the total for all firms in 1951 is shown in Row (3) of Table 2.1. After an examination of the firm's accounts and some discussion with its accountants, the Inland Revenue authorities generally have to reduce their estimate of the firm's profit to allow for any losses carried forward from previous years, for certain expenses such as interest not treated elsewhere, but above all to allow for the fact that the original assessment was deliberately on the high side. The latter deduction from gross income assessed is called 'overcharges' in Row (4). The total of these deductions for all firms is given in Row (7) of Table 2.1. The figure remaining after these adjustments is 'gross true income', and the total is shown in Row (10). 'Net true income' is 'gross true income' minus the statutory allowance for depreciation, called 'wear and tear allowance' in the period 1920–38, shown by Row (10) minus Row (13) equals Row (16). This deduction need not be the same as the figure for depreciation which is published in the firm's accounts. The total profit on which income tax is levied is called 'actual income', shown in Row (18), and is the sum of the net true incomes of all enterprises assessed minus exemptions such as charities or incomes below the exemption limit.

The final figure considered here is 'gross trading profit' which is the gross true income of a firm minus that part of its non-trading income which is not taxed at source. The remaining part of its non-trading income, which by definition is taxed at source, is not included in gross true income and is therefore automatically excluded from gross trading profit. The Inland Revenue reports analyse gross trading profit by industry, for individuals and firms, for companies and local authorities, for 1936–38 and for each year since 1947. But this analysis is not carried over into the Blue Books on national income. Gross trading profit is also the figure which is being used by the Oxford Institute of Statistics in their estimation of profits in British industries for 1927, 1932 and 1936–38. These figures supply

STUDIES IN PROFIT, BUSINESS SAVING AND INVESTMENT

the benchmarks for the present study. The relationship between total gross trading profit and total gross true income is also shown in Table 2.1. Gross true income in Row (10) minus gross true income of public corporations and other assessments shown in Row (19), minus the assessments on interest and occasional profits in Row (20), equals gross trading profit in Row (21). Full details of Row (19) and Row (20) are given in Cmd 9351, pages 51 and 54.

Gross trading profit is shown in the 92nd Inland Revenue Report, Cmd 8052, *after* the deduction of profits tax, but *before* deducting income tax. It is *before* deducting depreciation, debenture interest, royalties and long lease rents. For companies, gross true trading income is *after* deducting directors' fees but in the case of unincorporated enterprises the owners' remuneration is *not* deducted from gross trading profit. Another important point is that the imputed income assessed for income tax under Schedule A is also deducted before arriving at the figure of gross trading profit. There are many other relevant points of accounting, such as the allowances for capital expenditure and losses which may be charged against profit, but the definition of gross trading profit outlined here is sufficient for the purpose of economic research into industries' profits.

The task of constructing time-series of profits is easily formulated: the Oxford Institute figures of gross trading profit for 1927 have to be extrapolated back to 1920, while the corresponding figures for 1928–31 and for 1933–35 have to be estimated by interpolation. The extrapolation and interpolation are based on index numbers of profits constructed from a variety of sources of information on profit. The major primary source is a set of microfilms of accounts of companies quoted on the London Stock Exchange and deposited in its archives. It is true that such figures of profits relate to the larger enterprises in each industry, but there are good reasons for believing that the average year to year proportionate changes in the profits of large companies is the same as that for small companies and firms [51], [57] and one test of the technique of extrapolating from large to small brewing companies has given satisfactory results [50].

Another source is a collection of photostats of Inland Revenue 196.6 forms, summarized by industry group, giving the profits of a set of firms and companies, mainly those earning over £2,000 per annum in the inter-war period. At first sight these forms seem to give all the information required for an industrial analysis of profits 1920–38 and indeed the counterparts of these forms are used today in preparing the official estimates of profits in each industry [10] (p. 155). But close study of the fluctuations in profits estimated from

38

these forms reveals so many perverse movements that it is impossible to accept such series without knowing something about their constituent figures. Unfortunately, such information is made inaccessible by the Inland Revenue's confidentiality rules. It is probable that the idiosyncratic behaviour of profits series based on 196.6 forms is partly attributable to the acquisition of companies earning less the £2,000 per annum by companies earning profits above this limit, which could have the effect of increasing total reported profit between two years even though the separate profits of the companies involved in mergers declined. It is also likely that the exclusion of losses, which were a frequent occurrence in the depressed inter-war period, had the effect of making the figures of profits in the 196.6 forms atypical. Accordingly, it was decided not to use these forms, except in road motor transport for which no other adequate information on profit is available. In the latter case time-series were constructed from the 196.6 forms as explained in detail in Chapter 6.

2.3. COVERAGE AND INDUSTRIAL CLASSIFICATION

The coverage of the time-series of profit depends on the benchmarks estimated by the Oxford Institute of Statistics from Inland Revenue data, which relate to all companies and firms assessed for income tax under Schedule D for the years 1927, 1932 and 1936–38. The geographical coverage is, therefore, the present United Kingdom, because even the earliest benchmark excludes the Republic of Ireland. Accordingly, the profits generated in Southern Ireland 1920–22 are excluded, so that the time-series relate to the same geographical area throughout the period 1920–38.

The industrial classification of assessments by the Inland Revenue included a special category for companies operating mainly outside the United Kingdom, but which were assessed for taxation in this country. In the words of the Central Statistical Office,[10] p. 157: 'The separation of such companies is, however, to some extent arbitrary. Companies whose principal assets, except a head office, are situated abroad, are the most important cases and include most of the mining oil and plantation companies. But the activities of companies which operate both at home and abroad cannot be so easily segregated, and the whole profit is allocated to domestic or overseas operations on a judgment of the location of its principal activity. In making this arbitrary division each subsidiary company in a group is allocated individually.'

The industrial classification used in the present study depends

39

partly on the Inland Revenue industrial classification used in the benchmarks, and partly on the number of company accounts sampled in a particular industry. The Oxford Institute benchmarks are based on the pre-war Inland Revenue industrial classification, which differs from both the 1948 and the 1958 Standard Industrial Classifications. However, the Cambridge inquiry into investment in British industries 1920–38 had been faced with the same problem of industrial classification, and Dr Maywald kindly supplied a reconciliation between the pre-war Inland Revenue industrial classification and the Standard Industrial Classification, 1948, so that the precise industrial content of each Oxford Institute benchmark was known. In addition, the Inland Revenue had supplied the industrial classification of each company in the samples drawn by Dr Maywald in connexion with the Cambridge investment inquiry, namely all the companies quoted on the London Stock Exchange with an issued capital greater than £500,000 in 1920, 1930 or 1938, plus one-third of such companies below this size. This information made it possible to know the exact benchmark to which the profit of any company belonged, so that the interpolation between the benchmarks for any one industry could be based on the accounts of a sample of companies drawn from that industry.

When the number of company accounts for any one industry was below twenty, it was necessary to combine industries into larger categories in order to reduce the sampling error by increasing the number of company accounts available. For example, in the present study it was necessary to combine the paper and printing industries into one category, in order to have sufficient company accounts throughout the period 1920–38. The resulting time-series of profit for paper and printing is still consistent with the Inland Revenue and the Standard Industrial Classification, but relates to an Order rather than to separate minimum list headings. This is a weakness, but it should be noted that the current Inland Revenue reports[1] often resort to the practice of publishing figures of gross true income for groups of industries, including the present case of one figure for all the industries within the category of paper and printing.

In one respect the present study contains more industries than the Oxford Institute inquiry. A separate time-series of profit in agriculture is given in Chapter 3, whereas the Oxford Institute inquiry excluded this industry because in 1920–38 such profits were generally assessed for income tax under Schedule B, and because the Oxford Agricultural Economics Research Institute had made a separate investigation of agricultural profits in the period 1920–38. But the present study does not provide separate estimates of profit for each of the many categories investigated by the Oxford Institute of Statistics.

The time-series in Table 1.1 exclude profits in the finance sector, profits earned by adventures outside the United Kingdom, and the self-employment income of the professions, because the data available are less reliable than those derived from the other sources used in this study.

The income and expenditure of public authorities in the United Kingdom 1920–38 is being investigated by the Department of Applied Economics, University of Cambridge, and it is therefore unnecessary to make a separate study of the gross trading income of central and local government authorities in this volume. But one point of overlap must be mentioned at this stage. The profit of public corporations, such as the Central Electricity Authority and the London Passenger Transport Board, are included in the present time-series of profits, because they were assessed for income tax under Schedule D and therefore are included in the benchmarks. But the trading profits of local authorities have been excluded even though they were assessed under Schedule D.

The present investigation covers the following industrial sectors: agriculture; fishing; mining; manufacturing; construction; public utilities; transport; distribution. A variety of sources of information on profit is used but the major source, company accounts, must be described in detail at this stage.

2.4. COMPANY ACCOUNTS AND TAXATION, UNITED KINGDOM, 1920–38

The basic aim of Chapters 3 to 6 is to construct index numbers of the profit in each industry 1920–38 which can be used to interpolate between the benchmarks of absolute profit in each industry in 1927, 1932 and 1936–38, estimated by the Oxford Institute of Statistics. The primary sources used in compiling the index numbers are a microfilmed collection of the company accounts 1920–30 deposited in the archives of the London Stock Exchange, and a microfilmed set of Moody cards for the period 1930–38.[108] These sources have been supplemented by Wheeler's Tables[114] and by Porter's Financial and Statistical Service.[112]

The information given in these sources is very valuable, but far from ideal. Ideally, economists would like to sample from the trading accounts of companies which give full analyses of sales and

41

costs. But these accounts have not been published and, indeed, remain inaccessible to economists outside the Inland Revenue and the companies concerned. Profit and loss accounts were filed with the Registrar of Companies throughout the period 1920–38, and these contained the balance brought down from the trading account, giving the difference between sales and costs. But the various Company Acts which compelled public companies to make such returns did not specify the items to be included in published profit and loss accounts.

Sometimes taxation was given separately, especially in the period 1920–28, but at other times all figures were published after the deduction of taxation without the amount of taxation being shown. Sometimes depreciation was given but in general it was not published throughout the period. These are only two of the many limitations of published company accounts. The parts of profits after depreciation which were invariably published throughout the period 1920–38 were debenture interest and preference dividends. On the rare occasions when debenture interest was not given, it was always possible to obtain figures of outstanding debenture stock from published balance sheets and to calculate the gross debenture interest from the description of the debenture stock. Sometimes debenture interest and preference dividends were given after taxation had been deducted, in which case it was necessary to gross up these figures at the prevailing standard income tax rates to obtain this part of the appropriation of profits before taxation.

In the period 1930–38 ordinary dividends were usually published and presented no problems. But in the decade 1920–30 it was common to publish only the interim ordinary dividends in company accounts. The logic behind this policy was that the final ordinary dividend could not be declared until agreed by the annual general meeting of the company concerned, to which the profit and loss account was presented, and it seems to have been thought presumptuous for the directors to arrange for final dividends to be included in the accounts before their proposals had been voted upon by their shareholders. Fortunately, the Stock Exchange Year Book[113] and Wheeler's Tables[114] gave total ordinary dividends for most quoted companies throughout the 1920s, from information provided to them by the companies concerned, thus the problem of estimating final dividends from sets of company accounts for two successive years was avoided. When the ordinary dividends were declared net or free of taxation they were grossed up at the standard income tax rates to obtain gross ordinary dividends.

The remaining part of profit is corporate saving, after depreciation, and taxation incurred by the company, since the taxation borne by shareholders is contained in the gross dividends and debenture interest. For the period 1920–38 corporate saving was estimated by subtracting gross ordinary dividend from the item 'Earned for Ordinary' in Moody cards. 'Earned for Ordinary' was assumed to be before tax on dividends but after tax on corporate savings, so that the estimate of corporate saving was net of taxation. Net corporate saving, therefore, was grossed up for income tax and added to gross ordinary, preference and debenture interest to give an estimate of profits gross of income tax. The standard rates of income tax 1920–38 used to gross up published profits after taxation are shown in Table 2.2.

TABLE 2.2. *Standard Rates of Income Tax, United Kingdom, 1920–38, in Shillings Per Pound*

FROM	RATE	FROM	RATE
April 6, 1920 ..	6·0	October 15, 1931	5·0
April 6, 1922 ..	5·0	April 6, 1934 ..	4·5
April 6, 1923 ..	4·5	April 6, 1936 ..	4·75
April 6, 1925 ..	4·0	April 6, 1937 ..	5·0
April 6, 1930 ..	4·5	April 6, 1938 ..	5·5

Of the remaining taxes on profits, three may be considered at this stage: excess profits duty, corporation profits tax and national defence contribution. Income tax under Schedule A is ignored because the notional income under this heading is deducted from a company's profit when assessing its liability for income tax under Schedule D. For the purposes of social accounting, this notional income under Schedule A should be added back to Schedule D profits and Dr Feinstein is making this adjustment at the Department of Applied Economics, University of Cambridge, as part of the work on the reconciliation and summary of all the different parts of the United Kingdom's social accounts which have been constructed for the period since 1900. Income taxed under Schedule B is considered later in the section on profit from farming in Chapter 3. Income tax under Schedule C and E is irrelevant in the present study because it is levied on interest from Government securities and income from employment respectively, and both of these categories are outside the scope of the present study. The corporation duty (not the corporation profits tax) is ignored because the net receipts from this stamp duty were relatively small, fluctuating around £100,000 throughout the inter-war period. Overseas taxes on part of the profits of some companies sampled have been neglected simply because there is no way of measuring them. The assumption has to be made that their effects on the changes in the profits of such companies were small.

The excess profits duty was imposed in 1915 and was removed in 1921. For businesses which were started before the outbreak of the First World War, the liability for excess profits duty terminated at various dates between August 4, 1920, and August 5, 1921. For other businesses, liability terminated December 31, 1920. After January 1, 1920, the rate of duty levied on excess profits was 60 per cent, so that for the first year in the period studied the profits of the companies sampled must have been significantly affected by the excess profits duty. Details of the provisions for excess profits duty were not usually given in the company accounts sampled.

The definition of excess profit was exceedingly complicated; there were so many rules for determining the duty that it is impracticable to summarize them here. A brief description of the rules is given in the 64th Inland Revenue Report[1] (Cmd 1436), pages 142 to 149. Because of the extreme complexity of these rules, no attempt is made here to gross up the net profits of the companies sampled for 1920 and 1921 to allow for excess profits duty. It follows that the extrapolation of the benchmark of gross true income for 1927 back to 1920 on the basis of company accounts may underestimate profit in 1920, though any underestimation for 1921 is unlikely in view of the slump in that year, which had the effect of reducing or even abolishing *excess* profits for most companies.

Because excess profits duty cannot be estimated from published company accounts, an attempt must be made to measure its importance by using the Inland Revenue figures of the total net receipts from this tax. This is difficult. One of the consequences of the difficulties of measuring the excess of earned profits over standard profits was a substantial delay in payments of the duty while appeals were heard. Delay was also caused by the provision under the Financial Risks Committee Scheme which allowed those traders whose profits fell below the standard profit up to August 31, 1925, to obtain 80 per cent of the deficiency from the Exchequer, subject to certain conditions, in the form of *repayments* of excess profits duty. In fact, although the duty was removed as from August 5, 1921, at the latest, payment of the duty took place in each year during the period 1920–38. It is possible that some of the payments were made out of profits earned long after the year in which the excess profit was assessed. It is also possible that when the Exchequer made repayments to some companies, because their profits in or after 1921 fell below the standard profit used in computing excess profits liability, such repayments of duty were included in the income currently earned by these companies. Neither case would be shown by the published accounts. As explained in Chapter 6, it is known that the second case occurred in at least one company in the shipping industry, namely the Royal Mail Steam Packet Company, when the industry was experiencing a post-war slump.

TABLE 2.3. *Net Receipts by the Exchequer from the Excess Profits Duty and the Munitions Levy, United Kingdom, 1920–38 (£m.)*

YEAR	NET RECEIPTS	YEAR	NET RECEIPTS
1920	218·1	1930	2·3
1921	29·7	1931	2·1
1922	1·1	1932	2·3
1923	−1·9	1933	1·7
1924	2·8	1934	1·9
1925	2·4	1935	1·4
1926	4·6	1936	1·0
1927	−0·3	1937	0·8
1928	1·2	1938	0·7
1929	1·7		

Similar problems arise with the repayment of the munitions levy. This was imposed in 1915 and terminated on December 31, 1916, yet repayments took place throughout the inter-war period and could make for an increase in reported profits in company accounts.

The combined net receipts from the excess profits duty and the munitions levy are shown in Table 2.3. The timing of these tax payments is not certain, but there are reasons for supposing that on the average the excess profits earned in year t were assessed for taxation in year $t+1$ and that the actual payment of the tax occurred in year $t+2$. This is the clear implication of the 67th Inland Revenue Report[1] (Cmd 2227, page 111) which attributes the net deficit of £1·9 million in 1923–24 to the heavy repayments resulting from the trade depression of 1920–21. This supposition is also consistent with the descriptions of the time-lag in taxation payments of companies given by the Central Statistical Office,[10] page 166. In view of this average time-lag, it may be safely assumed that the large net receipts of £218 million in 1920 and £29·7 million in 1921 relate to the period before 1920. It may also be assumed that *excess* profits in 1921 were zero, since net receipts in 1923 were negative, so that no further adjustment to the 1921 figure of profit in Table 1.1 is required. However, it may be necessary to adjust the figure for 1920, the other year for which positive excess profits could be taxed, though repayments could be made by the Exchequer until 1925. It seems reasonable to attribute the net receipts of £1·1 million in 1922 to excess profits earned in 1920. After 1923 the net receipts throughout the remainder of the period summed to approximately £27 million. It is not known how much of this is attributable to 1920 but was delayed by litigation, but perhaps a figure of £20 million is a plausible guess. If so, this figure should be added to the estimate for 1920 in Table 1.1. This adjustment is of the order of 4 per cent of the total profits, and probably within the margin of error of the estimate in any case, so there seems little point in trying to obtain a more accurate measure of the effects of excess profits duty.

Furthermore, it is impossible to allocate this adjustment between individual industries so that the estimates of total gross profits for each industry have not been adjusted. The implicit assumption is that any adjustment would be within the error band which surrounds each estimate and which must be taken into consideration when using the estimates.

The second tax considered here is the corporation profits tax. This tax was imposed on companies in 1920 and repealed in 1924. The rates at which it was levied were 5 per cent of corporate profits from January 1, 1920, to June 30, 1923, and 2·5 per cent thereafter until June 30, 1924. Any excess profits duty paid was an allowable deduction in computing liability for corporation profits tax, just as it could be deducted in assessing income tax liability. Corporation profits tax paid was allowed as an expense in computing income tax liability. The definition of profit for the purpose of this tax was similar to that used for income tax purposes, except that Schedule A notional income was not deductible and interest on non-permanent loans was an allowable expense. Further details of this tax are given in the 64th and 68th Inland Revenue Reports[1] (Cmd 1436, pp. 150–1, and Cmd 2547, pp. 114–17). The published profits of companies in the sample from 1920 to 1924 were grossed up for this tax, but slight differences in the definition of profit were neglected. The extrapolation of gross true income from 1927 back to 1920, therefore, includes the corporation profits tax.

The national defence contribution was imposed on companies and unincorporated firms in April 1937. It therefore applied to the whole year 1938 and approximately half of the year 1937 in the period being studied. The rates of tax charged were 5 per cent on companies and 4 per cent on unincorporated firms. The main exceptions were public utilities, the railways and some professions. Further details of abatements and additional exemptions are given in the 81st Inland Revenue Report[1] (Cmd 5865, pp. 68–9). The estimates of profits in the years 1936–38 are based not on samples of accounts but on the Oxford Institute survey,[111] so it is necessary to increase the Oxford Institute's figures of gross true income to allow for the fact that the national defence contribution was a deductible expense when measuring profit for income tax purposes. Accordingly, corporate gross true income in 1937 was multiplied by 1,000/975 to allow for 5 per cent national defence contribution for roughly half a year, while the corresponding figure for 1938 was multiplied by 100/95. Non-corporate gross true incomes were multiplied by 100/98 and 100/96 for the same years. These adjustments neglect the abatements but exclude the exempted industries mentioned above. Another source of error is the fact that gross true income excludes the notional income assessed for income tax under Schedule A, whereas this item was not deductible for the purposes of assessing liability for national defence contribution.

Though some companies sampled gave figures of depreciation in their accounts during the period, it was not possible to obtain enough observations of depreciation for each of the years to construct a time-series of depreciation for each industry in order to interpolate between the Oxford Institute benchmarks of wear and tear allowances for 1927, 1932 and 1936. That is, when changes in gross profits in an industry had to be estimated from samples of company accounts, the proportionate changes in profits used were *after* depreciation though they were *before* taxation. The adjustments for tax described earlier in this section removed the effects of changes in the tax rates on the published figures of profits, but there is no way of measuring the effects of changes in the depreciation provisions made by companies. The assumption has to be made that the average of observed proportionate changes in profit *after* depreciation was similar to the corresponding average *before* depreciation. It is not argued that this assumption was true for *all* companies in the sample, but merely that it was true for the average, or more precisely the median, proportionate year to year change. Exceptionally large changes in the provision for depreciation may have a great influence on the changes in the profit of one company but such extreme changes do not influence the median change in any case, and the median is the measure of average generally used in this study, as explained in section 2.5. It is conceivable that the exclusion of

47

depreciation underestimates the long-term growth of profit in those industries which were increasing their capital equipment throughout the period 1920–38. On the other hand, the benchmarks of gross true income for 1927, 1932 and 1936, and the method of interpolation described in section 2.7, counteract any long-term downward bias in the estimation of gross profit. In short, the exclusion of depreciation from the company accounts sampled is unlikely to have any serious effect on the estimation of changes in gross profit of an industry, even though it could have serious effects on the estimation of such changes for a single company.

Company accounts are also affected by organizational changes such as a merger between two companies or the acquisition of one firm by another. It would be possible to correct for such changes by making detailed analyses of the accounts of the companies in question before and after the organizational change. But this procedure would be very costly and has to be avoided. Fortunately, an appropriate theoretical method of constructing a time-series of profit, which is explained in section 2.5, implies that we may use the *median* percentage change of profits in each company instead of the arithmetic mean percentage change and, of course, the median is not affected by the extreme values of percentage change in the profits experienced by the one or two companies involved in organizational changes in any one year. It was, therefore, considered safe to ignore the effects of organizational changes on company accounts.

Little is known about the importance of mergers in the period 1920–38. However, it is worth noting that between 1924 and 1939 mergers among quoted industrial companies in general, and among quoted brewing companies in particular, tended to increase the geometric mean size, although this increase was very slight, partly because relatively few companies were involved in amalgamations and therefore exerted relatively little effect on the geometric mean size (cf. [53], Tables 8 and 9, pp. 166–9, and [49], pp. 238–9). Since the geometric mean is similar to the median in the observed distributions of profit changes, there is some empirical justification for adopting the convenient working rule of ignoring the effects of organizational changes.

2.5. THE SAMPLING SCHEME

Gross profits in manufacturing, shipping, wholesale and retail distribution have been estimated partly from samples of the accounts of the relatively large companies quoted on the London Stock

48

Exchange. The reasons why it is possible to estimate the year to year changes of all firms' profits from observations of the changes of profits of large companies are based on distribution theory. A more complete explanation of the relationship between size, growth and change in profit is given in Chapter 9, but some explanation is necessary at this stage in order to justify the methods chosen to sample from company accounts.

TABLE 2.4. *Size Distribution of Companies by Trading Profit Assessed under Schedule D, United Kingdom, 1949*

| | COMPANIES | |
UPPER LIMIT £	NUMBERS '000	AMOUNT £M
250	62·8	6·0
500	16·8	5·9
1,000	21·1	14·3
1,500	12·0	14·1
2,000	7·9	13·6
3,000	10·9	26·0
4,000	7·1	24·2
5,000	4·7	20·8
10,000	12·2	84·1
15,000	5·2	62·1
20,000	3·1	52·1
25,000	1·9	42·4
30,000	1·5	40·9
40,000	2·1	72·5
50,000	1·3	56·5
75,000	1·9	110·6
100,000	1·0	83·8
200,000	1·4	196·4
1,000,000	1·1	424·8
Over 1,000,000	·2	466·7
All ranges	**176·3**	**1817·6**

A typical size distribution of companies by profit is given in Table 2.4 which is based on the Inland Revenue Schedule D assessments on profits earned in 1949. It can be seen that the size of profit ranges from under £250 to over £1,000,000 with some 36 per cent of companies earning less than £250 and some 26 per cent of the total profits earned by 200 or so companies earning above £1,000,000. Clearly, this distribution is highly skew and it would be difficult to plot it on a graph using absolute scales of profits. This difficulty may be removed by plotting the frequency of companies against the logarithm of profit instead of absolute profit. In Figure 2.1, the *cumulative percentage frequency distribution* of companies in Table

2.4 has been plotted using a logarithmic scale of profits on the abscissa. In addition, a *probability* scale is used on the ordinate; this is based on tables of the normal integral and has the effect of making the normal distribution function a straight line instead of the usual sigmoid curve. The points on Figure 2.1 lie close enough to a straight

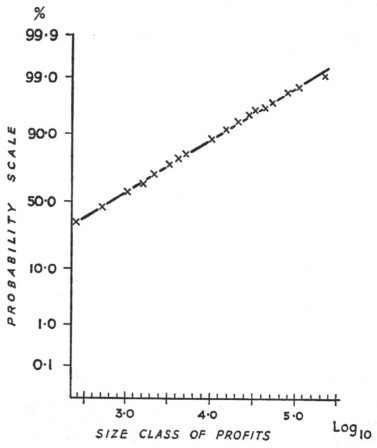

Fig. 2.1. Logarithmic probability graph for the data of Table 2.4.

line to suggest that this size distribution of companies assessed under Schedule D is from a population which is normal when the logarithm of profit is plotted on the abscissa. More simply, the distribution in Table 2.4 appears to be lognormal.

Unfortunately, Inland Revenue distribution of companies by profit is not published for each industry, but Tew and Henderson[92]

(Table C.1, page 280) have analysed the distribution of quoted companies by net tangible assets into twenty-one industrial groups. Chapter 8 shows that there is a high correlation between alternative financial measures of size, thus the shape of the distributions of companies by net tangible assets may be regarded as a reliable guide to the unknown form of the distribution of companies by profit within each industry. The twenty-one size distributions were subjected to the graphic test of lognormality used in Figure 2.1, and fifteen of them were approximately lognormal. The six exceptions were wool, other textiles, building and contracting, retail and wholesale distribution, and tobacco. Since the tobacco industry has only eleven quoted companies it is not surprising that its size distribution of firms does not fit a regular curve. The other five exceptional industries have a very high proportion of their total output and employment controlled by firms without a Stock Exchange quotation which consequently lie outside the observed size distributions. In view of the fact that these six observed size distributions are heavily truncated, it is once again not surprising that they do not give good fits to the simple two-parameter lognormal. In the circumstances, the approximation to the theoretical lognormal curve of the assets in fifteen industry groups is consistent with the hypothesis that the size distributions of profits within individual industries are approximately lognormal.

But a lognormal distribution is only one of many theoretical distributions which may be applied to the observed skew distributions of firms. In fact, Simon and Bonini[84, 85] argue that the lognormal is one member of the family of distributions, named after Yule, all of which are generated by a similar process. An essential part of this common generating process is Gibrat's law of proportionate effect, which states that the proportionate change in the size of a variable is independent of its absolute size. In view of the similarities between the members of this Yule family of distributions, it is largely a question of taste which particular distribution is used in practice. The lognormal is chosen here because of its simplicity, and because many of its properties are related to those of the normal distribution, which is familiar to economists, whereas the Beta and Gamma distributions, upon which the general Yule distribution is based, are perhaps less familiar.

An appropriate method of sampling from a skew, lognormal population would be to stratify and use a varying sampling fraction proportionate to the standard deviation of companies within each stratum. But this method is impracticable in the present case. The

51

accounts of private companies are inaccessible and have to be excluded from the sample even though many of them were larger than the smaller public companies quoted on the Stock Exchange.* Furthermore, the basic source of quoted companies' accounts 1920–38 listed at the beginning of section 2.4 excluded many small quoted companies because their shares did not have an active market and were therefore of little interest to investors. In short, the accessible population of company accounts, from which a sample can be drawn, consists of large quoted companies, where 'large' may be interpreted as over £500,000 issued capital. The sampling problem is therefore not one of drawing a stratified sample, but rather the question, 'How can a sample drawn from the upper strata be used to measure profits in the whole population?' This question may be answered along the following lines.

If the size distribution of firms by profit may be regarded as lognormal, it follows that large, medium and small firms have the same average proportionate change in profit, where proportionate change is defined as the ratio of profits in period t to profits in period $t-n$ where n can be 1, 2 or any other number of periods. It also follows that the distribution of proportionate changes in profits is *theoretically* another lognormal distribution, and that the mean and variance of the *logarithms* of proportionate changes in profits are the same for large, medium and small firms. Consequently, it is permissible to estimate the mean of the logarithms of proportionate changes in profits, and its sampling error, by sampling from the population of large firms only, and then to apply the result to all firms. By taking $n=1$ and estimating the year to year proportionate changes in profits of a sample of large firms 1920–38, it is possible to obtain the index number of profits required to convert the benchmarks of absolute profits into a time-series of profits throughout the inter-war period.

All this sounds reasonable in theory, but in practice a lognormal distribution does not describe the sizes of the few giant firms exactly, even if it is a very good summary of distribution as a whole [49]. It seems prudent therefore to pay special attention to the profits of the

---

* The earliest year for which information exists on the total gross profits of quoted and unquoted profits is 1949, when the largest 100 quoted companies earned over 25 per cent of total industrial profits, the remaining 2,449 quoted companies earned 35 per cent and the private companies and unincorporated firms earned 40 per cent (cf. [92], Table 8.1, p. 109). These figures are certainly compatible with the widespread belief that many private companies are larger profit-earners than many small quoted companies.

top few companies in each industry. Even in a low concentration industry such as brewing, which was chosen in a pilot study, the largest eight companies earned about 20 per cent of all brewing profits in 1938, showing that it would be dangerous to exclude any of these giants from a sample of profits in this industry, even though the general statement that proportionate changes in profits are independent of absolute size may be accepted. Accordingly, while the sample of profit changes in an industry may be restricted to large companies, say those with above £500,000 issued capital in 1920, it is desirable to have a complete count of the giant companies in each industry, plus a random sample of the other large firms above this limit. The number of giants to be enumerated depends on the degree of concentration in the industry, and a convenient working rule is to enumerate the profits of those giant firms which account for 20 per cent of the industry's profits, with the top three firms as a minimum.

Another practical qualification to the sampling scheme concerns the shape of the size distribution of proportionate changes in profits. Theoretically, this is *lognormal* because, after logarithmic transformation, it is a linear combination of normal distributions of profits in year t and in year $t-1$. But, in practice, the distribution of the ratio of two lognormal distributions often appears to be nearly *normal* (cf. [25], page 102). Consider the size distribution of profits in two adjacent years, t and $t-1$, and make the reasonable assumption that the variance of the logarithms of these two distributions is the same, say σ_1^2, since this variance is unlikely to change over such a short time. Then the variance of the logarithms of the ratio of the two size distributions, say σ^2, is $2\sigma_1^2 - 2\rho\sigma_1^2 = 2\sigma_1^2(1-\rho)$. But the correlation coefficient ρ will be high, because firms making large profits in year $t-1$ will usually make high profits in year t, so that σ^2 will be small. Since in a lognormal distribution the coefficients of skewness and kurtosis are governed by σ^2, it follows that the distribution of the ratio of the size distributions of profits in adjacent years will have low skewness and low kurtosis, and may therefore be regarded as approximately normal. Accordingly, the mean proportionate change in profits given in Table 2.5 is *before* logarithmic transformation even though the sample is derived from a theoretically lognormal population of proportionate profit changes.

Taking a random sample of the year to year proportionate profit changes of large companies, and adding a complete count of such changes in the case of the few very large firms, is an extremely simple technique of sampling from a highly skew distribution which has strong theoretical and practical justification. Indeed, it is difficult to see what else can be done, given the available sources of company accounts, even though the use of ratio-estimates may introduce a slight bias.

2.6. A TEST OF THE SAMPLING SCHEME

The next step is to test the sampling scheme just outlined by applying it to an industry with a fairly reliable existing time-series of profit which can be used as a standard. The only industry for which an official time-series is available 1920–38 is brewing, and even this series exists only because the Chancellor of the Exchequer was regularly questioned in the House of Commons during the inter-war period about the total profits earned in the brewing industry and it is possible to construct a time-series from his replies printed in Hansard.[16] This series is shown in Column (1) of Table 2.5.

TABLE 2.5. *Estimates of Profits in Brewing, United Kingdom, 1920–38*

	BREWING INDUSTRY PROFITS (HANSARD) £M	PROPORTIONATE CHANGE IN (1)	SAMPLE MEAN CHANGE PER CENT	STANDARD ERROR PER CENT	SAMPLE MEDIAN CHANGE PER CENT	NO. OF COS. IN SAMPLE
	(1)	(2)	(3)	(4)	(5)	(6)
1920	29·0	—	—	—	—	—
1921	19·8	68	54	6·3	41	20
1922	22·3	113	101	8·4	99	24
1923	23·3	105	102	2·5	103	26
1924	25·5	109	110	3·7	107	26
1925	26·5	104	117	5·3	115	29
1926	24·5	92	101	2·2	102	29
1927	24·0	98	101	2·2	102	29
1928	24·5	102	109	3·8	103	30
1929	25·0	102	107	4·7	103	29
1930	26·0	104	108	2·6	103	28
1931	23·0	89	92	2·4	92	28
1932	16·0	70	78	2·5	81	30
1933	18·0	113	102	2·9	102	30
1934	23·0	128	120	4·1	115	30
1935	26·0	113	110	14·6	108	30
1936	28·5	110	106	1·4	105	30
1937	31·5	111	106	2·5	105	29
1938	31·5	100	99	1·9	100	29

Since these figures were given to the House of Commons by the Chancellor of the Exchequer it may be assumed that they were compiled from Inland Revenue sources. Profits for later years are before national defence contribution and those for early years are before excess profits duty. But because it would have been impossible for the Inland Revenue to have given final figures to the Chancellor so soon after the year to which the profits related, the figures must have been estimated by the Inland Revenue from unknown samples of profits, plus unknown adjustments to include any likely difference between profits in the current and preceding years. However, even though they cannot be regarded as 100 per cent accurate, they are an exceedingly useful standard to set against the sample.

Column (3) of Table 2.5 shows the mean proportionate year to year changes in profits of a sample of quoted brewing companies. The basic sample consists of the largest eight brewing companies plus a random sample of twenty-two large companies with over £500,000 issued capital. In some years, especially at the beginning of the period, the accounts of a company selected in the sample were not available, or if available, did not give the required information. When this happened, a company of comparable size next in alphabetical order was chosen as a replacement. Even so, it was not always possible to obtain the required figures for all thirty companies throughout the period 1920–38 as can be seen in Column (6) in Table 2.5. Needless to say, though the constituents of the sample outside the giants change slightly over the period 1920–38, the figures in Column (3) are based on the same set of companies in adjacent years, as in a chain index. The ratio of gross profit in year t to that in year $t-1$ was calculated for each company in the sample and Column (3) shows the mean values of these proportionate changes. Thus, for example, between 1920 and 1921 the profits of brewing companies fell on the average to 54 per cent of their 1920 value, if we take the mean.

The simplest way of making an objective comparison between Columns (2) and (3) of Table 2.5 is to correlate them. In fact, the correlation coefficient is $r_{23}^2 = 0.76$, and the regression coefficients are $b_{23} = 0.88$, $b_{32} = 0.88$, where the subscripts refer to column numbers in Table 2.5. These results are very satisfactory and support the sampling scheme advocated in section 2.5. Howeyer, the general agreement between Columns (2) and (3) must not be allowed to mask important differences which occur in some years. In particular, between 1920 and 1921 the mean proportionate change in profits was 54 per cent whereas the Hansard figure for 1921 is 68 per cent of the 1920 figure. In this case of inconsistency it would be wise to choose the Hansard figure because the estimates of profits for 1920 calculated from the sample of company accounts are subject to unusually large errors of observation arising from the effects of excess profits on the information given in the accounts.

But in other cases of inconsistency it is difficult to choose between the official series and the sample estimate. The Hansard figures were invariably given in the following year. It is known that the Central Statistical Office regards such estimates nowadays as having a reliability of between 3 and 10 per cent, and the official pre-war profits series in Column (1) of Table 2.5 is likely to be less accurate than this. On the other hand, fifteen out of the eighteen means in Column (3) had sampling errors of less than 10 per cent, as shown by taking two standard errors in Column (4). Perhaps one safe course is to use the mean change and its standard error, except where the latter is excessive due to freak observations brought about by mergers and the like. There is certainly less likelihood of forgetting the standard errors of a sample estimate than there is of forgetting the errors present in an official time-series.

The usual method of counteracting the effect of extreme observations on the mean is to estimate the median. In the present case there is some theoretical advantage in favour of the median. Since the theoretical distribution of changes in profits is normal after logarithmic transformation it follows that the arithmetic mean of the logarithms coincides with the median of the logarithms of proportionate changes in profits. But the median of the distribution must be the same firm whether the distribution of profit changes is considered before or after logarithmic transformation. The observations, of course, have the same rank before and after taking logarithms, and the median is essentially a measure of rank. It follows that the median *before* logarithmic transformation corresponds to the mean of the distribution of proportionate changes in profits *after* logarithmic transformation.

The median proportionate change in profit is given in Column (5) of Table 2.5. Thus profits in 1921 were only 41 per cent of their 1920 value according to this measure of average, and in 1922 they were 99 per cent to their 1921 value. The series based on the median is similar to that based on the mean, which is not surprising in view of the theoretically low skewness of the distribution of proportionate changes in profit. But though both series have much in common, it is worth noting that the median is generally lower than the mean, indicating that some slight positive skewness is present in the sample of proportionate profit changes.

In so far as it is less likely to be affected by amalgamations and other organizational changes which tend to make for extreme in-

56

creases in the profits shown in the accounts of those companies involved, the median is a more reliable measure of central tendency than is the mean. Extreme changes in profits are reflected by the standard errors in Column (4) of Table 2.5 and it can be seen that the errors in 1921–22 and 1934–35 are rather high and it seems that the median should be preferred. Indeed, a preliminary inspection of proportionate changes in the profits of companies in other industries during the period suggested that one extreme change in a sample was a frequent occurrence and, for this reason alone, it would be advisable to use the median proportionate change of profits to construct the index numbers of profit for each industry.

The conclusion to be drawn from this test is that the lognormal sampling scheme proposed here has strong theoretical and practical justification and may be applied to other industries in order to construct a complete time-series of profits in British industries 1920–38. It must be recognized, however, that in some industries there may be special difficulties—such as losses—which did not arise in the pilot study of brewing, and which invalidate the techniques used so far. The lognormal sampling scheme cannot be applied to losses simply because the logarithm of a negative number is not defined. In fact, the working rule adopted in this study was that when only one company in a sample earned a loss, it was ignored and the median of the proportionate changes in the profits of the other companies in the sample was taken as a measure of the typical change in profit. But when two or more companies in a sample for one year earned losses, the differences between the *means* of the absolute profits and losses of the same set of companies in adjacent years was taken as a measure of the typical change in profits. When this alternative method was adopted because of two or more losses in year t, the mean of the absolute profits and losses was also computed for years $t-1$ and $t+1$ and the chain index between them was then spliced with the index based on the proportionate changes for all the other years. The resulting chain index number of profits is a theoretically unbiased estimate of the true change, but it is open to the practical objection that it may be unduly influenced by extreme changes. The major safeguard is the fact that the index number is used solely to interpolate between the Oxford Institute benchmarks: there is no question of attempting to estimate *levels* of profit in a particular industry by multiplying the mean of a sample by the estimated number of firms in an industry.

The decision to use the mean of the absolute figures of profit and loss, in those years when two or more companies in the sample made a loss, was made after various unsuccessful experiments with a linear transformation suggested by Klein[60] (page 49), and after a special study of losses in the iron and steel industry, carried out by Al-Atraqchi.[97] The latter study revealed that in years such as 1936 and 1937 when losses were infrequent, the size distribution of iron and steel companies by profit was lognormal, so that the method of using median proportionate changes in profit was appropriate. But in 1931 and 1932, when losses were frequent, the distributions of companies by profit were not lognormal; nor were they lognormal after removing losses by adding $p+1$ to each observation, where p equals the largest loss observed. They were unimodal, symmetrical, leptokurtic and had a very large range. In view of their symmetry it seemed reasonable to use either the median or the mean profit, including losses, since both measures were typical. In fact, the mean was used to construct index numbers for the years with losses, because it was found that such index numbers were more highly correlated with the year to year changes of the profits of unreconstructed iron and steel companies estimated in [98] than were index numbers based on the median of the proportion changes in profits, excluding losses.

2.7. INTERPOLATION METHODS

The index numbers of profit in each industry, obtained by the methods described in sections 2.5 and 2.6, then had to be reconciled with the benchmarks of absolute profit in each industry group estimated by the Oxford Institute of Statistics[111] from the Inland Revenue data for the years 1927, 1932 and 1936. The first step in this reconciliation was to subtract the gross profits of giant firms from the total gross true income of their industry in each of the benchmark years. As explained in section 2.5, for highly concentrated industries it is prudent to enumerate the profits of giant firms and add them to the estimate of the profits of the remainder of the industry obtained from the sample drawn for each industry.

The second step was to compare the index numbers based on the samples with index numbers based on the Oxford Institute's enumeration of gross true income for each industry, after these figures had been reduced by profits of the giant firms. Not surprisingly there were discrepancies between the two sets of estimates for the benchmark years. The index numbers based on samples included errors of observation and of non-response, in addition to sampling errors. The index of profits resulting from these samples is obviously less accurate than the Oxford figures based on Inland Revenue data, so the former index was adjusted to fit the Oxford Institute benchmarks.

The adjustments were made as follows. Let the Oxford benchmarks of *absolute profit* for the years 1936 and 1932 be denoted by Y_{36} and Y_{32}. Let the *index numbers* of profits based on samples of company accounts be X_{36} and X_{32} for the same years. Suppose that Y_{32}/Y_{36} was smaller than X_{32}, with $X_{36}=100$. Then the difference $X_{32}-(Y_{32}/Y_{36})$ was averaged over four years and the result, denoted by a, was added to each of the first differences in the sample index number 1932–36, e.g. $(X_{33}+X_{32})+a$, $(X_{34}-X_{35})+a$, so that the adjusted index number for 1932, X_{32}, equalled the ratio (Y_{32}/Y_{36}). That is, the interpolation between the Oxford benchmarks was proportional to, but not equal to, the fluctuations in the sample index number.

The resulting corrected index numbers of profits were then applied to the absolute figures of profit in 1936, excluding profits of giant firms, to obtain absolute figures for the years 1920–36. The profits of the giant companies were then added back to this series to give estimates of absolute profits in each industry 1920–36. The estimates for 1937 and 1938 were taken from the Oxford Institute figures without any modification, apart from the adjustment for national defence contribution.

CHAPTER 3

EXTRACTIVE INDUSTRIES

3.1. GENERAL REMARKS

EXTRACTIVE industries comprise agriculture, forestry, fishing, mining and quarrying, or Orders I and II of the 1958 Standard Industrial Classification. The gross profit of these industries in 1938 amounted to about 11 per cent of total gross profit earned in the United Kingdom, excluding the finance industries. Most of this was contributed by agriculture, as can be seen in Table 3.1, which gives the gross profit of the extractive industries in the United Kingdom 1920–38. Each of the four time-series shows large fluctuations during the period, but no industry had more varying fortunes than coal-mining. Coal-mining profits reflect the well-known economic history of the industry in this period with the strikes of 1921 and 1926–27, and the acute depression, 1929–33, superimposed on a chronic inter-

TABLE 3.1. *Gross Profit in the Extractive Industries, United Kingdom, 1920–38 (£m.)*

YEAR	AGRICULTURE	FISHING	COAL MINING	OTHER MINING AND QUARRYING
	(1)	(2)	(3)	(4)
1920	178	2·2	47·6	5·8
1921	137	2·1	−17·9	1·9
1922	108	1·5	20·1	3·2
1923	101	1·4	39·7	4·0
1924	93	1·7	24·4	5·5
1925	83	1·6	11·2	5·8
1926	80	1·4	9·6	5·0
1927	65	1·5	−3·1	4·6
1928	70	1·8	−2·9	5·0
1929	71	2·1	14·0	4·6
1930	80	2·3	13·3	4·3
1931	66	2·0	12·2	3·3
1932	68	1·0	11·0	2·7
1933	88	1·2	11·7	3·1
1934	101	1·5	14·4	4·9
1935	95	1·8	16·0	4·4
1936	107	2·0	21·2	5·3
1937	87	1·8	23·2	6·6
1938	85	1·5	24·8	5·6

DOI: 10.4324/9781003183266-4

war stagnation. The losses of 1921, 1927 and 1928 are all the more remarkable when it is borne in mind that they are computed *before* depreciation.

Gross profit in agriculture, and to some extent gross profit in fishing, contains a large element of reward for manual and managerial labour in addition to return on enterprise and capital. Many farms would have made losses during the period if the farm accounts had been debited with the full market value of the labour of farmers and their families. The same point is made in another way by Bellerby[33] who shows that the average farmer's *incentive income* per man-week was less than the industrial average weekly wage-rate throughout the period 1920–33. That is, farmers were living on the returns to their land and capital.

3.2. METHODS OF ESTIMATION—AGRICULTURE

Bellerby[33] has provided time-series of farmers' incentive income in the United Kingdom 1923–36. But the social accounting definition of farming income, as explained by the Central Statistical Office,[10] is different, because no deduction is made for depreciation or for interest paid on borrowed working capital. Consequently, it was necessary to add back the interest on occupiers' capital which had been deducted by Bellerby. In addition, estimates of depreciation of farmers' implements, kindly supplied by Mr Bellerby, were added back to get a time-series of gross profit in agriculture 1923–36. The corresponding figures for 1920–22 were estimated by assuming that the proportionate changes in profits were the same as the proportionate change in the total foods price index published in the Statistical Abstract.[23] Bellerby[33] estimated profits for the crop years 1937–38 and 1938–39 and an average for the calendar years 1937 and 1938. Gross profit for the calendar year 1938 was estimated by adding $\frac{5}{12}$ of the profit in 1937–38 to $\frac{7}{12}$ of that earned in 1938–39, following the method of the Central Statistical Office.[10] Profit for the calendar year 1937 was estimated from this figure for 1938 and the average for the two calendar years 1937 and 1938.

3.3. FORESTRY

It is believed that the gross profit derived from forestry for each year in the period 1920–38 was too small to be considered here. There are two reasons for this belief. First the 92nd Inland Revenue Report,[1] Table 42, estimated the total gross true income of forestry and fishing as £2·4 million, £1·8 million and £1·7 million for 1936, 1937 and 1938, whereas the Oxford benchmarks of gross true income in fishing alone for the same years are £2·0 million, £1·8 million and £1·4 million, which implies that the gross true income in forestry for these years was small or even negative. Secondly, after reviewing timber prices and wage rates in forestry, MacGregor[66] found little or no 'incentive income' in forestry during and since the Second World War even when prices in the war were fixed at 50 per cent above those ruling 1929–39, so it is probable that there was little or no incentive income in forestry throughout the depressed inter-war period.

3.4. METHODS OF ESTIMATION—FISHING

Time-series of the value of fish of British taking landed at ports in the United Kingdom were published in the Statistical Abstract[23] throughout the period. For the years 1920–22 inclusive the value of fish landed at ports in the present-day Republic of Ireland had to be excluded. This was done by assuming that the figure for Northern Ireland, which was published separately from 1923 onwards, fluctuated in proportion to the total United Kingdom figure 1920–22, and the estimates for Northern Ireland 1920–22 were then added to the values of fish landed in England, Wales and Scotland 1920–22. This time-series is shown in Column (1) of Table 3.2.

Chapman[36] provides estimates of wages and salaries earned in the fishing industry, and this series was subtracted from Column (1) to get the time-series of gross margin (gross profit plus fuel and other non-employee costs such as maintenance of equipment), shown in Column (2) of Table 3.2. This time-series was then used to interpolate between the Oxford benchmarks of gross true income in fishing and trawling for 1927, 1932 and 1936, as explained in section 2.7. The index-number based on the adjusted time-series of gross-margin is given in Column (3) of Table 3.2 and when applied to the absolute figures of profit in 1927, 1932 and 1936 gives the time-series of gross-profit in Column (2) of Table 3.1. The figures for 1937 and 1938 were extracted from the Oxford Institute's tables in [111].

3.5. METHODS OF ESTIMATION—COAL-MINING

The *Annual Reports of the Secretary for Mines* (Mines Department of the Board of Trade)[2] contain tables of the costs of production, proceeds and profits of at least 94 per cent of the coal-mining

EXTRACTIVE INDUSTRIES

industry for each year in the period 1920–38. Column (1) of Table 3.3 shows the commercially disposable output of coal in million tons for each of the years, and was obtained by increasing the published figures, which relate to proportions of the industry varying between 94 per cent and 97 per cent, so that the time-series of physical output relates to the whole industry. The description 'commercially disposable' should be noted: it means that coal given to the miners, and adjustments to the stocks of coal are excluded. It is, in fact, the physical counterpart to the figure of sales in Column (2) of Table 3.3.

TABLE 3.2. *Gross Profit in Fishing, United Kingdom, 1920–38 (£m.)*

YEAR	VALUE OF FISH LANDED £M. (1)	GROSS MARGIN £M. (2)	ADJUST INDEX OF GROSS MARGINS 1936=100 (3)
1920	28·5	12·2	112
1921	21·6	11·3	104
1922	18·4	8·0	74
1923	17·8	7·8	72
1924	20·4	9·4	86
1925	19·3	8·7	80
1926	17·7	7·8	72
1927	17·7	7·9	72
1928	18·4	8·3	88
1929	19·6	8·9	105
1930	18·9	9·0	114
1931	16·4	7·4	99
1932	15·5	6·9	47
1933	15·2	6·8	59
1934	16·0	6·9	75
1935	16·4	7·1	90
1936	16·3	6·8	100
1937	15·9	6·6	—
1938	16·6	7·5	—

The value of sales published has also been converted to 100 per cent. This estimate differs from the figure of 'sales' usually given in company accounts because selling and delivery costs have already been deducted from it.

Net profit in Column (3) is the difference between Column (2) and the total of other costs of production, including wages, stores and timber, and overheads. Net profit is calculated *after* the deduction of depreciation, and royalties and rents, and it includes losses. These three deductions are important and must be borne in mind when attempting to reconcile the figures in Table 3.3 with the Oxford Institute[111] figures of gross true trading income 1936–38. This reconciliation is attempted in Table 3.4.

63

Row (1) gives the net profit shown in Table 3.3 for 1936 to 1938. To this figure must be added the published figure of royalties, multiplied by 100/97 to allow for the fact that the statistics in [2] relate to 97 per cent of the industry in each of the three years covered. Royalties are not deductible from profits when assessing the income

TABLE 3.3. *Profits in Mining and Quarrying, United Kingdom, 1920–38*

YEAR	OUTPUT TONS M. (1)	COAL MINING SALES £M. (2)	NET PROFITS £M. (3)	OTHER MINING AND QUARRYING GROSS MARGIN £M. (4)
1920	217	—	36·1	12·1
1921	153	205·5	−21·8	4·0
1922	227	215·6	10·9	6·7
1923	254	250·9	27·7	8·4
1924	245	242·3	14·2	9·8
1925	224	190·6	2·9	10·2
1926	81	63·5	5·1	8·8
1927	231	174·5	−10·3	10·0
1928	219	145·3	−10·1	9·2
1929	238	165·6	4·4	10·2
1930	222	156·7	3·9	9·8
1931	188	131·8	2·7	8·1
1932	191	132·2	1·5	7·2
1933	185	125·3	2·2	7·5
1934	198	136·8	4·3	8·9
1935	206	138·9	5·4	9·1
1936	219	154·9	10·1	10·3
1937	224	177·6	13·8	11·9
1938	210	182·4	14·0	11·4

TABLE 3.4. *Comparison of Net Profit with Gross True Income in Coal-mining, United Kingdom, 1936–38 (£m.)*

	1936	1937	1938
1. Net profits	10·1	13·8	14·0
2. Royalties	5·0	5·3	5·1
3. Depreciation allowance ..	4·2	4·9	4·6
4. Total 1 to 3	19·3	24·0	23·7
5. Gross True Trading Income ..	21·2	22·5	23·6

tax liability of coal mines, simply because the Inland Revenue collects the income tax on royalties at their source. Again, because the profit published in [2] is after depreciation, it is necessary to add back some estimate of this figure before making a comparison with the Oxford Institute figure of gross true income. The estimates used in Row (3) of Table 3.4 are the wear and tear allowances made by the Inland Revenue. The total of Rows (1) to (3) given in Row (4) may be compared with the Oxford Institute figures of gross true trading income given in Row (5). There is little difference between Rows (4) and (5), which suggests that losses, which would make for such a difference since they are included in Row (1) and excluded from Row (5), must have been very small in comparison with positive profit in the years 1936–38. An inspection of the analysis of profit by regions given in [2] confirms this suggestion, because most coalfields made a positive profit for most quarters in the three years 1936–38.

Estimates of royalties obtained from [2] and adjusted for coverage were added to net profit in Column (3) of Table 3.3 for each year 1920–36. The Oxford Institute's survey[111] provided estimates of the Inland Revenue wear and tear allowances in the coal industry for 1927, 1932 and 1936 which may be regarded as a measure of depreciation. Figures of depreciation for other years in the period 1920–36 were estimated by linear interpolation. The resulting time-series of depreciation was added to net profit plus royalties to yield a time-series of gross profit 1920–36, which is shown in Column (3) of Table 3.1.

3.6. METHODS OF ESTIMATION—OTHER MINING AND QUARRYING

Unfortunately, the *Annual Reports of the Secretary for Mines*[2] do not contain detailed summaries of the accounts of firms engaged in other types of mining and quarrying. But they do provide figures of the value of the total product of each mineral for each year 1920–38. A careful comparison of these figures with the value of each of the principal products in these trades in the Census of Production for 1935[4] showed that they are reliable estimates of gross output, to use the Census term. It was therefore decided to construct an index number of gross profits in these trades based on the annual difference between the value of the production of minerals, other than coal, and the estimates of employee compensation for the same trades taken from Chapman.[36] The trades covered are salt mines, brine-pits, slate quarries and all other mines and quarries except coal, including lead, tin and iron ore, limestone, sandstone, sand and gravel, clay, igneous rocks and several other products. They correspond to trades covered by the Standard Industrial

B   65

Classification minimum list headings *102, 103* and *109*. The absolute gross margin, which includes gross profit and all costs other than employee compensation, is shown in Column (4) of Table 3.3.

For 1935 it is possible to obtain estimates of the costs of materials and fuel for these trades, in addition to obtaining a more reliable figure of the total value of the production of minerals, from the Census of Production. Indeed, the Census figures of net output (value added), being equal to the difference between gross output and material costs, are a close approximation to the sum of employee compensation and gross profits. It is true that the Census figures exclude the value added by small firms with less than eleven employees, but the Census gives figures of employment for all firms, say x, and for all firms with eleven or more employees, say y, so it was possible to estimate the total value added by all firms in these trades in 1935 by multiplying the estimates of value added for the large establishments by the ratio x/y.

The grand total of the value added by all these trades, after the adjustments just described, came to £16.5 million in 1935. The total employee compensation (wages and salaries) for these trades given in Chapman[36] is £11·9 million. The difference of £4·6 million is an estimate of profit before depreciation and before taxation for 1935. Estimates of gross profits in other years may be obtained by assuming they fluctuated in proportion to the series of gross margin in Column (4) of Table 3.3. This assumption implies that the materials and fuel costs in the index did not have any significant effect on the fluctuations in gross profits. This assumption has some justification: the 1936–38 figures derived in this way are £5·2, £6·0 and £5·8 million which may be compared with the estimates of gross true income for these trades made by the Oxford Institute,[111] namely £5·3, £6·4 and £5·3 million. Clearly the differences are small for each of these three years. But this encouraging result does not apply to a comparison made between the series in Column (4) of Table 3.3 and the Oxford benchmarks of gross true income in other mining and quarrying for the years 1927 and 1932. Since the Oxford figures exclude losses, a positive difference between the two estimates in favour of Oxford may be tolerated: but in the present case the Oxford figures of gross profit for 1927 and 1932 are *lower* than those derived from Table 3.3. In view of the greater accuracy of the Oxford figures in this case, it was decided to adopt the benchmarks for 1927 and 1932 and to interpolate for other years on the assumption that fluctuations in gross profits were proportional to, though not equal to, the fluctuations in the series of gross margin in Table 3.3, in accordance with the method described in section 2.7. The resulting time series of gross profits in other mining and quarrying is shown in Column (4) of Table 3.1.

3.7 RELIABILITY OF THE ESTIMATES

There is an important difference between the estimates for agriculture and those for all other industries: there are no Oxford Institute benchmarks for agriculture because most farming incomes were not assessed for income tax under Schedule D during the period 1920–38 and such assessments form the basis of the benchmarks. But the methods used by Bellerby[33] to estimate farmers' incentive income are similar to those used by the Central Statistical Office to estimate farmers' income in the current national income accounts, and it may be assumed that the degree of reliability is much the same. In fact, the Central Statistical Office places its estimates of farming income in category B, with errors of 3 per cent to 10 per cent, and it seems reasonable to assign the estimates in Column (1) of Table 3.1 to the same category.

The benchmark of profit in fishing for 1936 is reliable, being derived by the Oxford Institute from Inland Revenue sources. Its error is probably less than 3 per cent. The gross margin series in Column (2) of Table 3.2 is dependent upon the accuracy of Chapman's time-series of employee compensation in this industry [36], which has more than 10 per cent error. On the other hand, the year to year changes in employee compensation, and in gross margin, may well be more accurate. The main reason for this belief is that errors involved in this time-series, as in most economic time-series, are likely to have a systematic component in addition to a random component which would affect the accuracy of the absolute time-series but which would not affect the year to year changes or index form in Column (3) of Table 3.2. Moreover, the benchmarks of absolute profit for 1927 and 1932 limit the accumulation of errors in the time-series. For these reasons, therefore, it seems likely that the time-series of profit in fishing in Column (2) of Table 3.1 also has errors of between 3 per cent and 10 per cent.

Profit in the coal-mining industry in Column (3) of Table 3.1 is a very reliable estimate. The data in Table 3.3 are not subject to errors of interpolating, differencing, coverage, sampling and the like. They were derived from official sources and it is legitimate to regard their errors as being less than 3 per cent. The same is not true of the time-series of profit in other mining and quarrying. The techniques used in compiling this series were similar to those used in the case of fishing, so that similar arguments may be applied to the reliability of Column (4) of Table 3.1. Thus it is reasonable, and certainly consistent, to regard the time-series of profit in other mining and quarrying as having errors of 3 per cent to 10 per cent.

3.8 COMPARABILITY WITH OTHER ESTIMATES

A search for alternative estimates of profit in agriculture, in fishing and in other mining and quarrying has been unsuccessful, so that it is not possible to make any comparisons. For coal-mining, there is the index of profit compiled by Hope.[106] But this index is based on a sample of nineteen coal-mining companies and is subject to all the errors of interpreting company accounts in addition to sampling errors. Because of this, it seems preferable to use the time-series of coal-mining profit in Column (3) of Table 3.1, which is based on very reliable Board of Trade figures.

CHAPTER 4

MANUFACTURING INDUSTRIES

4.1 GENERAL REMARKS

IN THE present context, manufacturing industries are defined as those covered by Orders III–XVI inclusive in the 1958 Standard Industrial Classification, with the exception that storage, in minimum list heading *709* in the 1958 classification, is included in other manufacturing industry. But this item is relatively small, probably less than £12 million in 1936, so that the coverage of manufacturing industry as a whole in the present study is much the same as that in the 1958 classification. However, there are sometimes differences between a single manufacturing industry in the present study and its counterpart in the 1958 classification, and such differences are described in detail in the comments on each manufacturing industry in the next section.

It has been possible to estimate the gross profits of thirteen industrial groups within manufacturing. These groups generally correspond to the order level of aggregation in the Standard Industrial Classification, although for three groups it was necessary to combine orders, and for four other groups it was possible to estimate profits at the level of one or two minimum list headings. The level of aggregation chosen was the lowest level compatible with a sufficiently large number of company accounts available in the sample. For example, when too few company accounts were available to estimate profit for a particular order in the Standard Industrial Classification, this order was combined with a contiguous order with a similar deficiency of company accounts. The section on individual manufacturing industries includes some modifications of the general method of estimating profits described in Chapter 2.

The time-series of gross profit in each of the manufacturing industries is given in Table 4.1, with the industries arrayed in order of their appearance in the 1958 Standard Industrial Classification. On the average, total manufacturing gross profit in the period 1920–38 was £270 million so that each of the thirteen industries would have an average of about £21 million if the classification had been chosen so that each sub-division was the same size. An inspec-

 DOI: 10.4324/9781003183266-5

TABLE 4.1. Gross Profit in Manufacturing Industries, United Kingdom, 1920–38 (£m.)

YEAR	FOOD (1)	DRINK (2)	TOBACCO (3)	CHEMICALS ETC. (4)	METALS (5)	ENGINEER-ING (6)	VEHICLES (7)	METAL GOODS N.E.S. (8)	COTTON (9)	WOOLLENS ETC. (10)	LEATHER ETC. (11)	PAPER & PRINTING (12)	OTHER (13)	TOTAL MANUFAC-TURING (14)
1920	14·6	35·3	8·1	21·6	67·9	21·4	7·2	11·2	21·2	45·2	20·6	27·4	25·2	326·9
1921	17·0	24·3	8·8	12·5	39·3	20·7	2·6	5·4	3·8	12·6	6·6	13·0	12·6	179·2
1922	17·1	27·3	8·7	20·8	25·1	17·0	3·5	5·7	12·3	32·8	21·1	30·9	20·0	242·3
1923	18·6	28·7	9·0	22·8	31·8	19·2	3·7	5·3	10·8	39·0	20·4	32·6	19·9	261·8
1924	18·3	31·5	10·2	23·7	28·9	21·3	5·6	7·3	11·5	34·1	21·1	31·6	24·8	269·9
1925	18·9	32·4	11·0	23·8	17·9	25·4	6·4	8·1	10·2	26·7	20·8	31·3	25·6	258·5
1926	20·3	32·4	11·5	21·6	13·2	25·6	6·9	6·5	2·7	16·7	20·6	26·8	24·3	229·1
1927	21·0	31·8	12·2	24·5	16·8	28·4	10·7	6·2	11·9	25·5	22·8	28·2	27·2	267·2
1928	22·9	32·6	12·1	25·6	18·6	30·6	10·4	8·1	11·7	25·6	22·1	30·5	26·4	277·2
1929	26·4	33·2	12·9	26·9	20·1	32·0	12·7	8·4	4·7	21·5	21·2	33·1	21·7	274·8
1930	27·0	34·3	13·5	23·4	23·5	29·5	11·5	7·9	1·1	10·0	17·1	30·3	23·0	252·1
1931	30·0	31·5	13·3	23·0	14·8	25·0	8·1	5·1	2·9	6·2	12·6	28·3	19·4	220·2
1932	19·5	23·4	10·2	23·8	11·7	15·5	6·2	4·8	3·3	13·1	12·5	21·7	19·5	185·2
1933	20·1	24·6	9·6	26·6	14·7	16·5	7·3	6·9	6·1	20·1	16·5	25·1	24·6	218·7
1934	23·9	28·8	11·8	28·7	22·7	25·5	11·2	6·0	5·5	15·6	16·6	28·7	30·3	255·3
1935	28·4	30·8	13·2	32·3	28·1	39·5	14·7	9·0	5·5	19·3	17·2	31·7	34·7	304·4
1936	32·0	32·3	14·2	34·1	38·2	45·7	18·0	14·0	6·6	24·7	19·0	34·6	37·7	351·1
1937	29·3	32·8	15·7	38·4	54·8	61·7	20·6	15·7	9·9	21·7	19·1	36·5	36·3	392·5
1938	27·5	34·9	16·1	35·0	50·6	72·0	20·5	15·7	7·2	14·5	16·4	33·7	34·9	379·0
m	22·8	30·7	11·7	25·7	28·4	30·1	9·9	8·3	7·8	22·4	18·1	29·3	25·7	270·8

tion of the average profit in each industry shows that seven are above, five are below and one nearly equal to £21 million so that the distribution of industries by profit is roughly symmetrical. In fact, the range is from £7·8 million (cotton) to £30·7 million (drink) and neither of these limits is very far from the mean. It must be remembered that each of these time-series is subject to error, so that it would be undesirable to have an extremely skew distribution of industries by profit, because the time-series of profit for manufacturing industry as a whole would be heavily dependent on the errors in the profits of one or two very large industries in the upper tail of the skew distribution. With the present symmetrical distribution of industries by profit, an upward bias in the largest industry has a greater chance of being counteracted by an opposite bias in other large but slightly smaller industries. Thus the present choice of industries, made on the quite difference basis of availability of company accounts, has a further justification.

The time-series in Table 4.1 are plotted on a semi-logarithmic scale in Figure 4.1. Total manufacturing profits were high in 1920, a reflection of the post-war boom, fell sharply with the slump of 1921, and then increased until 1924. In 1925 their rise was halted and they then fell, possibly as a result of the return to the gold standard. A very sharp fall was experienced in 1926, due to the general strike of that year. The subsequent recovery lasted until 1929, when profits were not very far below their previous peak in 1920. But this boom was checked and the following downswing continued through 1930 to reach a nadir in 1932. In fact, the 1929 level was not approached until 1934. This recovery continued until 1937, no doubt aided by rearmament programmes, as indicated by the experience of the metals industry. But 1937 was a turning point; profits fell in 1938, though this movement was stopped by the onset of the Second World War in 1939. Even so, gross profits in the period 1936–38 were undoubtedly higher than in the early 1920s, so that there was an upward trend over the whole period. This trend may have been due in part to the installation of more capital equipment: it must be remembered that the time-series in Table 4.1 refer to profits, and by themselves do not throw any light on profitability, or on the rate of return on capital.

In general, the individual industries experienced fluctuations in profits similar to those just described for manufacturing as a whole. Exceptional behaviour is discussed in section 4.2. At this stage, comment is confined to overall trends and instability of profits. It can be seen that each of the industries experienced an upward trend

71

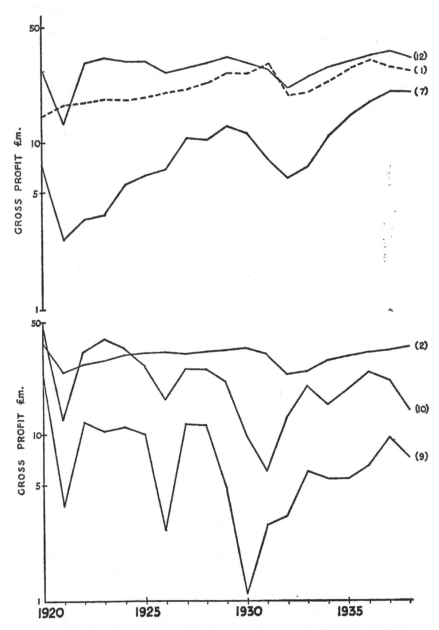

Fig. 4.1 (a). Time series of gross profit in manufacturing industries in columns
(1), (2), (7), (9), (10) and (12) of Table 4.1. Semi-logarithmic scale.

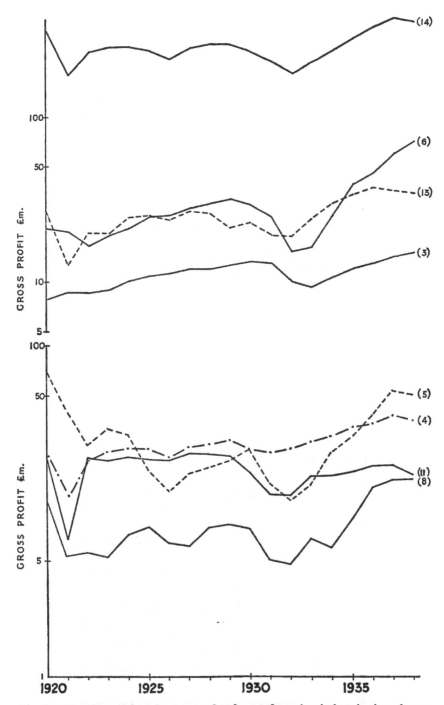

Fig. 4.1 (b). Time series of gross profit of manufacturing industries in columns (3), (4), (5), (6), (8), (11), (13) and (14) of Table 4.1. Semi-logarithmic scale.

TABLE 4.2. *Proportionate Changes in Gross Profit of Samples of Companies in Manufacturing Industries, United Kingdom, 1920–36*

YEAR	FOOD				BREWING				CHEMICALS				ENGINEERING			
	MEDIAN CHANGE	MEAN CHANGE	STANDARD ERROR	N	MEDIAN CHANGE	MEAN CHANGE	STANDARD ERROR	N	MEDIAN CHANGE	MEAN CHANGE	STANDARD ERROR	N	MEDIAN CHANGE	MEAN CHANGE	STANDARD ERROR	N
1920	—	—	—	—	—	—	—	—	—	—	—	—	—	—	—	—
1921	1·164	1·223	0·126	13	0·41	0·54	0·063	20	—	—	—	—	0·969	1·094	0·064	7
1922	1·009	1·098	0·096	15	0·99	1·01	0·084	24	—	—	—	—	0·823	0·988	0·103	13
1923	1·085	1·099	0·043	17	1·03	1·02	0·025	26	—	—	—	—	1·125	1·124	0·071	13
1924	0·984	0·981	0·055	20	1·07	1·10	0·037	26	—	—	—	—	—	—	—	—
1925	1·031	1·117	0·114	22	1·15	1·17	0·053	29	—	—	—	—	—	—	—	—
1926	1·075	1·116	0·069	25	1·02	1·01	0·022	29	—	—	—	—	1·009	0·983	0·046	22
1927	1·033	1·072	0·046	22	1·02	1·01	0·022	29	—	—	—	—	1·108	1·093	0·060	23
1928	0·989	1·042	0·047	22	1·03	1·09	0·038	30	1·030	1·118	0·051	24	1·044	1·102	0·046	21
1929	1·034	1·050	0·046	16	1·03	1·07	0·047	29	0·958	0·990	0·068	18	1·017	1·075	0·087	13
1930	0·946	1·021	0·086	12	1·03	1·08	0·026	28	0·886	0·895	0·041	12	0·903	0·904	0·054	13
1931	1·022	1·092	0·060	12	0·92	0·92	0·024	28	1·027	0·987	0·062	9	—	—	—	—
1932	0·929	0·824	0·128	15	0·81	0·78	0·025	30	1·068	1·149	0·119	12	—	—	—	—
1933	0·932	0·951	0·051	13	1·02	1·02	0·029	30	1·066	1·092	0·077	12	—	—	—	—
1934	1·042	1·078	0·074	15	1·15	1·20	0·041	30	1·079	1·116	0·070	15	—	—	—	—
1935	1·063	0·950	0·078	16	1·08	1·10	0·146	30	1·117	1·160	0·055	14	—	—	—	—
1936	1·030	1·044	0·076	17	1·05	1·06	0·140	30	1·050	1·144	0·059	14	1·084	1·165	0·071	15

TABLE 4.2. *Proportionate Changes in Gross Profit of Samples of Companies in Manufacturing Industries, United Kingdom, 1920–36—continued*

YEAR	LEATHER, ETC. MEDIAN CHANGE	MEAN CHANGE	STANDARD ERROR	N	PAPER AND PRINTING MEDIAN CHANGE	MEAN CHANGE	STANDARD ERROR	N	OTHER MEDIAN CHANGE	MEAN CHANGE	STANDARD ERROR	N
1920	—	—	—	—	—	—	—	—	—	—	—	—
1921	—	—	—	—	—	—	—	—	—	—	—	—
1922	—	—	—	—	—	—	—	—	—	—	—	—
1923	0·972	1·008	0·042	18	1·054	1·077	0·066	17	0·984	1·016	0·057	16
1924	1·027	1·110	0·074	22	0·972	1·074	0·066	24	1·217	1·204	0·062	24
1925	0·995	1·024	0·079	24	0·988	1·021	0·039	28	1·027	1·062	0·049	28
1926	0·987	1·001	0·061	24	0·989	1·022	0·036	31	0·952	0·933	0·050	26
1927	1·107	1·153	0·067	22	1·051	1·132	0·055	28	1·120	1·153	0·062	27
1928	1·025	0·991	0·049	26	1·053	1·053	0·021	37	1·019	1·059	0·048	28
1929	1·013	1·010	0·082	16	1·060	1·059	0·038	24	0·975	0·919	0·043	11
1930	0·831	0·903	0·080	10	0·905	0·904	0·031	16	1·025	0·984	0·058	10
1931	—	—	—	—	0·916	0·892	0·033	18	0·939	0·878	0·058	7
1932	—	—	—	—	1·003	0·996	0·037	16	1·021	1·077	0·112	9
1933	—	—	—	—	1·053	1·060	0·032	17	1·351	1·281	0·112	9
1934	1·020	1·052	0·056	10	1·058	1·047	0·083	18	1·121	1·248	0·138	9
1935	1·046	1·128	0·086	12	1·035	0·999	0·071	19	1·068	1·159	0·080	9
1936	1·120	1·132	0·062	12	1·035	1·044	0·047	18	1·083	1·092	0·083	9

in profits over the whole period, except woollens, leather and paper, whose profits had little or no trend, and cotton, whose profits experienced a clear downward trend, though there were some signs of recovery in 1937. Seven industries (metals, engineering, vehicles, metals not elsewhere specified, cotton, woollens and other manufacturing) had fluctuations which were greater than those for the whole of manufacturing, with the profits in the four metal-using trades especially volatile. At the other extreme, the most stable profits were those of the drink industry.

4.2. METHODS OF ESTIMATION

Food

The food industry includes all those trades covered by minimum list headings *211* to *219*, namely, grain milling, bread and flour confectionery, biscuits, bacon curing, meat and fish products, milk products, sugar, cocoa, chocolate and sugar confectionery, fruit and vegetable products, animal and poultry foods, plus the remaining food trades in minimum list heading *229*. The gross profit in the food industry in Column (1) of Table 4.1 was estimated by applying the year to year median proportionate changes in the profits of a sample of companies to the absolute figures of profit for 1936 estimated by the Oxford University Institute of Statistics, and then adjusting the time-series to fit the benchmarks in 1927 and 1932. There were no years when more than two companies in the sample made losses, so that it was permissible to use the techniques described in section 2.7, throughout the period. The median and mean proportionate changes in profit are given in Table 4.2, together with the standard error of the mean. All these estimates are *before* being reconciled with the Oxford Institute benchmarks.

There are detailed estimates of consumers' expenditure on each food product in Stone[90], but before making any comparison with the time-series of profit, it must be remembered that the final products have been purchased from retailers so that consumers' expenditure includes all the costs and profits of distribution, and taxes which are added to the foodstuffs after they have been manufactured.

It will be noticed that profit in the food trades increased between 1920 and 1921, contrary to the decrease in total manufacturing profit. This exceptional behaviour was checked by another detailed investigation of the published accounts of the companies in the sample for the period, and it was found that nearly all the companies reported a higher profit in 1921 than in 1920, so that the increase could not be attributed to the atypical behaviour of a few giant firms. Moreover, in the next downswing, 1929–31, profit in the food trades again increased slightly. However, before attempting an economic rationalization of the observed increases in food profits during downswings of trade, it is essential to note that profit in food manufacturing fell sharply between 1931 and 1932.

Further official information on gross profit in the food industry relates to sugar refining. Table 4.3 shows the losses made in the refining of beet sugar 1924–38, which relate to fifteen companies before 1935, and to their combination into one company, the British Sugar Corporation, for 1937–38. No allowance has been made for these losses in Table 4.1.

TABLE 4.3. *Losses in the Manufacture of Beet Sugar, United Kingdom 1924–38 (£m).*

YEAR				GROSS TRADING PROFIT (1)	STATE ASSISTANCE (2)	LOSS (3)
1924–25	..	..	..	0·31	0·56	−0·25
1925–26	..	..	..	0·27	1·34	−1·07
1926–27	..	..	..	1·73	3·98	−2·26
1927–28	..	..	..	2·26	5·02	−2·77
1928–29	..	..	..	1·34	3·54	−2·21
1929–30	..	..	..	1·78	5·33	−3·55
1930–31	..	..	..	1·37	7·76	−6·39
1931–32	..	..	..	0·44	2·95	−2·51
1932–33	..	..	..	0·65	4·06	−3·40
1933–34	..	..	..	1·04	5·73	−4·69
British Sugar Corporation						
1937	..	..	..	0·87	2·56	−1·69
1938	..	..	..	0·36	1·11	−0·75

Drink

The drink industry includes brewing and malting, spirit distilling and rectifying, soft drinks and other drinks, that is, all those trades covered by minimum list headings *231* and *239*. The brewing trade was chosen for the pilot study of the estimation of profits in an industry as a whole from samples of the large companies with quotations on the London Stock Exchange, because it is the one industry for which official estimates of profit have been made for each year in the period 1920–38. This supplementary time-series was compared with that compiled from samples of year to year proportionate changes in profit in Chapter 2, where it was concluded that the index based on the samples was reliable.

There is one adjustment to be made when moving from the brewing trade to the whole drink industry. The spirit distilling trade has a very high concentration ratio so it was decided to enumerate the gross profit of Distillers Ltd, which nowadays owns about 90 per cent of the total assets in the distilling trade. These enumerated gross profits were deducted from the Oxford Institute benchmarks of gross true income in the drink industry 1927, 1932 and 1936, to give a new set of benchmarks. The index number of gross profits in brewing was then applied to the new benchmark for 1936 and subsequently reconciled with the new benchmarks for 1932 and 1927, using the interpolation methods described in section 2.7. This technique resulted in a time-series of absolute gross profit in the drink industry, excluding Distillers Ltd. The gross profits of this giant company were then added back, to give the time-series of gross profit in the drink industry shown in Column (2) of Table 4.1. It is assumed that the profits of distilling firms other than Distillers Ltd were too small to affect the time-series of profits in the drink industry. It is also assumed that either the profits of the manufacture of cider, perry and soft drinks were highly correlated with those of the brewing companies, or that in the aggregate such profits were small compared with those of brewing companies. Consumers' expenditure on cider, perry and soft drinks in 1938 has been estimated as £19.3 million by Stone,[90] which is less than 10 per cent of the £199·9 million spent on beer in 1938, so that the second assumption is justified.

Tobacco
The tobacco industry comprises firms manufacturing tobacco, cigars, cigarettes and snuff. This industry has very few firms and is highly concentrated, with the biggest business unit, Imperial Tobacco Co., owning about 70 per cent of the total assets of the industry in 1953. Consequently, it was decided to enumerate the gross profits of Imperial Tobacco Co., Carreras, and three other firms 1920–38 which together, probably accounted for more than 90 per cent of the industry's profits. The British-American Tobacco Company was excluded because it is a subsidiary of Imperial Tobacco Co. and the American Tobacco Corporation and the double-counting of profits had to be avoided. The gross profits estimated from the published accounts are shown in Table 4.4. These published profits slightly over-estimated gross true income; for example in 1936 the gross true income in the tobacco industry was £14·2 million, compared with the

£15·5 million estimated from the accounts. Consequently, the inter-polation methods described in section 2.7 were applied in order to reconcile the total in Table 4.4 with the benchmarks for 1927, 1932 and 1936. The resulting time-series of gross profit in tobacco is shown in Column (3) of Table 4.1.

TABLE 4.4. *Published Profits of Domestic Tobacco Companies, United Kingdom, 1920–36 (£'000's)*

		IMPERIAL	ARDATH	CARRERAS	ABDULLA	PHILLIPS	TOTAL
1920	..	9148·8	83·3	30·5	51·7	−283·9	9030·4
1921	..	9531·1	149·9	77·7	62·9	23·5	9845·1
1922	..	9314·7	186·6	112·8	49·1	75·9	9739·1
1923	..	9397·3	232·5	328·1	55·0	68·0	10080·9
1924	..	10551·4	245·8	468·9	45·0	82·5	11393·6
1925	..	10893·2	349·1	858·4	68·8	174·2	12343·7
1926	..	11370·9	344·0	1093·4	65·4	238·3	13112·0
1927	..	11696·0	376·5	1310·5	64·7	152·9	13600·6
1928	..	11786·6	568·2	1097·5	77·3	172·0	13701·6
1929	..	12145·8	898·4	1265·9	82·8	203·6	14596·5
1930	..	12784·1	657·5	972·6	81·0	159·1	14654·3
1931	..	12784·0	638·9	910·3	61·6	163·6	14558·4
1932	..	11145·0	578·0	963·8	54·0	116·0	12856·8
1933	..	9993·0	569·4	1103·0	−23·2	123·5	11765·7
1934	..	12025·4	569·6	946·1	70·3	227·4	13838·8
1935	..	12901·7	561·9	1131·9	77·0	207·8	14880·3
1936	..	13176·4	543·9	1438·6	75·4	242·4	15476·7

Chemicals and Allied Trades

The chemicals and allied trades form a heterogeneous category which ranges from coke ovens and manufactured fuel to polishes, gelatine and adhesives. It includes all the trades with minimum list headings *261–3* and *271–7*. Two of the biggest business units in the country, Imperial Chemical Industries and Unilever, belong to this category. In the present study, Imperial Chemical Industries has been retained in this category. However, Unilever has been divided into Lever Bros Ltd, which has been assigned to chemicals, and Van Den Berghs and Jurgens, which have been assigned to the food industry. It is true that after 1929 the profits of these subsidiaries of Unilever must have been heavily dependent upon the policies laid down by the parent company, both in real terms, and in the way in which their separate accounts were presented. But the reason for separating the food interests from the soap interests of Unilever is that the Oxford Institute benchmarks are based on Inland Revenue assessments of *companies*, not business units, so that the gross true income for Lever Brothers is in the Oxford Institute benchmark for chemicals, while the gross true income of the Unilever margarine companies is in the food industry benchmark.

The first step in estimating the time-series of gross profit in chemicals and allied trades was to subtract the profits of ICI and Lever Brothers from the benchmarks in 1927, 1932 and 1936. Secondly, the year to year median proportionate changes in the profits of a sample of companies in this industry, given in Table 4.2, were then reconciled with the new benchmarks 1927, 1932 and 1936, using the interpolation technique described in section 2.7. This gave a time-series of absolute gross profit in this industry 1920–36, excluding the profits of the two giant firms. Finally, the gross profits of Imperial Chemical Industries Ltd and of Lever Brothers were added back to give the time-series of absolute gross profit given in Column (4) of Table 4.1.

Metal Manufacture

The major part of Order V, metal manufacture, is the iron and steel industry, including iron and steel (general), steel tubes and iron castings, etc with minimum list headings *311–13*. These iron and steel trades earned 76·9 per cent of total gross true income attributed to metal manufacture in 1936. The remaining 23·1 per cent was earned by the light metals, and copper, brass and base metals trades, with minimum list headings *321* and *322* respectively. The number of companies in these non-ferrous metals trades which were quoted in the London Stock Exchange was very small in this period. Indeed, the interpolation between the Oxford Institute benchmarks of profits in these non-ferrous metal trades has had to be based on a chain index of the means of absolute profits and losses of only seven sets of company accounts. This is a typical case where it is necessary to use inadequate information in an attempt to obtain greater coverage. The resulting time-series of profit is given in Column (1) of Table 4.5.

Fortunately, the year to year changes in the gross profit of metal manufacture as a whole are heavily dependent on the profits of iron and steel companies, and a large number of relevant accounts is available for the period 1920–36. The accounts of iron and steel companies 1926–35 were analysed by Coase, Edwards and Fowler,[98] and their time-series of net profit of unreconstructed iron and steel companies may be regarded as a reliable estimate of the year to year changes in profits. Their net figures were grossed up at the prevailing income tax rates to counteract the effect of different tax rates in different years. It was impossible to estimate depreciation and so the important assumption had to be made that year to year changes in depreciation were small compared with the changes in profit. Year to year changes in the profits of iron and steel companies 1920–26 and 1935–36 were estimated by Al-Atraqchi,[97] who spliced an index number based on the median of the proportionate changes in profits with an index number based on the net profit series in [98] after adjustment for income tax. The resulting index number of gross profits 1920–36 was reconciled with the Oxford Institute benchmarks in the manner of section 2.7. This reconciled index number was then applied to the 1936 benchmark of absolute gross true

TABLE 4.5. *Index Numbers of Gross Profit in the Metal and Vehicles Trades, United Kingdom, 1920–36, 1936=100*

YEAR	NON-FERROUS METALS TRADES (1)	IRON AND STEEL (2)	VEHICLES (3)
1920	168	102	30
1921	62	65	11
1922	27	44	16
1923	48	54	16
1924	58	46	24
1925	63	26	28
1926	47	18	30
1927	40	36	46
1928	57	34	48
1929	66	45	65
1930	57	38	61
1931	40	24	44
1932	34	24	36
1933	39	37	42
1934	57	64	63
1935	74	78	82
1936	100	100	100

income to give a time-series of profit in iron and steel which was added to the time-series of absolute profits of the non-ferrous metal trades to give the series of profits in metal manufacture in Column (5) of Table 4.1.

Engineering
This omnibus category comprises Orders VI and VII in the 1958 Standard Industrial Classification, or all the mechanical, electrical and marine engineering trades, including shipbuilding. Several companies made losses in the period 1930–32 so that the basic method of working in terms of proportionate changes could not be applied.

F

In these years a chain index was constructed from the mean of the absolute profits and losses of companies in the sample, which was applied to the index for the other years based on the median proportionate change in profit. The resulting index was reconciled with the Oxford Institute benchmarks, as explained in section 2.7, and then applied to the absolute gross true income of these trades in 1936 to give the time-series in Column (6) of Table 4.1.

Vehicles

This industrial category includes the manufacture of motor-cars, goods vehicles, motor and pedal cycles, aircraft, railway locomotives and wagons. Manufacturers of many component parts used in these vehicles are also included. Though this classification is based on pre-war practice, it corresponds to those industries with minimum list headings *381–5* and *389* in the 1958 Standard Industrial Classification. The introduction of mass-production techniques into these industries in the inter-war period meant that there were comparatively few companies in these industries by 1938. It is possible, therefore, to enumerate the profits of the few companies which produced most of the output and to construct a chain index number based on the mean of the absolute profit and loss of a set of companies. The chain index number of gross profit in vehicles is given in Column (3) of Table 4.5. After being reconciled with the Oxford Institute benchmarks for 1927, 1932 and 1936, this index number was applied to the 1936 absolute gross true income to give the time-series in Column (7) of Table 4.1.

Profits in the motor-car industry have been studied by Maxcy and Silberston,[69] whose estimates of the profits of the big six motor-car manufacturers, Austin, Ford, Morris, Rootes, Standard, Vauxhall, were used in the chain index number of profits in vehicles during the period 1929–36. But because Maxcy and Silberston estimated profit after interest, it was necessary to add debenture interest to their figures of profit in order to conform to the definition of profit used in the present study.

Metal Goods NES (Not elsewhere specified)

As its name suggests, this category is heterogeneous. It corresponds to Order IX in the 1958 Standard Industrial Classification, and ranges from tools and implements, *391*, to precious metals, *396*, and the remainder item in minimum list heading *399*. Most of the industries included are organized on a small scale, and it is certainly impracticable to enumerate the profits of more than a minute proportion of the firms in these industries. However, it was necessary to use an index number based on the mean of the absolute profits and losses of a sample in which, in most years, more than two companies made losses. After the adjustments described in section 2.7, the resulting index number was applied to the Oxford Institute benchmark for 1936, to give the time-series in Column (8) Table 4.1.

Cotton

The choice of industrial classification in the present study is partly dependent on the accounts available. In general, too few accounts are available to estimate profits at a level of aggregation less than the order level in the Standard Industrial Classification. The case of cotton is an exception. It corresponds to part of two minimum list headings, *412* and *413*, in Order X, and comprises the spinning, doubling and weaving of cotton.

TABLE 4.6. *Index Numbers* of Gross Profit in the Textile Trades, United Kingdom, 1920–36, 1936=100*

YEAR				COTTON (1)	WOOLLENS, ETC. (2)
1920	..	..	..	199	84
1921	..	..	..	58	36
1922	..	..	..	186	98
1923	..	..	..	164	120
1924	..	..	..	174	99
1925	..	..	..	155	71
1926	..	..	..	41	40
1927	..	..	..	180	66
1928	..	..	..	173	69
1929	..	..	..	63	63
1930	..	..	..	3	24
1931	..	..	..	26	17
1932	..	..	..	25	50
1933	..	..	..	75	77
1934	..	..	..	72	60
1935	..	..	..	77	77
1936	..	..	..	100	100

* Reconciled with Inland Revenue estimates for 1927, 1932, 1936

The decline of profit in the cotton industry over the inter-war period has already been noted in section 4.1. Indeed, there was no year 1920–36 when two or more companies in the sample did not make a loss. Consequently, the lognormal sampling scheme could not be applied, and the time-series in Column (9) of Table 4.1 is based on a chain index of means of absolute profit and loss, adjusted to fit the Oxford Institute benchmarks in the manner described in section 2.7.

Woollens and Other Textiles

This industrial category is equivalent to Order X minus cotton. Once again, there were always two or more companies in the sample which made losses during the period 1920–36, and so the mean of the absolute profit and loss of the sample of companies was used to construct the required index number. That is, the same procedure of estimating profit was used in the present case as was used in the case of cotton.

The resulting time-series in Column (10) of Table 4.1 is biased towards the financial experiences of woollen companies because they always formed more than half of the sample of companies in this category, whereas the total profit of woollen firms in 1938 was less than half of the total profits in the category 'woollens and other textiles'. The large relative size of Courtaulds in the category 'woollens and other textiles' was similar to that of Distillers in the drink industry or to that of ICI in the chemical industry. Consequently, it was necessary to adjust the time-series of profit in this particular textile industry group to allow for the fluctuations in the profit of Courtaulds in the manner described earlier in this section in the paragraphs explaining the adjustments made for giant firms in the drink and chemical industries.

Leather Goods, Clothing and Footwear

This industrial category corresponds to Orders XI and XII in the 1958 Standard Industrial Classification and includes leather, leather goods, fur and all forms of clothing and footwear. In addition, it contains the manufacture of tyres and other rubber goods which were included in the leather goods trade in the pre-war Inland Revenue classification, but which now appear in Order XVI, Other Manufacturing Industries. For the years 1920–22 and 1930–33, more than two companies in the sample made losses, so that the mean of the absolute value of profit and losses was used to estimate the movement in the profit of the same set of companies in adjacent years. In the remaining years in the period, the median of the proportionate changes in profit was used to construct an index number of profit which, after being reconciled with the Oxford Institute benchmarks in the manner explained in section 2.7, was spliced with the mean absolute changes 1920–22 and 1930–33 and then applied to the absolute figure of gross true income for 1936. The resulting time-series is shown in Column (11) of Table 4.1.

It must be remembered that the industrial classification of companies is based upon pre-war Inland Revenue practice, so that the many clothing and footwear companies with important retail outlets have been classified to this industry simply because the Oxford Institute benchmark contains the profits of such companies and it is convenient to maintain the convention that such profits may be allocated to manufacturing industry rather than to distribution.

Paper and Printing
This industrial category corresponds to Order XV in the 1958 Standard Industrial Classification, and includes paper-making, printing and bookbinding, publishing and newspapers and stationery. More than two companies in the sample made losses during 1920–22 so the mean of the absolute profits and losses was used for the index number of profit for these years. The resulting index number was spliced with the index of profit for the remaining years, based on the median proportionate changes in the positive profits of the sample of company accounts. The combined index number was reconciled with the Oxford Institute benchmarks as described in section 2.7.

Other Manufacturing Industry
This category differs from the corresponding Order XVI in the 1958 Standard Industrial Classification. It excludes the rubber trades in minimum list heading *491* but includes the trades in Orders XIII and XIV, namely bricks, pottery, glass, cement and other building materials, together with timber, furniture and other wood and cork manufactures. Apart from 1920–22, when more than two companies in the sample made losses, the median proportionate change was used to construct an index number of profit and then reconciled with the benchmarks.

4.3. RELIABILITY OF THE ESTIMATES

The accuracy of the estimates of profits in manufacturing industries depends partly on the interpretation of the company accounts in each sample and partly on sampling error. There are undoubtedly errors in the interpretation of the accounts simply because insufficient information was published by the companies sampled. For example, it is possible that in some company accounts the published profit was an *underestimate*, as a result of conservative accounting practices designed to plough back profit into the companies concerned, so that the first type of error, that of measurement, may be present. The influence of this error is reduced by the fact that the estimates are based on year to year changes in profit, and continuous conservative accounting practices would not have had much effect on the percentage *change* in profit. In addition, the estimates of changes in profit 1920–36 are checked by the absolute benchmarks 1927, 1932 and 1936. It is true that there are also the errors introduced by adjusting the net figure to estimate the taxation on profits, but on the whole it seems reasonable to follow the assumption of the Central Statistical Office[10] (page 166) and to regard the basic data on changes in profit as having an error of 3 per cent, subject to the additional error involved in basing estimates of the change in the profits of a whole industry on a sample of a relatively few companies within the industry.

The simplest solution to the problem of measuring sampling error is to assume that the distribution of the population of proportionate changes in profits is approximately normal, following an argument presented in Chapter 9, and to take the median plus or minus two standard errors as giving the 95·4 per cent confidence interval. Table 4.2 shows the median, mean and standard error of the mean proportionate changes in profits for those years when it was possible to use the lognormal sampling method to estimate changes in profit. The standard error of the median, which is equivalent to 1·25 times the corresponding standard error of the mean, measures the extent to which the median change is typical of the changes in profits of all companies in the sample. It must be remembered that the median changes in profits in Table 4.2 are before adjustment to fit the benchmarks for 1927, 1932 and 1936, as explained in section 2.7.

4.4. COMPARISON WITH OTHER ESTIMATES

Alternative estimates of profits for several industries in inter-war years were provided by Carruthers,[35] by the *Economist*,[100] and by Hope.[56, 106] In addition, there are estimates for individual industries, such as those for iron and steel, which have been described in section 4.2. Whenever such sources were regarded as superior to the samples of company accounts they were used to estimate profits in Table 4.1. It follows that whenever the alternative sources were not used—and for most industries in most years they were not—there were reasons for supposing that the present samples of company accounts were in some sense more reliable indicators of changes in profits. These reasons are explained in the present section.

There are at least five general reasons for preferring the time-series of profits developed here to other estimates. First, the latter were developed before the authoritative benchmarks were compiled by the Oxford University Institute of Statistics, whereas the present estimates make extensive use of the benchmarks. Secondly, as a result of the detailed industrial breakdown of the Oxford figures, the present time-series of profits are consistent with the Standard Industrial Classification. Thirdly, the present estimates have been made for the whole period 1920–38 instead of for parts of the period. They are thus consistent with the other items in national income estimated by the Department of Applied Economics, University of Cambridge, for the same period. Fourthly, the estimates based on samples of company accounts include a measure of the dispersion of profit changes around the mean as shown in Table 4.2, whereas the other estimates give no indication of the dispersion. Fifthly, in compiling the present time-series an attempt has been made to overcome the formidable problem of estimating the profits of an industry from a knowledge of only the largest firms' profits by the use of a lognormal sampling scheme. In the alternative estimates the problem of sampling from such skew distributions has been ignored.

There are also some specific reasons for preferring the present estimates, depending on the alternative source being considered. Carruthers[35] used profits after debenture interest, after depreciation and after taxation, so that his time-series are influenced by changes in the tax rates over time. Moreover, the time-period covered is only 1928–37. For these reasons alone, it is not permissible to compare his index numbers with the absolute figures in Table 4.1.

For some industries Carruthers used a similar industrial classification, namely for the drink, cotton, coal and paper and printing industries. He examined the accounts of thirty-two companies in the drink industry, which is about the same number used on the average to calculate the proportionate changes in drink profits in the present study, so that his figures do not have any advantage on this score. However, he used the accounts of only four companies in cotton and ten in coal, so that his estimates of profits in these industries are considerably less reliable than the corresponding figures in the present study. In the paper and printing industry he used fifteen company accounts, which is again a smaller number than used here.

For other industries a direct comparison between the estimates in Table 4.1 and those of Carruthers is made difficult, if not impossible, by the different definitions of industries. For example, Table 4.1 has nothing comparable to Carruthers' category 'building, contracting, sanitary engineers, decorating, etc.'. Carruthers combined the food and tobacco industries, examining eighteen accounts, but it is clear that the total must be heavily influenced by the results of the tobacco companies, especially if the Imperial Tobacco Company was included in his sample, even though total gross profit in the food industry was generally more than twice as great as the total profit in the tobacco industry 1928–37, as can be seen from Table 4.1. For this reason it seems preferable to separate the food and tobacco industries as in Table 4.1.

Carruthers stated that his index of profit in cotton is unreliable because it depends on the performance of one large company and three comparatively small companies. His separation of woollen manufacturing (nine companies) from other textiles (eight companies) does not seem justified in view of the small size of the two samples. His samples of ten coal and nine iron and steel companies are obviously less reliable than the estimates in Column (3) of Table 3.1 and Column (5) of Table 4.1. On the other hand he has large samples of companies (twenty-six and twenty-three) in his two classes of engineering industry. Unfortunately, these two categories overlap the Standard Industrial Classification minimum list headings and, because of this, are less useful than the estimates for the various engineering industries in Columns (6), (7) and (8) of Table 4.1.

The various sub-sections in Carruthers' category 'chemicals, etc.' presumably have much in common with the chemicals and allied trades in Column (4) of Table 4.1. But his 'leather, boots and shoes' category appears to exclude clothing and is not comparable with Column (11) of Table 4.1. Again, his category 'warehousemen, drapers, etc.' may have some firms in common with those with profits in Column (1) of Table 6.2, but he considered only ten companies compared with the average of twenty-one company accounts examined in the wholesale distributive trades in the present study. Finally, he listed forty-six companies, out of his total sample of 260, as 'all other classes', which has no counterpart in the present work.

It must be emphasized that these differences between the index numbers of Carruthers and the estimates in Table 4.1 are described in order to prevent invalid comparisons, and not to criticize the methods used by Carruthers; he did not have the advantage of working with the Standard Industrial Classification, with a series of Oxford Institute benchmarks for individual industries, or with a large sample of companies classified by the Inland Revenue so that they correspond to the benchmark industries.

During the inter-war period, the *Economist*[100] published the net profits of companies whose accounts it had received during the previous quarter. It also provided some industrial classification of the companies reporting their results, though this is not comparable with the classification used in the present study. The number of companies reporting to the *Economist* fluctuated over time, and

TABLE 4.7. *Index Numbers of Net Profit in Motor and Cycles Trade, Iron, Coal and Steel Trades, Textile Trades, and in Shops and Stores,* Economist *Linked Series, 1936=100*

YEAR			MOTOR AND CYCLE (1)	IRON, COAL AND STEEL (2)	TEXTILES (3)	SHOPS AND STORES (4)
1920	..	..	—	179	31	59
1921	..	..	—	115	78	31
1922	..	..	—	87	196	34
1923	..	..	58	103	223	72
1924	..	..	116	74	237	78
1925	..	..	106	30	221	84
1926	..	..	122	20	146	89
1927	..	..	130	36	208	94
1928	..	..	141	39	224	106
1929	..	..	157	57	156	109
1930	..	..	120	47	67	102
1931	..	..	33	24	46	83
1932	..	..	3	17	62	77
1933	..	..	51	31	94	78
1934	..	..	66	57	94	84
1935	..	..	78	75	92	92
1936	..	..	100	100	100	100
1937	..	..	112	131	107	105
1938	..	..	108	137	64	103

between the same quarters in different years, so it is not possible to use the raw figures as measures of the fluctuations in profit. Again, the *Economist's* figures relate to the time when it received the accounts from the companies and not to the year in which the profits were earned. These problems may be overcome by constructing a linked series or chain index number comparing the profits of the same set of companies in adjacent years, and by introducing an appropriate time-lag, say six months, between date of reporting and the relevant working year.

Such linked series of profits were constructed for four industries which appeared to have a counterpart in the present work: iron, coal and steel; motor and cycles (including aviation since 1934); textiles, and shops and stores. The index numbers are shown in Table 4.7 with 1936=100. The *Economist*'s profits figures are net of debenture interest, depreciation and taxation of company saving, so that the series cannot be used to interpolate between the benchmarks of gross true income. The changes in the tax rates during the period 1920–38 also affect the value of reported profits, so the figures cannot be used to measure the performance of different industries over time. However, they may be relevant for some economic problems and have been used, for example, by Lipsey and Steuer[62] in the context of the relationship between profits and changes in wages where they would appear to be the relevant measure of profit. But there is an important qualification to their reliability: as pointed out by Parkinson,[74] the *Economist*'s series are biased towards the more successful companies. This limitation is especially important when it is remembered that no adjustments have been made to the figures to reconcile them with the Oxford Institute benchmarks for 1927, 1932 and 1936.

There are many similarities between Hope's[106] work on profits and the present study. Both use the summaries of accounts in Moody cards, both use the Moody figure of 'earned for ordinary' in the estimation of gross profit, and both use the same convention of regarding the difference between this Moody figure and gross ordinary dividend as equal to net saving after taxation and depreciation. In one respect Hope's estimates of manufacturing profits are superior to those in Table 4.1; he was able to use the accounts of 378 companies in various manufacturing industries compared with the 241 used here. But this advantage is outweighed by the five factors listed at the beginning of this section. Hope developed his estimates not only before the Oxford Institute's figures were available, but also before the publication of the preliminary estimates for 1936–38 in the 92nd Inland Revenue Report.[1] Moreover, his industrial classification differs considerably from the standard form. In addition, he excluded the years 1920–23 and 1936–38 from his analysis so that there are important differences in coverage between the two studies.

The differences in the classification partly explain why he was able to use as many as 378 company accounts in manufacturing industry; many of these companies have to be placed in non-manufacturing industries if the Inland Revenue classification of companies is to be followed. For example, Hope used forty-eight company accounts in the food industry, but included many companies (such as International Tea Stores, Maypole Dairy, Lovell and Christmas) which ought to have been classified as companies engaged in the distributive trades. This is one reason why the present study uses 103 company accounts in wholesale and retail distribution whereas Hope used only fifty-eight company accounts in his three distributive categories, stores, hotels and restaurants, textile merchants.

For the drink industry Hope used forty-nine company accounts compared with the average figure of twenty-nine used in Table 4.1. But the estimates of gross profit in Column (2) of Table 4.1 are based on a sampling scheme designed to overcome the problems of sampling from the skew size distributions of brewing firms, and are also consistent with the Oxford Institute benchmarks for 1927, 1932 and 1936. Another advantage is that the present estimates include the profits of soft drink manufacturers which were classified to the food industry by Hope.

In the present study the British American Tobacco Company is excluded from the tobacco industry, partly because it operates primarily overseas and cannot be regarded as part of a domestic manufacturing industry, and partly to avoid double counting of the profits of this subsidiary which were passed on to the Imperial Tobacco Company. Hope included this giant company in the British tobacco manufacturing industry, and this is an important difference between the two studies, because the profits of the British American Tobacco Company were comparable with the *total* profits of *all* the tobacco manufacturing companies outside the Imperial Tobacco Company.

The number of companies in the chemicals, paper and printing, and textiles industries in each of the studies is much the same, so there is little to choose between them from this point of view. In Columns (5), (6), (7), (8) of Table 4.1 the profits of the metals and metal-using trades are based on the accounts of eighty-nine companies on the average. On the other hand, Hope used 148 company accounts for the same set of industries, but his classification once again has the disadvantage of not being comparable with the Oxford Institute benchmarks, which is particularly unfortunate when so many companies overlap several metal trades, and it is impossible to guess the industrial classification of a particular company used by the Inland Revenue. But this general disadvantage may be out-weighed in some cases where information is required for a particular subdivision for which profits are not published by the Inland Revenue. For example, the shipbuilding and locomotive and wagon trades are given separate treatment by Hope, whereas figures are not given in such detail in the present study, in the 92nd Inland

Revenue Report,[1] or in the Oxford Institute benchmarks. Another advantage of Hope's estimates is that he used more company accounts than does the present study for the leather and clothing industries, and he was also able to separate them. However, both these advantages must be set against the fact that his separate series are inconsistent with the Oxford Institute benchmarks.

CHAPTER 5

CONSTRUCTION AND PUBLIC UTILITIES

5.1. GENERAL REMARKS

THE present chapter estimates gross profit in the construction trades and in the public utilities, which correspond respectively to minimum list headings *500* and *601–3* in the 1958 Standard Industrial Classification, with the qualification that the building and contracting activities of local and central government authorities are excluded from construction. Public utilities comprise the electricity, gas and water supply establishments operated by local government authorities and by companies, though Table 5.1 excludes the profits of local authorities, which have to be kept separate for social accounting purposes. It must be remembered that the gross profit being measured

TABLE 5.1. *Gross Profit in Construction and Public Utilities, United Kingdom, 1920–38 (£m.)*

YEAR				CONSTRUCTION (1)	PUBLIC UTILITIES (2)
1920	..	..	..	11	14·4
1921	..	..	..	8	12·3
1922	..	..	..	6	17·3
1923	..	..	..	5	17·4
1924	..	..	..	6	16·6
1925	..	..	..	11	17·0
1926	..	..	..	15	15·9
1927	..	..	..	17	20·7
1928	..	..	..	6	22·0
1929	..	..	..	13	22·4
1930	..	..	..	9	25·6
1931	..	..	..	8	21·3
1932	..	..	..	9	23·2
1933	..	..	..	13	23·1
1934	..	..	..	15	23·4
1935	..	..	..	15	25·0
1936	..	..	..	19	26·6
1937	..	..	..	19	28·3
1938	..	..	..	20	28·4

 DOI: 10.4324/9781003183266-6

is *before* interest on loan capital so that even if these public utilities did not attempt to maximize their profits at all times, because of their social obligations, they had to earn at least enough profit to cover their loan charges.

The relevant time-series of profit 1920–38 are shown in Table 5.1. Supporting tables and explanations of the sources and methods used in compiling Table 5.1 are given in sections 5.2 and 5.3. The reliability of the estimates is assessed in section 5.4, but it may be said at the outset that the reliability of the estimates of profit in construction is low, indeed very low compared with the very reliable time-series of profits in the public utilities.

It is possible, therefore, that errors in the construction time-series cause some of the fluctuations observed in Column (1) of Table 5.1. The upswing 1924–27 and sharp fall in 1928 are not observed in the time-series of profits of other industries. On the other hand, the construction time-series is heavily influenced by the Lomax[63] index of physical production in building and contracting, and the fluctuations in this index, which are transmitted to the profit time-series, are the result of the careful research of many students of building cycles. In short, the present time-series of profit in building is the result of piecing together the results obtained by many scholars and reconciling them with the Oxford Institute benchmarks. The end-product may not be as reliable as one would wish, but it is difficult to see how a more reliable series could be obtained from the available facts.

Profit in public utilities did not fluctuate as much as in construction, which is not surprising. It showed a strong upward trend throughout the period, though this was primarily due to the growth of profit in the electricity supply industry over the period, which is shown by Table 5.4.

5.2. METHODS OF ESTIMATION—CONSTRUCTION

The primary source of information on construction, or building and contracting, in the inter-war years is the Census of Production,[4] though the figures contained in the reports for 1924, 1930 and 1935 require very careful interpretation, if only because such a large proportion of the value added in these trades was contributed by firms below the limit of eleven employees and was excluded by the Census.

The first step was to estimate the total number of employees in the building trades covered by the Census of Production. Table 5.2

94

shows the total employment in all firms. The number of working proprietors was estimated as the number of returns received from small firms plus the number of firms not making returns, following Chapman.[36] The total number of employees in Row (5) is the difference between total employment and the number of working proprietors. This figure multiplied by Chapman's estimate of average employee compensation gives the total of wages and salaries shown in Row (9).

TABLE 5.2. *Census of Production Data for Building and Contracting, 1924, 1930, 1935*

	1924	1930	1935
Employment ('000)			
(1) Firms with over 10 employees ..	419·05	453·57	502·28
(2) Firms with 10 or less employees..	95·34	155·84	243·98
(3) Total (1)+(2)	514·39	609·41	746·26
(4) Working proprietors	40·63	44·03	67·45
(5) Total employees=(3)−(4) ..	473·76	565·38	678·81
Value Added £m.			
(6) Firms with over 10 employees ..	80·6	94·0	100·0
(7) Firms with 10 or less employees	15·9	29·2	44·5
(8) Total (6)+(7)	96·5	123·2	144·5
(9) Employee compensation	73·6	89·1	102·6
(10) Gross margin=(8)−(9)	22·9	34·1	41·9

The value added for firms with employment greater than ten shown in Row (6) was extracted from the Census, as were the figures for small firms in 1924. But in 1930 and 1935 the value added by small firms was not estimated by the Census. The figures shown in Row (7) for these years were estimated by multiplying the total employment of small firms (including working proprietors) by the value added *per capita* of firms in the size class eleven to twenty-four employees, the smallest size class for which information is available in the Census.

The figure of gross margin in Row (10) is the total value added minus the estimate of employee compensation. This margin includes selling and transport costs in addition to gross profit and thus sets an upper limit to gross profit in the building trades covered by the Census. The trouble is that the coverage of the Census may be as low as 80 per cent, in terms of employment (cf. Bowen and Ellis[34]), and because of this Chapman increased the Census of Production figures of employment, using data provided by the Census of Population and by the unemployment insurance statistics. This explains why the figures in Rows (5) and (9) of Table 5.2 differ from those in Chapman.[36] The reason for not attempting to increase the gross margin in Row (10) to allow for the low coverage of Census of Production is that the primary object is to estimate an *index number* of profit 1920–36 in these trades, rather than the *absolute amount* of profit, and it seems reasonable to assume that the gross margin excluded by the Census fluctuated in sympathy with the recorded gross margin. The next task is, therefore, to estimate this gross margin for the years in the inter-war period not covered by the Census of Production.

TABLE 5.3. *Output, Employment and Gross Margin in the Building and Contracting Industry, United Kingdom, 1920–38*

YEAR	GROSS OUTPUT (MAYWALD) £M. (1)	EMPLOYMENT COVERED BY CENSUS OF PRODUCTION '000 (2)	VALUE ADDED £M. (3)	GROSS MARGIN £M. (4)	ADJUSTED INDEX OF GROSS PROFIT (5)
1920 ..	(444)	518	—	47·7	85·8
1921 ..	331	496	—	34·1	64·0
1922 ..	232	450	—	23·9	44·8
1923 ..	214	461	—	22·0	41·4
1924 ..	223	474	96·5	23·1	43·3
1925 ..	247	511	126·7	45·7	85·7
1926 ..	248	518	145·3	62·5	117·3
1927 ..	258	555	158·8	70·5	132·4
1928 ..	251	555	123·1	36·0	67·5
1929 ..	250	555	136·7	49·5	92·8
1930 ..	249	565	123·2	34·0	63·9
1931 ..	228	561	113·8	27·5	51·5
1932 ..	204	528	104·4	25·4	47·6
1933 ..	231	569	120·2	36·2	68·0
1934 ..	266	632	136·6	42·9	80·5
1935 ..	293	679	144·5	42·0	78·7
1936 ..	319	731	164·8	53·3	100
1937 ..	352	772	168·3	48·3	—
1938 ..	356	785	166·4	42·0	—

It is not difficult to estimate employee compensation for these years, thanks to the painstaking research of Chapman. It is true that her figures of employee compensation relate to the whole trade, whereas the present study is confined to that portion covered by the Census, but her figures of average employee compensation still apply. Thus the required estimate of employee compensation may be obtained by multiplying these averages by the figures of numbers of employees in Column (2) of Table 5.3, which were estimated by assuming that this series fluctuated in proportion to the total time-series of employees in the building trades given by Chapman.[36]

However, it is difficult to estimate value added in the inter-Census years, and such a series is necessary in order to obtain the required estimates of gross margin by subtracting employee compensation. Maywald[99] gives a time-series of gross output or sales in the building trade 1920–38, and has also estimated an index of building costs.[70] Lomax[63] has provided an index of physical production in the building and contracting trade. These results form the basis of the estimate of value added and of gross margin in Columns (3) and (4) of Table 5.3.

Maywald describes three different experiments in estimating gross output in this industry 1920–38 and the one represented in Column (1) enabled him to 'predict' the Census results of 1924 and 1935, using the known gross output in 1930 as a pivot, with great accuracy in the case of 1924 and with a tolerable error for 1935. Briefly, he started with the Chapman time-series of employee compensation, raised this throughout by the ratio of the 1930 value added to 1930 employee compensation, and then added estimates of raw material costs, based on a constant real consumption of material per employee, adjusted for price changes by his index of building costs. This technique yielded results which may be satisfactory for estimating one part of capital formation, but it is not used in the present study, apart from the period before 1924, because it was thought desirable to obtain estimates of profits independently of the estimates of employee compensation, so that a comparison between the two time-series might be made at a later stage. Instead, value added for the inter-Census years has been estimated by distributing the difference between the three Census years according to an index number obtained from the Lomax[63] index of physical production multiplied by the Maywald[70] index of building costs. The resulting series of value added in current prices is shown in Column (3), and the difference between this and employee compensation gives the required estimates of gross margin in Column (4).

Unfortunately, this method could not be extended to the years before 1924 because it yielded large *negative* estimates of gross margin. A glance at the values of the Lomax[63] index, which gives the mean annual physical production for 1920 as only one half of the 1926 figure suggests that Lomax's index for 1920–23 is too low. It is certainly inconsistent with Maywald's series of gross output for these years, even when the latter is adjusted for changing prices. In view of this conflict, it was decided to reject the negative estimates of gross margin derived from the Lomax index for 1920–23, and simply assume that the gross margin as a percentage of gross output in 1920–23 was the same as in 1924, the earliest Census year for which reliable information is available.

The time-series of gross margin in Column (4), in index number form with 1936=100, was used to interpolate between the Oxford Institute benchmarks in the manner described in section 2.7. Briefly, the index number based on Column (4) was adjusted so that it coincided with the Oxford Institute benchmarks for 1927, 1932 and 1936. The adjusted index number is shown in Column (5) of Table 5.3. No attempt has been made to allow for the exclusion of persistent losses by the benchmarks of gross true income: for each benchmark year the Oxford Institute figure is preferred to any other figure derived from Column (4), and because of this the index number in Column (5) differs from a previous estimate made in Column (3) of Table 1 in [52]. Corrections were made for the period before 1927 by reducing the index number based on Column (4) Table 5.3 for each year 1920–27 by the ratio of the adjusted 1927 index number to the crude index number for 1927, i.e. multiplying by 88·4/132.4. The index number in Column (5) when applied to the 1936 benchmark, gives the time-series in Column (1) Table 5.1 for 1920–36. The figures for 1937 and 1938 were extracted from the Oxford Institute survey[111] and adjusted for national defence contribution, as explained in section 2.4.

5.3. METHODS OF ESTIMATION—PUBLIC UTILITIES

In the period 1920–38 the electricity, gas and water industries occupied the borderline between private enterprise and public control; some areas were supplied by companies and others by local authorities. The financial results of the portion of these industries operated by local authorities in England and Wales were published in the *Local Government Financial Statistics* ,[13] and similar information is available for Scotland and for Northern Ireland in the *Local Taxation Returns* of these countries.[22] In the summaries of these results published in the *Statistical Abstract*,[23] the figures of expenditure include loan charges and transfers to reserves, which are not deductible from profits for the purpose of compiling gross true income, and are therefore inadequate for the purpose of estimating a time-series of gross profit.

The gross profit of all authorized electricity undertakings in Great Britain 1920–38, shown in Table IV in [52], was used to estimate an index number of electricity profits in the United Kingdom, on the plausible assumption that the profits earned by electricity supply in Northern Ireland either moved in much the same way as those earned in the mainland, or might be assumed to be too small to have any significant effect on the figure for the United Kingdom. The same assumptions apply to the rest of Ireland before 1922.

The basic source of information in [11] is not superior to the summaries in the *Statistical Abstract*[23] which gave figures of working receipts and expenses for each year from 1921 to 1937. The result for

TABLE 5.4. *Gross Profit in the Electricity, Gas and Water Supply Industries,* 1920–38 (£m.)*

YEAR			ELECTRICITY (1)	GAS (2)	WATER (3)	PUBLIC UTILITIES (4)
1920	..	..	8·4	5·7	0·28	14·4
1921	..	..	6·0	5·9	0·37	12·3
1922	..	..	7·3	9·2	0·81	17·3
1923	..	..	7·9	8·7	0·77	17·4
1924	..	..	8·3	7·5	0·76	16·6
1925	..	..	8·3	7·9	0·80	17·0
1926	..	..	8·1	7·0	0·76	15·9
1927	..	..	9·8	10·0	0·85	20·7
1928	..	..	11·6	9·4	0·96	22·0
1929	..	..	12·7	9·2	0·53	22·4
1930	..	..	15·2	9·2	1·18	25·6
1931	..	..	10·8	9·4	1·13	21·3
1932	..	..	12·5	9·3	1·35	23·2
1933	..	..	12·7	8·9	1·54	23·1
1934	..	..	12·9	8·9	1·64	23·4
1935	..	..	14·1	9·0	1·87	25·0
1936	..	..	15·6	8·9	2·12	26·6
1937	..	..	17·0	9·1	2·16	28·3
1938	..	..	17·2	9·0	2·15	28·4

* Excluding local authorities.

the financial year 1937–38 includes those of companies for the year ending December 31, 1937, of Local Authorities in England and Wales for the year ending March 31, 1938, and of Local Authorities in Scotland for the year ending May 15, 1938. In the present study all these results are regarded as being primarily attributable to the previous calendar year, 1937, and the corresponding assumption is made for the results of every other financial year in the period 1920–38.

The difference between total revenue from working and total working expenses was regarded as the required figure of gross profit. It does not equal the published figure of gross surplus from working, because the latter includes some non-trading income. Two adjustments have been made to the figures in [23]. First, the figures published for the years before 1931 are after the deduction of income tax, so this has been added back at the prevailing standard rates. Secondly, no financial figures are available for 1920, but since the output figure is published for all years, it was possible to estimate profits in 1920 by multiplying the mean profit per million units generated for 1921 and 1922 by the output for 1920.

The resulting time-series of gross profit in the electricity supply industry was then reconciled with the Oxford Institute figures in the manner of section 2.7, to give a time-series of gross true income over the period which may be denoted by p. The next step was to estimate the proportion of such profits earned respectively by companies and local authority undertakings. The *Annual Reports of the Ministry of Health*,[12] and the summaries of local government finance in the *Statistical Abstract*,[23] provide estimates of the profit from electricity supply accruing to local authorities. These estimates were subtracted from the time-series denoted by p to give the figures of profits in electricity shown in Column (1) of Table 5.4.

Column (2) of Table 5.4 gives a time-series of gross profit in the gas supply industry 1920–37 which was extracted from the Board of Trade *Returns Relating to Authorized Gas Undertakings*.[3] The figures of gross profit are before loan charges and the timing of the results is the same as in the electricity supply industry.

This time-series was used to interpolate between the Oxford Institute benchmarks, using the technique described in section 2.7, to obtain a time-series total gross true income earned by the gas supply industry 1920–36. The basic source in [3] gives estimates for companies and for local authorities, which may be denoted by c and by a respectively. The required time-series of gross true income earned by *companies* in the gas industry was then estimated by multiplying the time-series of total gross true income by $c/(c+a)$.

Gross profit in Column (3) of Table 5.4 is derived from the difference between the working receipts and working expenses of water supply undertakings operated by local authorities in England and Wales. The primary source is *Local Government Financial Statistics*,[13] but the relevant figures were in fact abstracted from the appendices to the *Annual Reports of the Ministry of Health*,[12] where the figures are available at the required level of aggregation. The summaries in the *Statistical Abstract*[23] also relate to all local authorities in England and Wales but give no details of loan charges which have to be excluded from expenditure when estimating a gross profit equivalent to gross true income.

100

The differences between local authority profits and the corresponding Oxford Institute benchmarks for 1927, 1932 and 1936 were regarded as estimates of gross true income earned by water supply companies in those years. Estimates of gross true income earned by companies in other years during the period 1920–38 were obtained by assuming that it fluctuated in the same way as the reported profits of local authority water supply undertakings, after the latter had been reconciled with the Oxford Institute benchmarks, using the techniques of section 2.7. Column (3) of Table 5.4 gives the results.

The three time-series of gross true income earned by companies in the electricity, gas and water supply industries were then added to give the time-series shown in Column (2) of Table 5.1 for the period 1920–36. The figures for 1937 and 1938 are those in the Oxford Institute report[111] minus the estimates of local authority profits.

5.4. RELIABILITY OF THE ESTIMATES

The time-series of profit in building and contracting is subject to the errors of measurement, of estimation and of coverage: even the year to year changes of Column (5), Table 5.3, are only rough estimates. But it would be wrong to regard the figures as merely conjectural. They are dependent on the careful research of economic statisticians and certainly have more justification than have informed guesses. Nevertheless, they are undoubtedly less accurate than the estimates for public utilities. In short, they should be classified as category C, with more than 10 per cent error.

The estimates of profits for electricity and gas supply in Table 5.4 are firm figures and may be placed in category A, with less than 3 per cent error. They are not subject to any type of error to any significant extent. On the other hand, the absolute figure for the water supply industry in Table 5.4 refers to local authorities in England and Wales and the use of this series to estimate corporate profit in the water supply industry may introduce several errors. But in the case of the water-supply industry, which was relatively free from fluctuations in profit, it is safe to assume that such errors are unimportant. Consequently, corporate water supply profits may be placed in category B, with less than 10 per cent error.

5.5. COMPARABILITY WITH OTHER ESTIMATES

The estimates of profit in the public utilities were derived from official summaries of accounts, so there is no point in comparing the results with any unofficial summary of accounts, such as *Field's Analysis of the Accounts of the Principal Gas Undertakings in England, Scotland and Ireland*[102] or *Garcke's Manual of Electricity Undertakings*.[104] On the other hand, it would be highly desirable to compare the estimates of profit in construction with another time-series, possibly one based on a sample of company accounts. At first sight, the Hope[106] index of profit in building 1924–35, based on twenty-five company accounts, appears to be just the comparable time-series required to check Column (1), Table 5.1. Unfortunately, a closer examination reveals that Hope's sample of building company accounts is heavily weighted by the cement manufacturers, and other ancillary trades outside building and contracting, so that the two time-series are not comparable.

CHAPTER 6

TRANSPORT AND DISTRIBUTION

6.1. GENERAL REMARKS

THE present chapter provides estimates of profit earned by the transport and distributive trades. Transport includes railways, road transport, shipping, docks and canals, and approximates to those trades which now have minimum list headings *701* to *705* in the 1958 Standard Industrial Classification. Small differences arise in the cases of telephones, air transport and storage: in the pre-war Inland Revenue classification adopted here, there is a small item of profit earned by the telephone industry, presumably at Hull, outside the Post Office,* which is ignored in the present chapter. Profit in the air transport industry in the inter-war period was also considered too small to be included. Finally, the category 'storage', *709.2* in the 1958 Standard Industrial Classification, is nowadays included in 'miscellaneous transport services', whereas the pre-war Inland Revenue classification excluded storage from transport and allocated it to 'miscellaneous trades' in manufacturing.

Distribution may be divided into the wholesale and retail trades. The wholesale trade comprises merchants, warehousemen and other agents connected with the distribution of goods, or all those trades now covered by minimum list heading *810* in the 1958 Standard Industrial Classification. In the present study, retail distribution covers more than the trades with minimum list heading *820*. The Oxford Institute benchmark of profit is based on pre-war Inland Revenue practice and includes not only the purely distributive shops but also those engaged in semi-industrial activities such as bakers' shops. In addition, it includes a few trades such as laundries, catering and hotels, which appear in 'miscellaneous services', Order XXIII in the 1958 Standard Industrial Classification. In 1938 about 53 per cent of the total profit in retail distribution was earned by the purely distributive shops, 10 per cent by the catering and hotel trade, and no less than 37 per cent by retailers engaged in semi-industrial

---

* The telephone system in Kingston-upon-Hull is municipally owned and its annual telephone accounts are published. Cf. Hazelwood.[54]

 DOI: 10.4324/9781003183266-7

activities. Some of the latter remain in the 1958 minimum list heading *820*, but because a few trades have been reclassified it is impossible to obtain a completely accurate comparison between the time-series of profit in the retail trades 1920–38 and the corresponding time-series since 1949. However, some comparison can be made between profit in retail distribution 1936–38 and the corresponding post-war time-series by using the 1949 Inland Revenue Report,[1] Cmd 8052, which reclassified a 1 in 5 sample of assessments on retailers' profits 1936–38 according to the 1948 Standard Industrial Classification.

The transport and distributive trades are very important. Together they earned about 40 per cent of total gross true income, excluding the gross true income of the finance industries, in the United Kingdom in 1938. This percentage may be compared with the 35 per cent earned by all manufacturing industries together. In spite of the great emphasis traditionally placed upon manufacturing firms in economic analysis, the manufacturing sector was not much larger in terms of profits in 1938 than the distributive trades which by themselves earned about 29 per cent of total gross true income. Moreover, this percentage excludes the surpluses earned by the Co-operative Movement, which are treated separately here, since they were not assessed for income tax, and are excluded from the benchmarks of profit in the distributive trades.

Table 6.1 gives estimates of the gross true income 1920–38 earned by four transport industries, namely, railways, road transport, docks and canals, and shipping. Corresponding time-series for the distributive trades are given in Table 6.2, together with the surpluses of the wholesale and retail sections of the Co-operative Movement. The sources and methods used in compiling these time-series are described in sections 6.2 and 6.3, while sections 6.4 and 6.5 examine their reliability and their comparability with other estimates.

A comparison of Columns (1) and (2) of Table 6.1 shows the opposite fortunes of the railways and road transport 1920–38. From 1922 gross profit earned by the railways had a clear *downward* trend, whilst profit in road transport had an *upward* trend throughout the period, in spite of the Road and Rail Traffic Acts of 1930 and 1933 which were aimed at restricting the growth of road transport at the expense of the railways. Indeed, it is apparent that, in terms of profit, road transport had overtaken the railways by 1938. It is true that both industries were adversely affected by the acute depression 1929–33, but the forces making for the growth of road transport appear to have been strong enough to have enabled it to recover more quickly than the railways, though it is possible that the restric-

TABLE 6.1. Gross Profit in Transport Industries,* United Kingdom, 1920–38 (£m.)

YEAR			RAILWAYS (1)	ROAD TRANSPORT (2)	DOCKS HARBOURS, ETC. (3)	SHIPPING (4)
1920	..	..	6·8	11·6	0·6	28·6
1921	..	..	−8·8	13·0	0·6	26·0
1922	..	..	43·5	11·0	0·7	24·6
1923	..	..	39·0	13·2	0·7	23·9
1924	..	..	35·7	17·2	0·7	23·9
1925	..	..	33·9	18·1	0·7	22·1
1926	..	..	17·5	18·9	0·7	22·5
1927	..	..	39·0	19·0	0·8	24·1
1928	..	..	37·7	21·8	0·7	24·4
1929	..	..	41·3	20·5	0·7	25·3
1930	..	..	34·4	21·1	0·7	25·8
1931	..	..	30·5	24·6	0·6	14·5
1932	..	..	24·4	19·7	0·5	9·9
1933	..	..	26·5	21·3	0·6	18·0
1934	..	..	28·8	26·0	0·6	19·5
1935	..	..	30·3	27·9	0·6	23·9
1936	..	..	33·4	30·4	0·5	24·6
1937	..	..	35·3	35·2	0·6	39·9
1938	..	..	27·1	34·5	0·6	33·9

* Excluding undertakings operated by local authorities.

TABLE 6.2. Gross Profit in the Distributive Trades, United Kingdom, 1920–38 (£m.)

YEAR			WHOLESALE (1)	RETAIL (2)	CO-OPERATIVE SOCIETIES WHOLESALE (3)	RETAIL (4)	TOTAL WHOLESALE (5)	RETAIL (6)
1920	..	..	106·8	159	−0·08	25·70	106·7	185
1921	..	..	66·9	182	−4·50	18·27	62·4	200
1922	..	..	93·0	188	0·71	14·28	93·7	202
1923	..	..	85·7	194	1·13	16·24	86·8	210
1924	..	..	88·5	211	1·65	19·30	90·2	230
1925	..	..	85·9	213	1·90	20·26	87·8	233
1926	..	..	83·7	207	2·01	20·85	85·7	228
1927	..	..	84·1	225	2·64	23·20	86·7	248
1928	..	..	89·9	228	2·47	24·59	92·4	253
1929	..	..	84·6	226	2·65	25·94	87·3	252
1930	..	..	80·4	203	2·36	26·74	82·8	230
1931	..	..	69·8	195	4·25	26·42	74·1	221
1932	..	..	50·6	186	3·53	24·89	54·1	211
1933	..	..	54·1	199	2·82	23·73	56·9	223
1934	..	..	64·2	207	4·51	25·32	68·7	232
1935	..	..	71·1	220	4·10	26·71	75·2	247
1936	..	..	82·6	227	4·55	28·36	87·2	255
1937	..	..	89·8	226	5·31	29·75	95·1	256
1938	..	..	77·9	219	5·97	30·89	83·9	250

tions of entry into road transport under the 1930 and 1933 Acts may have contributed to the growth of profit in this industry by reducing competition.

Gross true income in the shipping industry, shown in Column (4) of Table 6.1, was much larger than that earned by the docks and canals industry, but it was more unstable, showing a much greater percentage fall in the downswing of the depression 1929–33. This apparent instability was probably real, even though the sources of shipping profits, namely company accounts, are less reliable than the accounts of local authorities used to compile the time-series docks and canals.

The benchmarks of gross true income in 1927, 1932 and 1936 are reliable enough for these two transport industries, but it is worth noting a special reason for the inaccuracy of the published accounts of some shipping companies in the 1920s, which came to light in the Kylsant case. Lord Kylsant was chairman of one of the largest shipping companies, the Royal Mail Steam Packet Company, which was able to show profits in its published accounts which bore little or no resemblance to the profits it was actually earning in the 1920s. During the First World War the company accumulated vast reserves for taxation, and was able to use these reserves in the period 1920–28 to hide losses which were being earned from current working. In 1922 the Government gave shipping companies a special obsolescence allowance to compensate them for replacing their war losses at high post-war prices. This allowance was set against the excess profits duty which the company was liable to pay to the Inland Revenue but for which it had already provided, so that the obsolescence allowance was another source for hiding current losses. The misleading information in the published accounts of this company came to light in the trial of Lord Kylsant,* but it is important to remember that he was found *not guilty* on the part of the charge relating to publishing deceptive accounts but *guilty* on the part relating to the publication of a misleading prospectus. Since it was not illegal to include repayments of excess profits duty from the Treasury in profit figures published in the accounts of shipping companies, it is possible that some of the other shipping companies' accounts used here are also misleading, so that biased estimates of year to year changes in profits may have been made. Unfortunately, the extent of this bias is not known; the only safeguard is that the benchmarks, being Inland Revenue figures of gross true trading income, would exclude such repayments and reflect profits earned

* A description of this case is given by Vallance[94], Chapter 12.

from current working. Even so, the benchmarks tend to under-estimate losses, for reasons given in Chapter 2, so that the time-series of shipping profits in the 1920s must be used with special care. The most that can be said in favour of the time-series of shipping profits in Table 6.1 is that it looks plausible, and that it is highly cor-related with the Chamber of Shipping's index of freight rates [58], the zero-order correlation coefficient being 0·71, excluding the freak year 1920, and 0·57 including it.

When comparing the profit of the wholesale trade with that of the retail trade in Columns (1) and (2) of Table 6.2, it is essential to remember that in the present context profits are gross of stock appreciation. Purely monetary changes in the value of stocks are likely to influence the gross true income of wholesalers more than that of any other trade, and this influence could easily explain the greater fluctuations of wholesale profits compared with profits in retail distribution. Because of this, the correlation between whole-sale and retail profits is not very high, the zero-order correlation coefficient being given by $r_{12}=0·41$, where the subscripts refer to the columns in Table 6.2. The extreme observations for 1920 were omitted from this calculation, so the low correlation cannot be attributed to the exceptionally high wholesale profits in 1920.

6.2. METHODS OF ESTIMATION—TRANSPORT

Railways
The railway companies made annual financial and statistical returns to the Ministry of Transport, including a detailed breakdown of working expenses and receipts, together with an analysis of these results for railway working, and for each ancillary business such as canals, docks and road transport operated by the railway companies. Figures of net receipts from railway working, equal to the difference between working receipts and working expenses of railway working, are given in the summary tables in the *Statistical Abstract*.[23] A time-series of net receipts from railway working is given in Column (1) of Table 6.1. There is one adjustment to the published figures which relates to the period before 1927. The method of compiling railway companies accounts was changed in 1928, but the former 1927 figures were recalculated on the new 1928 basis, enabling the series of net receipts 1920–26 to be multiplied by the ratio of the new 1927 figure to the old 1927 figure, so that the whole series 1920–38 could be made internally consistent.

The figures for 1936–38 of £33·4, £35·3 and £27·1 million may be compared with the Inland Revenue figures of gross true income of £28·2, £29·5 and £27·0 million for the same years. The discrepancy for 1936 and for 1937 is surprisingly large, though there is hardly any difference between the two sets of figures for 1938. An inspection of the details of working receipts and expenses reveals that net receipts increased by some £2 million between 1936 and 1937 primarily because both passenger and goods receipts increased more than did working expenses. The increase in gross true income of £1·3 million is consistent with this, though the absolute level of gross true income seems on the low side. But the difference between the two sets of figures between 1937 and 1938 is striking in the present context when both sets of data are from official sources. The railway returns show quite clearly that while passenger receipts were much the same in 1938 as in 1937, goods train receipts fell by £6·8 million, working expenses increased by £1·6 million and net working receipts fell by £8·2 million. Yet the Inland Revenue gross true income fell by only £2·5 million. This inconsistency makes it necessary to choose between two figures from reliable sources. The figures in the railway returns are to be preferred because their constituents are known. It is assumed that the figures of gross true income in this case are a less reliable guide to current profits because they have been compiled after various unknown adjustments, possibly including losses of some ancillary services in previous years, to meet the requirements for levying taxation and not to measure the financial performance of the railways in the years in question.

Road Transport

The road transport industry (*702–3*) includes road passenger transport operators, road hauliers, furniture removers and car-hire firms, in addition to tramways and omnibus firms. The financial results of tramways, light railways and trolley vehicles are conveniently summarized in the *Statistical Abstract*.[23] In 1936 the total gross profit of such undertakings was £3·4 million. But this is small compared with the Inland Revenue gross true income figure of £33·6 million for all road transport and, consequently, this series cannot be used as an index of road transport profit.

The accounts of local authorities, summarized in [13], [15], [22], give the profits of tramways, trolley buses and omnibuses operated by local authorities. For England and Wales the total gross profit from this source in 1936 was £5·3 million. This series is also too small to be used as an index of road transport profit and in any case it duplicates, to some extent, the profit of tramways in the £3·4 million in the previous paragraph. The accounts of road transport under-takings operated by the railways, summarized in [14], are a further source of information, but gross profit of such road transport in 1936 was only £122,800, and again is very small compared with the figure of £33·6 million to be explained. It appears that this type of official source does not help to estimate profit in road transport 1920–38.

There remains the possibility of using a sample of the accounts of road transport companies to estimate profits 1920–38. Unfortunately,

TABLE 6.3. *Gross Profits in Transport Industries,*
United Kingdom, 1920–36 (£m.)

	PROFITABILITY IN ROAD TRANSPORT (PORTER)	DOCKS, HARBOURS LOCAL AUTHORITIES	SHIPPING			
YEAR			MEDIAN PER CENT CHANGE	MEAN PER CENT CHANGE	STANDARD ERROR	N
	PER CENT	£M.				
	(1)	(2)	(3)	(4)	(5)	(6)
1920 ..	—	4·67	—	—	—	—
1921 ..	—	4·04	0·88	0·88	0·038	26
1922 ..	—	4·26	0·94	0·91	0·057	26
1923 ..	—	4·01	0·97	0·94	0·045	21
1924 ..	—	4·44	1·00	1·04	0·049	22
1925 ..	—	4·37	0·92	0·86	0·043	25
1926 ..	—	4·38	1·01	1·06	0·056	28
1927 ..	—	4·69	1·08	1·16	0·058	26
1928 ..	7·49	4·95	0·98	0·95	0·034	26
1929 ..	7·61	5·10	1·00	1·03	0·061	23
1930 ..	8·22	4·44	0·98	0·96	0·064	17
1931 ..	9·32	4·70	—	—	—	—
1932 ..	8·80	4·39	—	—	—	—
1933 ..	7·47	4·69	—	—	—	—
1934 ..	8·69	4·87	—	—	—	—
1935 ..	8·94	4·71	—	—	—	—
1936 ..	8·86	4·79	1·04	1·16	0·085	19

there were comparatively few public companies in road transport: most firms were unincorporated or were private companies with no obligation to file copies of their accounts with the Registrar of Com-panies. However, *Porter's Financial Statistics*[112] estimated the mean profitability of a sample of thirteen road transport companies which were quoted on the Stock Exchange. This is given in Column (1) of Table 6.3, but no figures are available for the period before 1928 because this statistical service was not operating then. Profitability is defined as net profit as a percentage of net assets, so this figure differs considerably from the gross profit which is required. But the main reason for not using this interesting time-series, derived from a rarely used source, is that the number of companies in the sample is too small. Moreover, there seems little chance of increasing the size of sample either for the period 1928–38 covered by Porter's or in the period 1920–27.

The general absence of information on profits in road transport made it necessary to use the Inland Revenue 196.6 forms described in section 2.2. The relevant category of the Inland Revenue 196.6 forms in this instance was heterogeneous; it included profits of electric power and light and telephone in addition to those of road transport. Profits in 'telephones' during this period were very small and may be ignored, but the same is not true for electricity. The year to year changes in the total gross true income of all firms in the electricity and road transport industries earning more than £2,000 per annum are given in these summaries for 1920–38. These changes in percentage form were applied to the sum of the gross true income of road transport and the gross profits of authorized undertakings in electricity for 1936, in order to estimate gross profits in both industries 1920–36. The total profits in road transport were then estimated by subtracting the gross profits in electricity from this sum 1920–36.

The final step in the estimation of gross profit earned by the road transport industry was to exclude the profit accruing to road transport undertakings operated by local government authorities. The summaries of local government finance in [12], [23] provided estimates of gross profit earned by local authorities in road transport, which were subtracted from the gross profit of the whole road transport industry previously estimated. The resulting time-series, after being reconciled with the Oxford benchmarks in the manner described in section 2.7, is shown in Column (2), Table 6.1.

Docks, Harbours, Canals, etc.
In 1936 the total gross true income earned in the docks and canals group of industries was about £6 million. The summaries of local government finance in [12], [23] reveal that the gross working receipts of docks, etc., operated by local authorities in England and Wales alone were about £4·8 million in 1936, so that most of the profit in this industrial sector was, in fact, earned by local authorities. Indeed, a previous study [52] used the local government results to estimate an index number of profit in this industry. But because of the need to exclude the profits accruing to local government, some revised method must be used which will estimate solely the *company* profits earned in docks, canals, wharves and the other industries included in the minimum list heading *705*, though in view of the relatively

small magnitude involved—less than £1 million—it would be un-economic to develop very elaborate estimation techniques.

The first step was to extract from [12] the difference between the working receipts and expenditure of docks, harbours and the like operated by local authorities in England and Wales. The results are given in Column (2) of Table 6.3. The required information for Scotland and Northern Ireland was not readily accessible for all years, so it was decided to increase the figures for England and Wales by one-seventh to allow for the other countries. This size of increase was chosen because it was the ratio of the expenditure on harbours, etc., by local authorities in Scotland to the corresponding expenditure in England and Wales, including loan charges.

Then, on the assumption that movements in the profit of companies followed those of local authorities, the resulting time-series was used to interpolate between the Oxford Institute benchmarks for 1927, 1932 and 1936, in the manner described in section 2.7, to give a time-series of total gross true income earned by local authorities and companies in docks, harbours, etc. A *provisional* estimate of the gross true income of companies in this industry was then made by subtracting the adjusted time-series of profits in Column (2) of Table 6.3 from the time-series of total gross true income. But this time-series, being subject to all the errors of differencing, was not regarded as sufficiently reliable to publish, though it had to be used to estimate the absolute level of company profit in this industry in the benchmark years 1927, 1932 and 1936–38. A completely different source of information, however, was used to interpolate between the estimates of absolute company profit in the benchmark years.

For the period 1924–35 it was possible to substitute the index of company profits in docks, harbours and canals compiled by Hope.[106] This index was used to extrapolate from the figure for 1935 to give the estimate of profit earned in docks, canals, etc., excluding the profits accruing to local authorities, which is shown in Column (3) of Table 6.1. The estimates for 1920–23 were obtained by applying an index number of profits based on the net receipts of docks, harbours, wharves and canals operated by the railway companies, as reported in the Railway Returns,[14] to the profits figure for 1924 derived from Hope's index number.

Shipping
The final transport industry considered here is shipping. The number of shipping companies with Stock Exchange quotations is large enough for their proportionate changes in gross profits to be esti-

mated by the lognormal sampling scheme. The theoretical and practical difficulties are reviewed in Chapter 2. Briefly, it is postulated that the proportionate change in profit is independent of the size of the company, so that the mean of a sample of proportionate changes drawn from the larger quoted companies is a reliable measure of the mean proportionate change in profit of companies of all sizes. Proportionate change in the present context means the ratio of company's profit in the year t to its profit in the year $t-1$. In order to counteract the effect of extreme proportionate changes in profit, and for other theoretical reasons explained in Chapter 2, the median change is used instead of the mean change. The median and mean change in profit, together with the standard error of the mean, are given in Columns (3)–(5) of Table 6.3. From these year to year changes it was possible to compute time-series of absolute gross profit, using the 1936 benchmark. In years when two or more companies in the sample made losses, namely 1930–34, a chain index number was constructed based on the mean of the absolute figures of profits and losses of the same set of companies in adjacent years. The results were then spliced with the index numbers for 1920–30 and 1935–36 based on the median proportionate changes in Column (3) of Table 6.3. The combined index number of gross profits for 1920–36 was then used to interpolate between the Oxford Institute benchmarks, as explained in section 2.7, and the resulting time-series of gross profit is given in Column (4) of Table 6.1.

6.3. METHODS OF ESTIMATION—DISTRIBUTION

As for shipping, the number of companies in the distributive trades with Stock Exchange quotations is sufficiently large for the year to year changes in profit to be estimated by the lognormal sampling method described in Chapter 2. It is true that the proportion of the total profit in distribution earned by the distributive companies quoted on the Stock Exchange was, and is, very low. It is also true that the number of distributive firms quoted on the Stock Exchange was minute compared with the total number of firms in distribution. But the sampling error of the median proportionate change in profit does not depend on the number in the sample as compared with the number in the population, it depends on the square root of the number in the sample. The median, mean and standard error of the mean proportionate changes in profit for wholesale and retail distribution are given in Table 6.4 for all years 1920–36 except those in which more than two companies in the samples earned losses, when the alternative method of using the difference between the means of the absolute values of profit was used to construct the required index numbers, for the reasons given in section 2.6. The index numbers of gross profit derived from Table 6.4 were then reconciled with the Oxford benchmarks, using the techniques explained in section 2.7, but with one modification to the results obtained for 1920–23. The Minutes of Evidence in Volume III of the Report of the Royal Commission on Food Prices[21] include the results of an Inland Revenue investigation into the profit of the wholesale and retail food distributive trades for the years 1920–23. The proportionate changes in the mean profit of companies and firms in these Inland Revenue samples were applied to one-third of each of the estimates of profit in wholesale and retail distribution in 1923, to give estimates of profit in the food sections of these trades for 1920–23. The assumption that profit in food distribution was one-third of all profit in distribution in 1923 is very crude, but it has some justification; the first year for which estimates of all types of consumers' expenditure are available is 1938, and in that year the expenditure on food was about one-third of the expenditure on all goods sold through the distributive trades [9], [90].

Profit in the non-food distributive trades was then estimated in the usual way by applying the median proportionate changes in Table 6.4 to two-thirds of the total figure for wholesale and retail profit in 1920. The estimates of profit in the food and non-food distributive trades were then added back to give revised series for wholesale and retail distribution 1920–23, which are included in the final series in Columns (1) and (2) of Table 6.2. Since profit in food distribution was remarkably stable in the period 1920–23, in spite of the sharp changes in the levels of prices and employment, and since companies distributing food were under-represented in the samples obtained from the Stock Exchange archives, it is not surprising that the inclusion of separate estimates of profit in food distribution tended to reduce the fluctuations in distributive profits.

The surpluses earned by the Co-operative Societies given in Columns (3) and (4) of Table 6.2 were extracted from the *Reports of the Chief Registrar of Friendly Societies*.[17] A comparison of Co-operative surpluses with the Inland Revenue gross true income series 1936–38 shows that the Co-operative Wholesale Societies earned about 6 per cent of total profits in wholesale distribution 1936–38, while the corresponding percentage earned by Co-operative Retail Societies was over 17 per cent. The sums of Co-operative surpluses and corporate profits are given in Columns (5) and (6) of Table 6.2.

TABLE 6.4. *Proportionate Changes in Gross Profit in the Distributive Trades, United Kingdom, 1920–36*

YEAR	WHOLESALE				RETAIL			
	MEDIAN (1)	MEAN (2)	ERROR (3)	N (4)	MEDIAN (5)	MEAN (6)	ERROR (7)	N (8)
1920	—	—	—	—	—	—	—	—
1921	—	—	—	—	1·15	1·09	0·070	15
1922	—	—	—	—	1·09	1·14	0·069	22
1923	0·91	0·96	0·056	26	1·02	1·06	0·030	27
1924	1·03	1·01	0·044	28	1·08	1·13	0·033	39
1925	0·97	1·03	0·049	34	1·01	1·02	0·030	40
1926	—	—	—	—	0·97	0·98	0·030	40
1927	—	—	—	—	1·09	1·16	0·038	43
1928	—	—	—	—	1·02	1·02	0·027	45
1929	0·98	0·99	0·039	20	1·00	1·01	0·032	36
1930	1·00	0·93	0·046	15	0·90	0·93	0·029	35
1931	0·91	0·94	0·055	16	0·96	0·95	0·051	34
1932	0·77	0·88	0·090	11	0·96	0·97	0·036	37
1933	0·94	0·97	0·029	12	1·06	1·13	0·041	39
1934	1·01	1·01	0·081	16	1·04	1·09	0·027	38
1935	0·97	0·92	0·043	17	1·06	1·13	0·029	40
1936	1·03	0·98	0·033	18	1·03	1·06	0·026	41

6.4. RELIABILITY OF THE ESTIMATES

At this stage it is necessary to examine the estimates in Tables 6.1 and 6.2 for evidence of four types of error: error of measurement, estimation, coverage and of sampling. In addition, an attempt must be made to indicate the likely size of the error, using the categories of error denoted A, B and C by the Central Statistical Office.

The profit of the railway companies given in Column (1) of Table 6.1 is a firm figure and its error category is A, less 3 per cent error. On the other hand, the estimates of road transport profit in Column (2) of Table 6.1 are less reliable because they are based on differencing 196.6 form data and these are subject to fluctuations which are highly erratic, difficult to interpret, and therefore suspect. Accordingly, road transport profit is placed in category C, with more than 10 per cent error, though this does not modify the general picture of a strong upward trend in the profits of road transport over the period 1920–38. The profit of docks, harbours and canals in Column (3) of Table 6.1 is based partly on results of local authorities in England and Wales, but subject to errors produced by differencing. Even so, the basic data are fairly reliable, and so is Hope's index, and it seems reasonable to allocate this time-series to category B.

The profits of shipping, wholesale and retail distribution are based on samples of company accounts. The figures in the accounts are subject to errors of the first, second and fourth types. However, in spite of the shortcomings of published company accounts and the subsequent adjustments to add back income tax, it is likely that the first and second type errors are not large, so that the basic data on proportionate change may be placed in category A. But there is still the sampling error to be considered. The simplest solution to this problem of error is to regard the distribution of proportionate changes in profit as nearly normal, following an argument given in Chapter 9, and take the median proportionate change plus or minus two standard errors, each of which is approximately 1·25 times the standard error of the mean given in Table 6.3 and 6.4, so that the true median proportionate change will lie within this range more than 95 times out of 100.

6.5. COMPARABILITY WITH OTHER ESTIMATES

The main difficulty which arises when comparing the present estimates of profit with those made by other research workers is that there is no reliable method of assessing which estimate is the more accurate.

A comparison of some of the present results with those obtained by Hope[106] for 1925–35 is possible. The relevant industries in common are railways, shipping and retail distribution. The profits of railways in Table 6.1 are very reliable estimates standardized over time, and are to be preferred to any independent analysis of the published accounts of the four main-line railway companies, though there is not much to choose between them. Hope's index for shipping is based on the accounts of thirty-eight companies, while his index for stores is based on sixty-eight companies. He considered more companies than the twenty-four included in the figures for shipping and the forty-two for the distribution in Table 6.3 and 6.4, and this is one reason for preferring Hope's index numbers. Against this must be set the fact that the index numbers for shipping and retail distribution in the present study allow for the extreme skewness of the size distribution of companies in these industries, and the use of the *median* proportionate change counteracts the effect of organizational changes, such as mergers and acquisition, which generally affect total profit in aggregates of company accounts. Moreover, the fact that fewer companies have been considered in the present study is allowed for in the standard errors of the proportionate changes in profit in Tables 6.3 and 6.4. Consequently, it is legitimate to argue that the time-series of profit in Tables 6.1 and 6.2 are to be preferred to those estimated by Hope.

CHAPTER 7

THE APPROPRIATION OF COMPANY PROFITS IN MANUFACTURING INDUSTRY

7.1. INTRODUCTION

CHAPTERS 1 to 6 have been concerned with the estimation of time-series of gross profit. It would be valuable to have corresponding time-series for each constituent part of gross profit, namely, gross ordinary and preference dividends, gross debenture interest, depreciation and gross business saving. In addition, a time-series of the taxation borne by the dividends and by undistributed profits would also be interesting. The Blue Book on National Income[9] presents a corporate income appropriation account for 1938 and for each year since 1946. The gross trading profits of companies and trading services of public corporations, together with other corporate income, are allocated between (*a*) dividends and interest, (*b*) taxation and (*c*) undistributed profits after taxation but before providing for depreciation and stock appreciation. There is a further analysis of this appropriation account between companies, non-nationalized companies, and public corporations. But there is no analysis by industry, except for a separate treatment of the appropriation of the profits of companies in the insurance, banking and finance sector.

This deficiency is partly made good by the annual Inland Revenue Reports[1] which estimate the appropriation of companies' *sales*, including gross profit, in each industry from large samples of company accounts. This analysis is available for 1936–38 and for each year since 1948. In the early years, the total sales figure, or turnover, of each industry was broken down into material costs, personnel costs, other costs, increase in stocks, trading profit, depreciation allowances, losses allowed for income tax purposes, non-trading income, gross dividends and loan interest, royalties, profits tax, income tax and the balance representing net undistributed profit. Each item was expressed as a percentage of turnover. The current (1963) analysis is less detailed, but profits, dividends and undistributed profits as percentages of turnover are still published.

DOI: 10.4324/9781003183266-8   116

The Oxford Institute survey[111] did not examine appropriation of income in 1927 and 1932, so that the most that can be done is to extrapolate the Inland Revenue estimates for 1936–38 back to 1920 using the appropriations of profit in the samples of accounts drawn to estimate changes in profits 1920–36. This extrapolation is confined to manufacturing industries, partly because the corporate sector is more important in manufacturing than in distribution, the other major sector for which accounts could have been used to estimate appropriation, and partly because the traditional economic theory of the firm, which is the source of various hypotheses about firms' propensities to save, is formulated with manufacturing in mind. It is possible to estimate the appropriation of profits earned in the railways and in the shipping industries and in the corporate sector of the distributive trades, but it is impracticable to estimate such appropriations for any of the other industries considered in Chapters 3 to 6.

The methods used to estimate the appropriation of company profits in the manufacturing sector as a whole, and in individual manufacturing industries, are described in section 7.3. A comparison is made in section 7.4 between the results and the estimates made by the *Economist* and by Hope.[106] These sections are preceded by a general commentary in section 7.2 on the present results of estimating the appropriation of profit 1920–38.

7.2. GENERAL REMARKS

In the present study, the economic analysis of the appropriation of manufacturing profit is carried out at successively lower levels of aggregation: the analysis for all companies in manufacturing is followed by a breakdown into individual manufacturing industries, which in turn is followed by an analysis of the variations of the appropriation of profit between different companies in the same industry. A systematic inquiry is conducted in Volume II of this study, but at this stage it is worthwhile making a few brief remarks on the appropriation of profit at the highest levels of aggregation.

Row (1) in Table 7.1 shows the total gross true income of companies in manufacturing industry and Row (2) gives estimates of the wear and tear allowances made to these companies by the Inland Revenue. The methods of estimation are described in section 7.3. Row (3) is net true income and is the difference between Rows (1) and (2). In fact, net true income was on the average 87 per cent of gross true income during the period 1920–38.

TABLE 7.1. *The Appropriation of Company Profits in Manufacturing Industry, United Kingdom, 1920–38 (£m.)*

	1920	1921	1922	1923	1924	1925	1926	1927	1928	1929	1930	1931	1932	1933	1934	1935	1936	1937	1938
(1) Gross true income ..	254·7	151·4	204·8	221·2	228·1	218·4	187·9	225·8	249·3	240·3	221·0	192·6	161·1	193·0	227·9	275·3	320·3	363·8	354·2
(2) Wear and tear ..	19·5	16·2	17·5	20·8	29·1	21·5	20·1	26·0	30·9	33·9	25·3	23·7	28·6	28·1	35·6	41·0	50·1	57·2	59·7
(3) Net true income= (1)−(2) ..	235·2	135·2	187·3	200·4	199·0	196·9	167·8	199·8	218·4	206·4	195·7	168·9	132·5	164·9	192·3	234·3	270·2	306·6	294·5
(4) Other income— losses ..	92·6	53·2	73·7	78·7	78·2	77·3	66·0	78·5	85·7	81·0	76·7	66·1	51·5	64·3	74·8	91·0	105·0	101·3	149·8
(5) Total income= (3)+(4) ..	327·8	188·4	261·0	279·1	277·2	274·2	233·8	278·3	304·1	287·4	272·4	235·0	184·0	229·2	267·1	325·3	375·2	407·9	444·3
(6) Dividends and interest (gross) ..	146·9	130·7	161·0	181·7	151·6	162·3	146·4	174·3	176·7	162·7	177·3	169·4	138·2	152·6	169·1	203·0	222·9	261·9	333·5
(7) Royalties (gross) ..	7·0	7·0	7·0	7·0	7·0	7·0	7·0	7·0	7·0	7·0	7·0	7·0	7·0	7·0	7·0	7·0	7·0	7·0	7·0
(8) Gross Business Saving ..	173·9	50·7	93·0	90·4	118·6	104·9	80·4	97·0	120·4	117·7	88·1	58·6	38·8	69·6	91·0	115·3	145·3	139·0	103·8
(9) Taxation on business saving ..	52·2	15·2	23·2	20·3	26·7	21·0	16·1	19·4	24·1	23·5	19·8	14·6	9·7	19·2	20·5	25·9	35·9	50·2	66·4
(10) Net business saving=(8)−(9) ..	121·7	35·5	69·8	70·1	91·9	83·9	64·3	77·6	96·3	94·2	68·3	44·0	29·1	50·5	70·5	89·4	109·4	88·8	37·4

The next item in Row (4) is most important. It consists of other income minus losses, and on the average was some 35 per cent of gross true income over the period. Other income comprises that part of profit which the Inland Revenue authorities impute to the ownership of property and tax under Schedule A, plus interest and dividends received whether directly assessed for taxation or taxed at source. An inspection of the 94th Inland Revenue Report,[1] Cmd 8436, pages 66 to 73, shows that in most industries 'other income' fell sharply relatively to gross true income between 1938 and 1947. Part of this decline may be attributed to the fall in property income derived from overseas, and another part to the stability of the notional income assessed for income tax under Schedule A. Both types of income are included in the Inland Revenue category 'other income' and both may be included in the national income. But 'other income' also contains interest received from United Kingdom government securities and dividends from the non-manufacturing sector, which may be regarded as transfer payments to be excluded from the national income. However, 'other income' in Row (4) is so large compared with gross true income that it is clear that it must have influenced companies' decisions on dividend policy and so it cannot be excluded from the analysis of the appropriation of profit. That is, the relevant profit to be appropriated is not the gross true income in Row (1), which is used for estimating the contribution of profit to gross national income, but the total income in Row (5), which is the sum of Rows (3) and (4).

The figure for royalties in Row (7) is treated separately by the Inland Revenue authorities because such payments are not deductible from companies' gross true income: companies automatically pay income tax on royalties, which is deducted before paying the royalties to their owners, so that the Inland Revenue collects the tax on royalties at source. For the study of the appropriation of profit it is convenient to subtract this small item from total income. The dividends and interest item in Row (6) is *before* taxation and includes payment of debenture interest and preference dividends, which generally have to be paid by companies, in addition to the dividends on ordinary shares, which are the result of decisions made by the companies in the light of the income available for distribution. The income tax on this item which is paid by the company is recovered from the shareholders. The balance remaining in Row (8) is gross company saving, and over the whole period this item was about 38 per cent of the total income available for distribution, namely Row (5) minus Row (7). The taxation of company savings, shown

119

in Row (9), was some 10 per cent on the average, so that the net amount ploughed back by companies in manufacturing was about 28 per cent of total income.

But this figure of net company savings is subject to two major qualifications. First, though some losses are included in Row (4), where they have been offset against positive profits, there were undoubtedly many losses which occurred during the benchmark years 1936–38 which are excluded from the Inland Revenue's item 'other income less losses' because many companies earned insufficient positive profit to offset their losses and were thus not assessed for income tax. Such losses should be regarded as dissaving and subtracted from the net saving in Row (10), for the purpose of estimating the total internal funds available for investment in corporate manufacturing. Secondly, the estimates of profits include stock appreciation, and it is possible that the downward trend in prices throughout the period may have produced underestimates of profit by the Inland Revenue as the result of purely monetary declines in the value of stocks. The effects of the second qualification counteract those of the first, but though the net result is not known, it is assumed to be small on the average throughout the period.

An inspection of Row (10) supports those who believe that business saving is very much a residual item. In the downswings of 1921, 1929–32 and 1938, net business saving fell more sharply than dividends and increased more in the upswings which followed. It is also interesting to note that the increased taxation resulting from imposition of the national defence contribution in 1937 and 1938 seems to have been borne by business saving in those years. If it is legitimate to regard business saving as a residual item, it follows that dividends rather than savings is the variable to be explained in any econometric analysis of the appropriation of profit.

The variation of dividends between different industries is shown in Table 7.2, which gives the ratio of gross dividends and interest to total income in the thirteen industrial groups for which profits were estimated. It is impossible to estimate absolute figures because of the absence of information on non-trading income and depreciation in most of the company accounts sampled, as explained in section 7.3. The unweighted average ratios for each industry are given in the bottom row of Table 7.2, and range from 112·6 per cent for the cotton industry down to 44·6 per cent for the vehicles industry. The figure for the cotton industry does not mean that over the whole period this industry was able to pay out in dividends and interest more than its total income, because the average is not weighted by

120

TABLE 7.2. Ratio of Dividends and Interest to Total Income for Companies in Manufacturing Industries, United Kingdom, 1920–38, per cent

YEAR	FOOD (1)	DRINK (2)	TOBACCO (3)	CHEMICALS (4)	METALS (5)	ENGINEERING (6)	VEHICLES (7)	METAL GOODS (8)	COTTON (9)	WOOLLENS ETC. (10)	LEATHER ETC. (11)	PAPER & PRINTING (12)	OTHER (13)	TOTAL (14)
1920	69·5	44·4	72·8	76·9	54·2	53·0	36·8	75·8	93·0	17·4	23·9	45·6	36·8	44·8
1921	73·2	62·3	66·9	99·1	72·9	74·8	86·5	145·2	248·6	74·5	71·5	68·1	57·2	69·4
1922	52·7	61·0	79·3	80·6	84·8	88·5	47·2	56·8	70·2	37·4	43·4	47·1	50·0	61·7
1923	49·5	65·1	86·9	81·9	65·8	82·2	40·5	49·0	77·1	37·7	41·0	45·6	46·3	65·1
1924	49·0	63·6	86·2	83·5	72·1	75·4	29·7	42·6	75·7	41·4	36·7	46·7	45·5	54·7
1925	57·7	63·9	83·8	82·4	110·7	70·4	33·3	41·5	75·0	49·5	43·8	54·1	48·8	59·2
1926	48·8	66·9	82·2	93·8	151·7	83·7	32·0	50·1	108·7	59·4	60·8	55·4	51·2	62·6
1927	50·9	68·3	83·3	85·0	88·1	88·4	40·8	47·5	68·4	46·1	64·6	58·6	48·1	62·6
1928	52·0	66·4	84·7	82·1	86·6	70·6	44·6	44·2	80·7	46·1	75·5	63·3	48·5	58·1
1929	49·9	66·3	88·0	81·2	75·3	52·3	44·2	42·9	87·0	56·9	68·2	63·6	53·2	56·6
1930	74·2	66·5	90·2	90·8	73·9	61·7	38·4	55·8	218·0	75·4	80·9	73·3	53·3	65·1
1931	72·6	68·0	90·7	79·9	96·6	71·7	42·5	64·7	176·4	133·2	78·0	70·0	60·3	72·1
1932	77·1	74·3	92·7	88·4	100·9	64·2	49·2	54·0	269·8	63·4	79·9	63·2	60·6	75·1
1933	78·5	71·0	102·3	72·7	77·8	68·4	47·9	48·3	92·8	48·2	63·9	63·8	56·4	66·6
1934	79·5	68·9	93·2	46·7	64·7	59·6	43·3	63·9	92·2	65·5	59·9	67·3	56·0	63·3
1935	69·9	68·0	92·6	71·8	58·8	50·8	45·1	68·9	86·9	64·2	65·7	66·2	55·1	62·4
1936	63·5	66·9	91·5	78·8	58·1	54·2	47·8	51·3	71·1	59·8	60·1	66·1	52·9	59·4
1937	59·7	65·5	86·7	77·6	51·3	47·8	43·5	48·9	57·7	59·2	61·2	58·8	52·8	65·3
1938	56·1	67·9	85·7	76·7	49·5	50·8	54·3	53·9	89·4	121·9	52·4	65·4	52·5	76·3
m	62·3	65·5	86·3	80·5	78·9	66·8	44·6	58·2	112·6	60·9	59·5	60·1	51·9	63·1

the amounts of total income and dividends in each year. A glance at Column (9) of Table 7.2 shows that in 1921, 1926 and 1930-32 the cotton industry paid dividends out of reserves, and these extreme observations produce a high arithmetic mean proportion of total income distributed. In short, although the cotton industry generally distributed a higher proportion of its profit than did other industries, this should not be attributed to the generosity of the cotton companies, but to the persistently low trading profits in the industry. Conversely, the low proportion of total income distributed in the vehicles industry should not be attributed to the parsimony of companies in the industry, but to the high profits and rapid expansion of the industry during the period. These examples suggest that any model designed to explain the propensity to distribute dividends should include profits and growth of the firm among the determining variables.

It would be very convenient if it were possible to reach reliable conclusions on the propensity to distribute dividends simply by an inspection of the figures, combined with an intuition based on training in economic theory. However, it must be admitted that such an approach is generally invalid: a plausible economic interpretation of time-series can all too often be contradicted by an equally plausible, equally ingenious, but diametrically opposed interpretation of the same figures. It is true that such short-cut methods are used in practice when economic decisions have to be reached quickly and long before any formal theory can be postulated and tested, and that the right conclusions are often reached using such techniques. But it is also true that wrong conclusions are also reached, and on other occasions correct conclusions are based on invalid theoretical models, so that the makers of economic policy do not really know why they are right. For these reasons, a discussion of the determinants of dividend policies is postponed until Volume II when a systematic analysis of the available data will be given. Econometric techniques are used, but it must be stressed that this does not mean that institutional influences are ignored. On the contrary, the type of industry, the degree of owner control and other institutional forces listed by Florence[46] are likely to be important, and are included in the analysis.

7.3. METHODS OF ESTIMATION

The basic method used to estimate the appropriation of company profits in manufacturing industries was to obtain benchmarks from the 94th Inland Revenue Report for the year 1936, and to estimate the appropriations for the years 1920–35 from the *changes* in the profit appropriations in the samples of company accounts used in Chapter 4 to estimate profits in manufacturing.

It would be possible to apply a lognormal sampling scheme to the estimation of changes in the *appropriation* of profit similar to that used to estimate changes in the *level* of profit. It could be assumed that the distribution of companies by dividends is lognormal, so that the distribution of companies by the ratio of dividends to profit is also lognormal, and that year to year changes in this average ratio for an industry could be estimated from the observed changes in the ratio for a sample of large companies drawn from all companies in the industry. In spite of its plausibility, such a sampling scheme was not used primarily because of insufficient evidence to support the assumption that the distribution of companies by dividends is lognormal. This is in contrast to the strong evidence in Figure 2.1, which shows how close the observed distribution of companies by gross profit is to the theoretical lognormal curve.

Consequently, it was decided to construct a chain index of the proportion of profit distributed in dividends from the samples of company accounts. That is, the appropriation of profit into ordinary dividend, preference dividend, debenture interest and saving was estimated for each company in a sample which was constant for each pair of adjacent years in the period 1920–36, but which varied over the period as a whole. The mean proportion of total income distributed as gross dividends and interest was then estimated for each sample for adjacent pairs of years. The proportionate year to year changes in this mean gave the required chain index number of the percentage of profit distributed as dividends and interest. In this context, dividends and company saving are *before* taxation, but corporate saving is after depreciation. Profit is the total of these items and includes non-trading income: it corresponds to the Inland Revenue's concept of total income.

The actual computations were simpler than this description of the method. Writing O for gross ordinary dividend, Q for gross preference dividend, D for gross debenture interest, S for gross corporate saving and P for total income, the following computations were made for each set of companies ($i=1, 2, \ldots, n$):

$$\frac{\Sigma (O_i+Q_i+D_i)}{\Sigma P_i} \bigg/ \frac{\Sigma (O_i'+Q_i'+D_i')}{\Sigma P_i'}$$

where the prime denotes the second of two adjacent years. That is the *weighted* mean proportion of profits distributed was calculated for each sample so that the results of the large companies were allowed to dominate the mean value.

The unweighted proportion would be written

$$(1/n) \sum_{i=1}^{n} \{(O_i + Q_i + D_i)/P_i\}$$

but there are at least three reasons for preferring the weighted mean. First, since it is desirable to know the total amount distributed and saved in each industry, the giant firms *should* be allowed to have an influence on the final result which is proportional to their large dividends and profits. Thus the appropriation of profit made by the typical firm is less interesting than the total made by all firms in an industry. Secondly, the weighted mean appropriations of profit in the samples sum to unity,* which is very convenient for the allocation of the time-series of gross profits. Thirdly, the use of unweighted mean proportions produces freak results in those cases where a company earns little or no profit and yet pays some dividend out of reserves. In some years, such ratios can be very large for some companies, often greater than unity, and indeed, in the extreme case where profit is zero and some dividend or debenture interest is paid, the ratio is infinite, whereas such freak results do not occur for the total of all firms in an industry.

The 94th Inland Revenue Report,[1] Cmd 8436, analyses the turnover of large companies within each industry for the years 1936–38 and so, the chain index numbers having been completed, the next step in the present estimation of profit appropriation was to calculate from this Inland Revenue data the proportion of total income distributed as gross dividends and interest in each manufacturing industry in 1936. The corresponding proportion for manufacturing industry as a whole was next estimated by taking a weighted average of the proportions for individual industries, using as weights the estimates of net true income for each industry published in the 92nd Inland Revenue Report[1] Cmd 8052.

The benchmarks of dividends and interest as a proportion of total income of each manufacturing industry were then extrapolated back to 1920, using the chain index numbers described earlier, to give a time-series of the proportion of total income appropriated as

* $\Sigma O_i/\Sigma P_i + \Sigma Q_i/\Sigma P_i + \Sigma D_i/\Sigma P_i + \Sigma S_i/\Sigma P_i$
$$= (\Sigma O_i + \Sigma Q_i + \Sigma D_i + \Sigma S_i)/\Sigma P_i = 1.$$

124

dividends in manufacturing industries shown in Table 7.2. A weighted average of these proportions was then calculated to give the proportion of total income in the corporate manufacturing sector which was distributed as dividends and interest, as shown in Column (14) of Table 7.2. The gross profits in Table 4.1 had to be used as weights, because there is no information on total income in each industry during the period 1920–35. The percentage appropriations of profit for the years 1936–38 were taken directly from the 94th Inland Revenue Report.

The next step was to convert the percentages in Column (14) of Table 7.2 into absolute figures of dividends and interest required for Table 7.1. The conversion for the years 1936–38 was simple enough, because the 94th Inland Revenue Report provided the detailed appropriation of profit in percentage form, while the Oxford Institute survey[111] provided absolute figures of corporate gross true income, wear and tear allowances and net true income for each industry which could be used to estimate absolute value of Rows (4) to (10) in Table 7.1. For example, consider the estimation of the absolute level of total income in Row (5) for 1936. Denote the weighted average ratio of total income to turnover by t and the weighted average ratio of net true income to turnover by n. Both ratios are given in the 94th Inland Revenue Report for each manufacturing industry, and the weighted averages for the whole of manufacturing were obtained by using as weights the net true incomes for the individual industries published in the 92nd Inland Revenue Report, Cmd. 8052. These weights were used because the industrial classification is exactly the same in both reports. The industrial classification in the Oxford Institute survey[111] is slightly different, as explained in Chapter 2, but since the time-series of profits in the present study are based on the Oxford classification, it was necessary to use the absolute figures in [111], instead of those in [1], to convert the percentage appropriations into absolute figures. Denoting the absolute level of net true income of manufacturing companies in 1936 by N, a figure extracted from [111], the absolute figure of total income, denoted by T, was found by evaluating $T = Nt/n$. The absolute figures in the other rows in Table 7.1 for 1936–38 were obtained by a similar procedure.

The absolute appropriation of profit in manufacturing for years 1920 to 1935 was then estimated as follows. The time-series of gross true income in manufacturing companies in Row (1) of Table 7.1 was obtained by interpolating between the benchmarks for *corporate* gross true income in [111], using the time-series for the whole manufacturing sector in Column (14) of Table 4.1 and the technique described in section 2.7. The difference between Column (14) of Table 4.1 and Row (1) of Table 7.1 provides an estimate of non-corporate profit in manufacturing, but it is subject to all the errors involved in differencing.

The Oxford Institute survey [111] also provided estimates of total wear and tear allowances in manufacturing for the benchmarks years 1927, 1932 and 1936–38. The wear and tear allowances for companies in the manufacturing sector were estimated for these years by multiplying the total figure by the ratio of corporate gross true income to total gross true income in manufacturing. Estimates of wear and tear allowances for the remaining years in Row (2) of Table 7.1 were obtained by interpolating between the benchmark years using the time-series of total wear and tear allowances published in [1] and the techniques explained in section 2.7. The key assumption in this part of the estimation is that changes in the wear and tear allowances for manufacturing industry as a whole were similar to those for all the industries covered by the Inland Revenue. In fact the wear and tear allowances for manufacturing were only half of the total so that it would be possible for changes in the allowances for manufacturing industry to be hidden by the grand total figure. But in the absence of sufficient information on depreciation in published accounts, there is no alternative to making this assumption. In view of its possible limitations, however, there would be no case for extending the measurement of depreciation to individual industries within manufacturing. The time-series of depreciation in Row (2) of Table 7.1 was then subtracted from Row (1) to give the time-series of net true income in Row (3).

The Inland Revenue appropriations of turnover show a separate percentage for royalties. The absolute level of this small item was estimated as approximately £7 million in 1936–38 and, in the absence of any further information, it was decided to assume that this amount was constant throughout the period 1920–38.

The Inland Revenue authorities, in their evidence to the Colwyn Committee,[18] estimated that net business saving (after depreciation and taxation) in companies in the mining, manufacturing and productive sector was about £87·2 million in 1922 and £85 million in 1923. However, these estimates were subject to a margin of error 'which might be considerable' and were in fact inconsistent with subsequent Inland Revenue estimates, relating to companies in maufacturing but excluding those in the mining and productive industries, of £90·4 million gross business saving in 1923 and £97·0 million in 1927, shown in Row (8) of Table 7.1. No revised figures for 1922 are available, but it was assumed that the proportionate change between 1922 and 1923 was the same as that observed between the earlier estimates presented to the Colwyn Committee, so that the figure of 93·0 in Row (8) for 1922 was found by evaluating $(90·4 \times 87·2)/85$. The estimates of taxation in Row (9) were found by multiplying the figures in Row (8) by the standard rates of income tax.

The sum of Rows (8) and (7) as a proportion of total income, equals the complement of the percentages in Column (14) of Table 7.2 after dividing by 100. It was therefore possible to estimate *absolute* total income in these three years from the percentages in Table 7.2 and the absolute figures of the sum of Rows (7) and (8) in Table 7.1. That is, dividing the percentages in Column (14) of Table 7.2 by 100 and denoting the result by d, and denoting the absolute sum of Rows (7) and (8) in Table 7.1 by B, the estimates of total income in the three years were made by finding, $T=B/(1-d)$. The appropriation of profit for 1922, 1923 and 1927 was completed by subtracting net true income in Row (3) from total income in Row (5) to get other income minus losses in Row (4). In view of losses contained in Row (4) it seems reasonable to regard it as a residual or balancing item.

Estimates of total income in the remaining years in the period were then obtained by interpolation, on the assumption that the fluctuations in total income were the same as those observed in net true income in Row (3). Estimates of other income in Row (4) were then obtained by subtracting Row (3) from Row (5), while estimates of dividends and interest in Row (6) were found by multiplying Row (5) by the proportions in Column (14) of Table 7.2. Dividends and royalties were then subtracted from Row (5) to give estimates of gross business saving in Row (8). Taxation was then estimated by multiplying gross business saving by the prevailing standard rates of income tax and the estimates of net business saving in Row (10) were found by subtracting Row (9) from Row (8).

7.4. RELIABILITY AND COMPARABILITY

The estimates of the appropriation of profit for the years 1936–38 in Tables 7.1 and 7.2 are very reliable because they are based entirely on Inland Revenue analyses of company accounts submitted to the Board. It would be fair to place them in the official error category A, with less than plus or minus 3 per cent error. But the estimates for the other years are based on observed *changes* in the appropriations of profit in samples of company accounts, and while it is true that such *changes* are a more reliable guide than the *absolute* figures published in company accounts, the fact remains that the estimates for the years 1920–35 are less reliable and should probably be placed in category B, with less than 10 per cent error.

The alternative estimates of the appropriation of profit have also been based on samples of published company accounts and cannot be more reliable than the estimates presented here. Indeed, the fact that the present estimates are in part based on the Inland Revenue benchmarks for the years 1936–38 makes them more accurate than the estimates made by the *Economist*,[100] by Radice,[81] by Clark[37] and by Hope.[106]

TABLE 7.3. *Comparison of Estimates of Net Business Saving as a Percentage of Profit, United Kingdom, per cent*

YEAR	NET SAVINGS AS PER CENT OF PROFIT IN TABLE 7.1 (1)	NET SAVINGS AS PER CENT OF PROFIT— RADICE (2)	NET SAVINGS AS PER CENT OF PROFIT— CLARK (3)	NET SAVINGS AS PER CENT OF PROFIT— HOPE (4)
1920 ..	45·3	—	—	—
1921 ..	21·4	—	—	—
1922 ..	30·2	—	—	—
1923 ..	27·8	18·0	—	—
1924 ..	37·7	20·0	22·3	13·3
1925 ..	34·1	18·9	21·1	6·2
1926 ..	30·8	16·0	17·9	−8·7
1927 ..	30·8	18·5	20·6	10·8
1928 ..	35·3	18·2	20·3	10·2
1929 ..	36·7	16·7	18·6	12·0
1930 ..	27·8	13·9	15·8	2·4
1931 ..	20·6	4·6	5·5	−0·5
1932 ..	17·4	7·3	8·8	−1·6
1933 ..	27·3	14·7	17·2	1·2
1934 ..	29·4	18·4	20·9	5·6
1935 ..	30·6	22·0	24·0	10·1
1936 ..	32·9	25·0	—	—
1937 ..	25·3	—	—	—
1938 ..	10·1	—	—	—

The estimates of net business savings as a proportion of profit in Column (3) of Table 7.3 were made by Clark[37] from samples of company accounts received by the *Economist*.[100] Profits are the sum of gross ordinary and preference dividends plus net business saving (after taxation and after depreciation). These estimates were revised

by Radice,[81] who added debenture interest to profits in the denominator, which explains why his figures are lower than Clark's. He
also extended the series to 1923 and to 1936. Both series are therefore
based on the *Economist*'s samples of companies which included
many non-manufacturing companies and even some which were
operating primarily overseas, so that these estimated appropriations
are not comparable with those in Table 7.1. Column (1) of Table 7.3
shows Row (10) as a proportion of Rows (5)−(7)−(9) in Table 7.1,
and is equivalent to Radice's measure of the appropriation of
profit. It can be seen that the estimates derived from Table 7.1 are
persistently higher than those made by Radice in Column (2) of
Table 7.3. But the figure of 32·9 per cent in Column (1) for 1936 is
based on Inland Revenue data, and is unquestionably more reliable
than the figure of 25 per cent estimated by Radice. This suggests that
similar differences in other years are also justified, and that the
estimates in Table 7.1 are to be preferred to those based on the
Economist's samples.

A summary of the appropriation of the profits of 510 companies
in a sample drawn by Hope[106] is given in Column (4) of Table 7.3.
This sample included 141 non-manufacturing companies, the four
main-line railway companies among them, so once again the results
are not comparable with those in Table 7.1. However, the measures of
appropriation are the same: the numerator in the percentage is net
saving after depreciation and after taxation, and the denominator is
profit after depreciation and after taxation on company saving, but
before gross interest and dividends. It can be seen that Hope's
estimates of the percentage of profit saved are persistently below
those made by Clark and by Radice, in addition to being below
the percentages in Column (1) of Table 7.3. Moreover, while the
estimates in Columns (1) to (3) fall sharply in 1926 and 1931 they
remain positive, whereas those made by Hope for these years are
negative. The difference between Columns (4) and (2) may be
attributed to the differences between the *Economist*'s sample and
that drawn by Hope. It is possible that the latter was heavily
influenced by a few giant companies with large negative saving. At
least, an inspection of Table XV in Hope[106] suggests that the large
negative saving of the railway companies in 1926 was primarily
responsible for the negative figure for 1926 in Column (4) of Table
7.3. In view of the nature of Hope's sample of companies it seems
reasonable to prefer the results in Column (1) of Table 7.3 as a guide
to the undistributed profits of manufacturing companies.

PART II

THE EFFECTS OF THE SIZE OF THE FIRM

CHAPTER 8

ALTERNATIVE MEASURES OF THE SIZE OF FIRMS

BY JAMES BATES

8.1. OBJECTIVES AND METHODS

ECONOMICS, like many other disciplines, contains several areas in which it would be convenient to have ideal criteria, but in which there are so many conflicting considerations that the ideals cannot be achieved. One such area, in which there has been a great deal of debate over the years, is the problem of defining and measuring the size of a firm: there are several possible measures, none of them ideal in the sense that it could be employed with confidence in any conceivable situation, but all of which may be said to measure size in some way or another. In this situation it is necessary to choose that criterion of measurement most suitable for a particular purpose.

The objective of this chapter is to spell out the main considerations affecting various possible measures, to discuss their advantages and their disadvantages, and to demonstrate what many economists have long believed to be true: that it does not matter very much in practice which measure is chosen, since most measures give approximately the same result. The latter proposition is not universally accepted, and it is sometimes argued that the apparent size of a firm depends very largely on the measure chosen: it is claimed for example, by Harris and Solly[105] that 'except when attention is confined to a small number differing greatly in size ... companies appear "greater" or "smaller" according to the yardstick applied'. (Harris and Solly were in fact making a particular case: that one cannot say that the largest n firms are of particular importance to the economic life of a nation, if there is no agreement about which *are* the largest firms. They go on to state that this would depend on how one measured size.) Later in the chapter this particular statement is shown to be untrue as a generalization. The important point is that it is always possible to find extreme examples where the precise measure chosen may well make a considerable difference—for example a wholesaling firm may have a very large turnover, but small value added and relatively small employment—and generally this is likely to be true of any statement of tendencies; but the interesting question is: does it make any difference on the average which measure is chosen? It is the *central tendency* which is important: if it is generally true that there is a high correlation between various measures of size, then in general one can say that it does not matter much which one is used, and the choice of a measure may then depend on convenience. And if in general a firm is large or small by any of the measures chosen, then it is likely to be true that it will be possible to attribute a size measure to individual firms, and further to classify them into size groups with a fair degree of confidence that the groupings will be realistic, and of some practical use.

There are several reasons why it may be necessary to measure the size of firms. In the academic field, a size classification is frequently required in research: it may be argued for example that many economic variables depend on size of firm. One variable frequently mentioned in this context is profitability: and although there may be nothing in this or in many of the other hypotheses that some variable or other may depend on size (it is not the task of this chapter to pronounce), unless size can be measured in some satisfactory way the hypotheses cannot be tested. Since some size measures may be influenced by or may influence (arithmetically) the variables being considered (for example profit is part of value added, and a measure of size based on value added may not be the most appropriate if one is testing a statement that profits depend on size) it may from time to time be necessary to consider a few alternative measures. At an early stage in the Oxford Small Business Survey (see [30]) the problem arose of what was a small business, and several alternative suggestions had to be considered. Eventually a measure in employment terms was used, partly because this information was readily available, and this was used in sample selection. But it turned out to be much more convenient in practice to use other size measures in analysis, and in the consideration of financial problems a measure based on net assets was employed.

Size measures may also be needed for administrative reasons. The Small Business Administration in the United States for example was set up in order to give specific help to small businesses: in order that it can do so it has to decide what is a small business. Small firms have several special problems, some of which stem from their size—they have problems in the field of finance, innovations, research and development, management and many other fields (see [30]) and to the extent that these problems may require legislation and special help, some criteria of size may be necessary. Qualitative measures of size are sometimes suggested for dealing with such problems: it has been suggested for example (see [101]) that from the point of view of credit availability some such criterion might be 'too small to float securities in the public market', 'unknown to lenders and investors outside one area'. Such measures are of doubtful practical value and are subject to differences of interpretation; they may help in identifying problems (although even here they may imply pre-judgment of the problem), but they can do little else, and they certainly do not permit any accuracy in observation or measurements. In some circumstances it is possible to avoid the problem of definition of a size measure by defining the problem in different terms: the Industrial and Commercial Finance Corporation for example tend to define the size of help (in money terms) which they will give to a small firm. Relative size measures are also suggested (for example, the smallest 10 per cent, next 10 per cent, etc.), and such measures are simple, precise and consistent; but since they too depend either on the measurement of absolute size with some accuracy or the ranking of subjects in some reasonable size order, they do not overcome all of the problems.

It is also suggested that public policy may be concerned with the relation of efficiency to size, and with such matters as monopolistic tendencies in certain industries and sectors of the economy, the share of large firms in investment, employment, etc. In fact it is not usually size *per se* which matters in such contexts so much as relative sizes, concentration and shares of the total: in the United Kingdom, for example, the major proportion of profits, employment and assets is accounted for by quoted public companies and nationalized industries (see [110]), and in many cases policy may effectively be concentrated on them. There have been several good studies of the concentration of industry both here and abroad (see, for example, [39], [49], [53]), and it is not necessary to concern ourselves with these problems here; but even in this context it is legitimate to observe that all such studies of concentration, relative sizes, etc., are helped by the existence of reasonable size criteria. Similarly, consideration of the economic aspects of the growth of firms relies on being able to measure size; if a size measure is acceptable, it is not unreasonable for many purposes to use it as a growth measure also.

Not all of these arguments are important, but they are frequently brought up in discussion; and, since size may be a matter of debate, it is as well to look at the problem systematically.

8.2. THE MAIN TYPES OF MEASURE

The attempt to measure absolute size is subject to considerable difficulties. Ideally, absolute size measures should be precise, objective and relatively simple both to calculate and explain and they should overcome most of the problems connected with qualitative and relative measures; but the ideals are not easy to achieve. One major snag is simply that sufficiently detailed information is not always readily available. It is sometimes argued further (see [101], p. 155) that a large number of absolute size classes are cumbersome to handle and costly to achieve: neither of these are inescapable difficulties, and they are in any case administrative rather than conceptual problems.

A more important difficulty arises over inter-industry differences; whatever the size measure chosen it is unlikely to mean the same thing for all firms in all industries. Industries differ with respect to capital intensity, composition of labour force, the ratio of material cost to total cost and many other variables, and these factors affect different size measures in different ways.

When grouped frequency distributions are used, problems arise over the top open-ended class interval of absolute size distributions; this does not happen in the case of relative size distributions. Such problems may be particularly important when comparisons over time are being considered, since, whilst firms may graduate from one class interval to another, they cannot graduate out of the top one; and it has been argued (see [101]) that this may be a particularly serious problem in analysing long-run differences between small and big firms. Similarly the use of grouped data may not be suitable for inter-industry comparisons, since in some industries all of the firms may fall into (say) the lowest class interval.

Essentially, however, these are arguments against grouped frequency distributions rather than against absolute size measures, and the difficulties are not insuperable. Since grouped distributions are frequently the only information available however, it is as well to make sure that they are as good as possible and particularly that the choices of measures and class intervals are sound.

A major advantage of absolute size criteria is that once the difficulties (of making sure, for example, that measurement is on the same basis for all firms) have been overcome, it is relatively easy to classify businesses by the criteria chosen.

In addition to these general difficulties, there are problems which are specific to individual measures. Several types of measure have

136

been suggested and used: these fall into readily recognized groups. The broadest distinction to be made is between physical measures of one kind or another and financial measures.

Physical Measures

Many of the physical measures which are used in practice are appropriate for particular industries only (a coal mine, for example, may be classified by tons of coal produced, whereas a weight measure would not be appropriate for the products of an electronics firm); another difficulty of such physical measures is that they cannot take account of differences in quality (such as grades of coal). Measures of productive capacity are of essentially the same type, and suffer from similar disadvantages; they also frequently contain a large subjective element in their assessment which makes comparisons even more difficult. For particular purposes such measures as these may be useful, but they are so specific in nature and serve such limited purposes that it is not profitable to discuss them in detail. The problem of comparisons by such physical output measures is analogous to the problem of adding up heterogeneous components in compiling index numbers; it is usually necessary to try to overcome such problems in practice by converting physical output measures to some form of value-of-output measure, multiplying output by some price measure.

The physical measure of size most frequently used is *employment*: from many points of view (for example, in studies of the social impact of firms, employment policies and other behavioural characteristics which are closely related to labour) this may be the most suitable measure of size. A major advantage claimed for employment as a measure is that it is free from monetary influences, and can therefore be used for international comparisons, and for comparisons over periods during which there may have been considerable fluctuations in prices (it is, of course, possible to make allowances for these implied disadvantages of financial measures). It has also been argued that an advantage of employment as a measure is that it does not vary over time and between societies according to the general productive power of a society: the argument goes on that when output per head doubles, and a firm produces twice as much at the end of a period, it has not doubled in size. This argument is not entirely valid, since in some senses such a firm will in fact have doubled in size and importance, and its share of the incomes and output of the society to which it belongs may have changed. The ratio of capital to labour, or of output to labour, may change over time; capital and output are both measures of size in their own right, and in general employment is no better and no worse than either of these measures. Thus an argument that employment is a superior measure of the importance to society of a business often depends on the assumption that labour is the most important element in productive capacity: there is a circularity in this form of argument which reduces its appeal and force.

But the measure has its limitations. Problems of definition arise— are male and female employees equivalent, how does one treat part-time staff, does one merely include manual workers, direct labour, clerical staff, supervisory staff and managers, and so on? These are real problems whose solution may require arbitrary decisions, but once a decision has been reached it can be consistently applied to all firms, and it is unlikely that the measure chosen will cause major discrepancies to arise from this source. More serious difficulties arise as a result of inter-industry differences, since different industries have different labour intensities and capital intensities: in the clothing industry, for example, firms which employ relatively large numbers of workers may have relatively small fixed assets—are they, therefore, small or large firms? The answer may depend on the terms of reference of the study which requires the size classification: from the point of view of a financial study they may be small.

Within the smaller size ranges there may be further difficulties associated with the employment measure: these were illustrated by the experience of the Oxford Small Business Survey (see [30]). There was a tendency for turnover to be proportionately higher than employment the larger the firm: this was due to the fact that turnover per man tended to be higher the larger the firm, partly because of the higher labour productivity of larger firms. There was also a tendency for employment to be proportionately higher than assets the larger the firm; this was partly due to the tendency to undervalue assets in small firms, and partly due to the fact that small firms in the Oxford Survey were usually less capital-intensive than large public companies.

A major practical virtue of the employment size measure is that it is fairly readily ascertained. In Britain the half-yearly Earnings Inquiries of the Ministry of Labour ask firms to specify the number of people in their employment in certain well-defined categories. For the purposes of Government research this information is available; for private purposes it is not so easy to obtain from the various Government departments (a fact which makes it hard to draw up reasonable sampling frames based on employment statistics), but the firms themselves usually keep the data and will frequently be prepared to provide the necessary information to research workers. Employment is the measure of size of establishments employed in the Census of Production; it is also one of the measures used by the American Small Business Administration; and it is frequently the measure chosen for research projects (the Oxford Small Business Survey, see [30], for example, defined small firms as any employing less than 500 people but concentrated effectively on firms employing fewer than 100 people). It is probably the commonest published size measure and the only one which is relatively freely available (subject to the limitations mentioned) over the whole size range of businesses. Table 10.1 in Chapter 10 provides an illustration of the use of an employment size measure.

Financial Size Measures
Financial measures of size are of two main types; one based on stocks, or amounts recorded at a moment of time, the other based on financial flows. The stocks type of measure is usually in terms of the assets of the firm, and may represent such quantities as net assets, total assets, working capital, or market value of assets; the main flow measures are turnover (sales), value added (or net output), measures based on profits, and—a measure occasionally employed in certain circumstances—payroll (or cost of labour).

Perhaps the main advantage of asset measures is that all firms are required to place a value on their assets at the end of the financial year; these book values are readily available from the published accounts of public companies; for the remainder of the business sector the information is not generally available but, since the firm itself records the information, it may frequently be elicited by inquiry. All measures based on the book value of assets are, however, subject to difficulties arising from the differing valuation practices of firms. In practice most firms value their assets on an original cost basis, and this is the value at which the assets normally stand in the balance sheet of the firm; from time to time firms may revalue their assets as changes in price levels enforce a realization that book values do not necessarily reflect the true value or earning capacity of the business. But the fact that all firms do not revalue simultaneously, and do not revalue on the same basis, means that size comparisons based on assets are not being made on the same basis for all firms. A further complication arises from the fact that balance sheets show the written-down value (the value net of accumulated depreciation) of fixed assets (since the Companies Act of 1948 they have to show original cost as well, but this provision applies only to assets acquired since 1948). Again, this complication might not matter much in practice if there were some uniformity between firms, but in fact this is seldom the case. The Inland Revenue is rather strict about the amounts which it will allow firms to charge as depreciation (or, more strictly, wear and tear allowances) as costs against tax; but the permitted allowances are not necessarily the amounts actually charged by the firms and written off. There is a strong suspicion too that firms tend on the whole to write down their assets prematurely, resulting in a downward bias for assets measures; this need not matter very much for purposes of comparison if the practice were common to all firms, but it clearly has some effect on aggregate measures of the assets of the business sector.

Book values are, however, the only readily available source of information on the size of assets. Most economists would argue that some sort of replacement cost basis* would be appropriate for asset valuations, since these take account of changes in price levels; but the concept of replacement cost is by no means unambiguous. Does replacement cost mean the cost of an identical replacement, or of a more up-to-date model, or even of something completely different (production methods do not remain unchanged over the years), or does it mean cost of replacement with new or second-hand assets? The latter to some extent overcomes the problem of whether or not one replaces with identical units, since a second-hand valuation would usually imply that similar units were used for replacement, but, since little is generally known about the second-hand value of business assets, it is not easy to measure. Second-hand values may depend also on whether the valuation is to be on a going-concern basis or on a scrap-value basis—accountants normally eschew the former and, implicitly if not avowedly, place a value on assets which is between the scrap value and the second-hand value of an asset to an intending purchaser who will use the asset himself. Uncertainty about what values mean makes life difficult for the research worker.

A way round this particular problem is to ascertain fire-insurance values of assets: most firms insure their assets against fire, and there are strong incentives to ensure that valuations for insurance purposes are realistic. If assets are over-valued premiums are unnecessarily high, and recompense for loss will be on market value, not assessed value; if assets are under-valued, premiums may be low but insurance companies will only pay up to insured value, and the firm may lose. Under-insurance is probably more common than over-insurance and

* For full discussion of this and related concepts see Barna.[27]

in periods of rising prices there may be a tendency for firms to allow insured values to lag behind prices; but even so it is likely that for large and efficiently managed firms insured values will provide a closer approximation to replacement cost than will book values.

Barna[27] used fire-insurance values in his estimate of the replacement cost of fixed assets in manufacturing industry for 1955. He did not make a direct comparison with book values, and it is impossible from available data to correlate replacement costs and book values. The book value of fixed assets of manufacturing industry in 1955* was probably between £8,000 million and £9,000 million; Barna's estimate of replacement costs for manufacturing industry as a whole was £15,100 million (about 50 per cent higher than another estimate by a different method by Redfern[82]); but not much reliance should be placed on this comparison.

Respondents in the Oxford Small Business Survey were also asked the insured value of their physical assets (fixed assets plus stocks). The correlation between these, shown in Table 8.2, is high (0·80). This may be explained partly by the fact that stocks are usually valued annually at something like current values; but it is also likely that insurance values of fixed assets may not be reviewed in small firms as frequently as is desirable. The differences between book values and insured values of Survey companies are shown in Table 8.1.

TABLE 8.1. *Balance Sheet Value of Physical Assets Expressed as Percentage of Insured Value*

PERCENTAGE				NUMBER OF FIRMS
0·–49·9 ..	..	..	..	77
50–74·9 ..	..	..	..	61
75–99·9 ..	..	..	..	58
100 and over	..	..	..	98
Total	..	..	..	294

It may be argued that even replacement cost is not the ideal figure for the size of assets, since it does not accurately reflect the earning

* Calculated as follows: book value of fixed assets of quoted public companies in Britain in 1955 was £3,603 million (see [7]); these companies accounted for 43 per cent of paid up capital in the company sector (see [110]); assuming that this percentage may also be applied to fixed assets, and applies equally to manufacturing and other industries, the book value of assets of companies in manufacturing was $\frac{£3,603m.}{43} \times 100$, or £8,400 million approximately. Assets of unincorporated businesses cannot be estimated, but it is unlikely that they would approach £1,000 million.

capacity of the firm, which may depend on the efficiency with which the assets are utilized. Market valuations might be thought to overcome such difficulties, since these might be claimed to reflect the earning capacity of the firm, and to represent the discounted future earnings of the firm. All of this might be true if stock exchanges were perfect markets and if earning capacity were the only thing which affected market values; but in fact market values may be influenced at least as much by temporary disturbances and irrational factors as they are by earning capacity. Another shortcoming of market valuations is that they are not strictly valuations of a business by the market: current stock exchange prices merely reflect the value of shares which happen to change hands at the time of the valuation; these could possibly reflect the value of the firm if it were to be sold as a going concern, but there is no good reason why this should be so at any one time. Valuations may also fluctuate considerably, and this may reduce their usefulness as a size measure. A further limitation of market valuations is that they can only be employed for quoted public companies, since these are the only businesses which have their shares traded on stock exchanges in any quantity. Nor is it necessarily true that earning capacity is a good measure of size for all purposes; it is a subjective measure dependent on market forces, and it may not be an accurate reflection of the economic weight or significance of an enterprise.

In their analysis of business concentration Hart and Prais[53] considered market valuation of assets along with other potential measures of size, and found in fact that it was highly correlated with other measures: r^2 (of logarithms) of market valuation with total fixed assets was 0·86; with nominal value of share capital and debentures it was 0·92; with net assets, 0·93; with profit for the same year, 0·87; with average profits for five years, 0·86.

There are other problems associated with individual size measures based on assets. Total assets of a firm (fixed assets plus current assets) are not a very good measure, because they include highly volatile items in the shape of cash and other liquid assets. These items may fluctuate considerably over time—cash, for example, may accumulate at the end of a month as debtors pay their bills, it may fall as stock purchases are paid for—and, since measurement can only normally be made from a balance sheet (which is only a snapshot of the assets structure of a firm), the date on which the information is published may have a large, and possibly arbitrary, influence on the apparent size of the firm. There is no reason why the level of these items at a particular date should reflect the typical level. But to take the less volatile items (i.e. the fixed assets) alone still would not give an accurate picture, since a business needs more than fixed assets if it is to conduct its operations successfully.

Probably the best available measure based on assets is net assets, which may be defined as share capital, plus reserves, plus long-term liabilities; or alternatively as the total fixed assets of a firm, plus its current assets, but net of current liabilities. This is analogous to personal net worth since it represents the assets of the firm net of current outside debt, or, approximately, the owners' interest in the firm. The advantage of this measure is that it excludes more volatile elements, and in a sense represents the continuing or permanent element in the assets of the firm. The measure does not, however, avoid the difficulties of valuation common to all asset measures; and there is a further snag which may arise in that net assets may be negative (if losses are carried to the balance sheet for a number of years). In small companies, it is arguable that net assets may be an underestimate of size, since paid up capital is normally small, both in total, and as a proportion of reserves. On the other hand, issued capital is usually relatively stable.

There are further disadvantages of asset measures in general. Minor difficulties may arise over the choice of a date—does one choose the beginning or the end of a time period for example?—but provided that the basis is consistent over the field of comparison, this is not a particularly serious problem. Measurement of size by value of assets does not necessarily provide a reliable indication of relative importance in terms of employment: in industries where there is a large amount of capital per person employed an assets size measure will give a false impression if comparisons are made with industries in which amounts of capital per employee are relatively small. Further, assets measures do not tell us much about the output capacity of the assets, or the efficiency of their use; and generally assets are not necessarily in any close functional relationship with outputs.

A major virtue of asset measures, however, is that they are fairly readily available from the balance sheets of firms and, valuation problems apart, they do represent a consistent approach to the problems of measuring size. They may not be ideal measures, but frequently they are the best available.

Flow measures of size may be more appropriate for many purposes, but they too have their limitations. The sort of size measure which most economists would probably accept for many purposes is one based on value added (the difference between sales and cost of materials, representing the value added to materials by the processes of production, or, as it is frequently called, net output). Such measures represent the true contribution to national output of individual firms, or alternatively the income originating in the firm. They do not suffer from valuation problems (save in as much as depreciation is part of value added), but they do suffer, in common with all other financial measures, from difficulties arising from price changes over periods of time. One minor difficulty may arise over the use of this measure in small firms: as is shown in Chapter 10, management costs and costs of directors may be a large part of value added, and these may lead to an overstatement of net output and a consequent overestimation of size. Unfortunately this is usually the most difficult measure to ascertain for the individual firm—firms have no obligation to publish such figures, and are reluctant to disclose them to outsiders—and perforce it can rarely be employed. The Census of Production does ascertain this measure for all establishments; it would be useful if size distributions were published from time to time. On an industry basis Barna[27] found that value added and physical assets (fixed assets plus stocks) were highly correlated, with $r = 0.726$.

Turnover (or sales) is another flow measure which may be useful in certain circumstances. A major objection to the use of the measure is a purely practical one: few firms are willing to divulge the information. The reasons for this reluctance are not easy to see—the information is not particularly useful to competitors—but attitudes of secrecy die hard. A few of the bigger firms in Britain are now starting to publish the information, but their number is still small (116 in 1960).

There are other objections. One problem arises through inter-industry differences and differences of input-output structure between firms in the same industry. In the wholesaling industry, for example, turnover may be high, but firms may be small by other measures: the reason is that purchases are a high proportion of total costs, and net output and employment are correspondingly low; in the coal-mining industry wages are a high proportion (about 70 per cent) of total costs, and turnover may be a more realistic measure of size in this industry. Within industries and for firms of similar capital and output structures, this problem may not be serious; but the general argument, that net output, employment and turnover are not necessarily in any constant relationship within the firm or between firms still holds, and may be a powerful argument against the measure. Similarly there are difficulties which arise from vertical integration, and a major shortcoming of the turnover measure is that it disregards the extent of the latter: for example, if there are two firms in an industry, A and B, both of which have equal shares of total sales in the industry, but A buys components and adds a 'lick and a promise', whereas B makes all of its own components, they may both appear to be the same size; whereas in fact, by other measures, such as employment and output, B would be much the larger firm. In a similar fashion, the ratio of capital to turnover in different firms and industries may be affected by the degree of capitalization.

Harris and Solly made a great deal of these difficulties, and claimed to demonstrate that the nationalized industries appear significantly different in size when ranked by turnover, employment and net assets. In fact, the rank correlations are high: using the ranks provided by Harris and Solly, the rank correlations are: turnover and employment, 0·8858; turnover and net assets, 0·7143; employment and net assets, 0·8286.

Despite these arguments, in fact, turnover is highly correlated with other measures of size (see also Table 8.2), and for certain purposes (for example, for ascertaining shares of a market and testing hypotheses about market shares) it might be a reasonable measure.

Measures based on profits provide further examples of the flow type of measure: they only represent part of the income flow of a firm, but, differences in efficiency apart, they might be expected to be influenced by similar factors in similar firms. But one cannot, of course, ignore differences in efficiency, and in fact most measures of size based on profits turn out to be measures of efficiency in one way or another. An objection to the profits type of measure is that profits are fairly volatile and tend to vary a great deal from year to year: this objection may be overcome in practice by taking averages over a period of years during which such variations might be expected to cancel themselves out.

The precise profits measure to use is a matter of dispute: in order to overcome the difficulties associated with different dividend policies, different impact of taxation between firms, and definitional problems about what is profit, it is desirable on the whole that the measure used should be as gross as possible. Difficulties, mainly associated with the problem of directors' remuneration, arose in the Oxford Small Business Survey over the measurement of profit (see Chapter 10). The shape of size distributions may depend on such factors, although the ranking of firms within the distribution may not be significantly affected.

In principle, one would argue that profits are better as a measure of relative size than of absolute size; but since some measures of profit are fairly generally available (for public companies at least) there may be occasions when it is necessary to use them for both purposes.

Several other flows of funds may be ascertained; wages and salaries, for example, are a type of employment-based financial measure appropriate in certain circumstances (for example, in examining fringe benefits and their importance); these may be expected to be highly correlated with employment. The major snag with all flow measures is that they are not easy to ascertain; another disadvantage is that flow concepts are usually closely related to each other (value added is part of turnover, so is profit, so is payroll). This latter disadvantage may be important: if, for example, one wished to discuss the effects of size on profits, the fact that profit is part of turnover and part of value added would mean that one could naturally expect a high correlation between profits and these other measures, and it might be preferable to use other size measures. In practice, since profit on turnover varies a great deal from firm to firm and over time, this disadvantage may be less serious than it is in theory. There is a corresponding advantage: since many flow measures are closely related to each other, they tend to provide similar answers, and ascertaining one of them may well be sufficient for many practical purposes.

8.3. MEASUREMENT AND RESULTS

Sources and Methods
In order to examine the force of all of these arguments in practice, I have taken all the size measures which could be readily ascertained, for as many different firms and groups of firms as possible, and have compared them with each other. The sources of the information are various. A by-product of the Oxford Small Business Survey was the availability of a number of possible size measures which could be determined accurately. For quoted public companies, the Central Statistical Office and Board of Trade publish certain data from time to time (see, for example, [6]); information about assets, profits and turnover is available for 116 of these companies. For American companies the list of the 500 largest American companies published annually by the magazine *Fortune* has been used: this contains several possible measures, and a sample of seventy-two companies has been used as a basis for calculations. *Fortune* also publishes a list of the 100 largest foreign industrial companies, with various

possible measures: these proved to be of little use, largely because of the difficulties of international comparisons, and the fact that different firms use the same names to mean different things.

The methods used are extremely simple: where absolute measures could be made, correlation coefficients of the logarithms of the size measures have been calculated; when rankings only were available, rank correlation coefficients have been calculated.

Results

The results are shown in Table 8.2.

TABLE 8.2. *Correlations of Alternative Size Measures*

CORRELATIONS BETWEEN		CORRELATION COEFFICIENTS (R²) OF LOGARITHMS			RANK CORRELATION COEFFICIENTS		
		(1)	(2)	(3)	(1)	(2)	(4)
Value Added & Payroll		0·92	—	—	(a)	—	—
,, ,, Net Assets		0·80	—	—	(a)	—	—
,, ,, Gross Profits		0·71	—	—	(a)	—	0·86
,, ,, Employment		0·24	—	—	0·61	—	—
,, ,, Turnover		0·84	—	—	(a)	—	0·95
Payroll & Net Assets		0·70	—	—	(a)	—	0·80
,, ,, Gross Profits		0·50	—	—	(a)	—	—
,, ,, Employment		0·23	—	—	0·64	—	0·96
,, ,, Turnover		0·76	—	—	(a)	—	—
Net Assets & Gross Profit		0·60	0·95	—	(a)	—	0·94
,, ,, Employment		0·18	—	0·58	0·52	0·69	0·81
,, ,, Turnover		0·73	0·87	0·75	(a)	(a)	0·90
,, ,, Net Profits		(a)	—	0·84	(a)	(a)	0·73
,, ,, Total Assets		(a)	—	0·97	(a)	(a)	—
Gross Profits & Employment		0·21	—	—	0·53	—	—
,, ,, Turnover		0·57	0·88	—	(a)	—	0·85
,, ,, Net Profits		(a)	—	—	(a)	—	0·92
Turnover & Employment		0·20	—	0·76	0·50	(a)	—
,, ,, Total Assets		(a)	—	0·91	(a)	(a)	—
,, ,, Net Profits		(a)	—	0·64	(a)	(a)	—
Employment & Net Profits		(a)	—	0·54	(a)	0·65	—
,, ,, Total Assets		(a)	—	0·66	(a)	0·75	—
Total Assets & Net Profits		(a)	—	0·82	(a)	(a)	—
Book Value of Physical Assets and Insured Value		0·80	—	—	(a)	—	—

(a) Not calculated.
— Not ascertained.
(1) Small Business Survey Sample [30].
(2) 116 British quoted public companies [6].
(3) Sample of 72 from 500 largest American companies [103].
(4) Calculated from data in [105].

Rank correlation coefficients of each measure against the other (using data from [105]) are all high: the lowest, between net assets and profits, is 0·73. The contention that a firm's ranking depends on the measure chosen is therefore not verified: generally speaking, it makes little difference which measure is used.

Correlations between various absolute size measures for American firms are also high: the highest, between total assets and net assets is perhaps not unexpected, but it is interesting that the next highest correlation is between turnover and total assets—between a flow and a stock measure—this may throw some doubt on the arguments against turnover as a size measure. The two lowest correlations are between employment and assets and profits respectively: this reflects the fact that capital/labour ratios are different in different industries; and also points to the fact that profits and employment measure different things—output and input respectively—and there is not necessarily any close relationship between inputs and outputs in different firms. Profits of American firms in this study are expressed net of tax, and therefore do not conform to the ideal that the profit measure should be as gross as possible. Only three correlations are possible for British quoted public companies; these are all high. Gross profits and turnover would be expected to be highly correlated, since the one is part of the other (although gross profits may differ between firms more than turnover because of different efficiencies), but the high correlation of a stock measure (net assets) with two flow measures (profit and turnover) is interesting.

In the Small Business Survey sample the one thing that stands out is that employment is not highly correlated with other size measures. The reasons for this have been discussed earlier—(see section 8.2)— these arise partly because of inter-industry differences in capital/ labour ratios and input-output ratios and partly because of the tendency to understate assets in small firms. Even so it is interesting that rank correlations between employment and other measures are high: this is largely because all of the firms in the example were small in employment terms (less than 100 employees), and there was not much difference between any of them in absolute, quantitative terms; ranking introduces an element of difference, and these new differences correspond fairly closely to differences in rank by other measures. It may also be true that the correlation between employment and other measures in small firms is not linear in logarithms, so that a linear correlation coefficient is not the appropriate measure. A further factor which may help to depress employment, and therefore lead to understatement of size by the employment measure in small firms, is the fact that most small firms and nearly all very small ones, have working proprietors and small clerical staff. There is even a low correlation between employment and payroll, which may indicate wide differences in practices relating to employment and remuneration.

In a more restricted field, Florence[46] compared the larger companies in Britain by two size measures—net tangible assets and issued capital—and found that it did not much matter which measure was used, since there was little displacement from given size classes as a result of the choice of one measure or another. The classifications used for this comparison were rather coarse, but the comparisons do lend further force to the arguments of this chapter.

8.4. CONCLUSIONS

The conclusions of this chapter may be stated briefly. Although there are several theoretical reasons why certain size measures are less than ideal, and several arguments may be advanced against the use of any measure; in practice it does not seem to matter very much which measures are used, since they are mostly highly correlated with each other. In practice, therefore, choice of a measure can depend largely on convenience and ease of ascertainment. There may of course be good reasons why certain measures are not the most suitable for certain purposes, and these may lead to a preference for other measures. But it is encouraging that it does not seem to matter very much if one is forced to use a measure which is less than ideal.

CHAPTER 9

GROWTH AND THE SIZE OF FIRM

9.1. INTRODUCTION

THE extrapolation of changes in the profits of large companies on the Stock Exchange to smaller unquoted companies, and even to unincorporated firms, was justified in Chapter 2 by an appeal to lognormal theory, to the shape of the observed size distribution of all companies by profits in Figure 2.1, to the results of four tests of the hypothesis that the average proportionate change in profits is independent of size [51], and to tests of the sampling method in the case of the brewing industry [50]. The present chapter examines this lognormal sampling theory more closely. The basic hypothesis of independence of size and proportionate change in profits, or in assets, employment or any other measure of firm size, is interesting in its own right and is given closer scrutiny in section 9.2. Moreover, there has been further work on this topic since [53], particularly in the United States, and section 9.3 is devoted to a review of some of the American researches. Finally, the Board of Trade[7] has now published distributions of proportionate changes in assets which permit the direct tests of the basic hypothesis using data for recent years which are conducted in section 9.4.

9.2. THE LAW OF PROPORTIONATE EFFECT

The typical size distribution of firms is positively skew. This skewness can often be removed by plotting the frequencies against the logarithms of size, so that the original distribution may be deemed to be lognormal. The widespread occurrence of this type of distribution is interesting because it suggests that an equally widespread law of growth of firms is producing it.

A normal curve is generated when a large number of small, independent random forces act on a variate in an additive manner; and a lognormal curve can be generated if they act multiplicatively. In the present context this means that the determinants of the growth of firms tend to change the size of firms by randomly distributed proportions. Some forces make for an increase, some for a decrease, but all act randomly in the sense that there is no tendency to favour or disfavour firms of any particular size. Gibrat[48] referred to this process of equiproportionate growth as 'la loi d'effet proportionnel.'

The law of proportionate effect may be stated as follows:

$$X_t - X_{t-1} = \varepsilon_t X_{t-1} \tag{9.1}$$

where X_t denotes the absolute size of a firm at time t and ε_t denotes a proportion drawn at random from a set of proportions which are mutually independent and also independent of X_{t-1}. Aitchison and Brown[25] give the following heuristic treatment of this theorem before developing it more rigorously.

They rewrite (9.1) as

$$(X_t - X_{t-1})/X_{t-1} = \varepsilon_t \tag{9.2}$$

so that

$$\sum_{t=1}^{n} (X_t - X_{t-1})/X_{t-1} = \sum_{t=1}^{n} \varepsilon_t \tag{9.3}$$

and they then suppose that each time interval is small,

$$\sum_{t=1}^{n} (X_t - X_{t-1})/X_{t-1} \sim \int_{X_o}^{X_n} (1/X)dX \tag{9.4}$$

$$\sim [\log X]_{X_o}^{X_n} = \log X_n - \log X_o \tag{9.5}$$

That is,

$$\log X_n - \log X_o = \sum_{t=1}^{n} \varepsilon_t \tag{9.6}$$

or,

$$\log X_n = \log X_o + \varepsilon_1 + \varepsilon_2 + \ldots + \varepsilon_n \tag{9.7}$$

By the additive form of the central limit theorem, the variate $\log X_n$ is normally distributed. This is true even if $\log X_o$ and the ε_t are not normally distributed, providing that n is large. Equation (9.7) is simply a more formal statement of the theory that firms grow by randomly distributed proportions and therefore tend to be log-normally distributed. The weakness of the conditions necessary for the generation of a lognormal curve explains why they are observed so frequently in practice.

Let us now impose slightly stronger conditions on this theorem of proportionate effect and assume that the bivariate distribution of $\log X_t$ and $\log X_{t-1}$ is a normal surface. Simplify the notation, denoting $\log X_t$ by y, and $\log X_{t-1}$ by x, and $f(y, x)$ is assumed to have the bivariate normal distribution specified in scalar form, for example, by Hoel,[55] equation (15) page 198. Hoel also shows that the two marginal distributions of this surface are normal univariate distributions. That is, the theoretical size distributions of firms at time t and $t-1$ are lognormal and it certainly seems reasonable to assume that this is the case in practice, judging by the univariate distributions observed in [53]. It also follows that the conditional distribution of y given x, denoted by $f(y|x)$, is another normal curve with the probability density function shown in equation (20) of Hoel[55] on page 200, and with variance $\sigma_y^2 (1-\rho^2)$, where σ_y is the standard deviation of y and ρ is the coefficient of correlation between x and y. It can be seen that all the conditional distributions of y must have the same standard deviation, because σ_y and ρ are constants. In other words, the bivariate normal distribution $f(y, x)$ is homoscedastic.

Hoel also shows that the locus of means of the conditional distributions of y, which gives the regression of y on x, is the linear equation

$$\bar{y}_x = \mu_y + \rho\sigma_y (x-\mu_x)/\sigma_x \tag{9.8}$$

with regression coefficient given by $\beta = \rho\sigma_y/\sigma_x$. \hfill (9.9)

This result appeared in the form $\sigma_y^2/\sigma_x^2 = \beta^2/\rho^2$ in equation (9) in [53] and was used to show that in the lognormal model of the growth of firms the variance of the logarithms of the sizes of firms could increase or decrease over time, depending on the ratio of the regression coefficient to the correlation coefficient. It was found that estimates of β were generally not significantly different from unity and that they were generally higher than estimates of ρ over the period 1885 to 1939 so that business concentration, measured by the variance of the logarithms of size, increased. That is, $(\sigma_y^2/\sigma_x^2) > 1$.

Figure 9.1 is a hypothetical scatter diagram showing the observations of y and x about the regression line $\hat{y} = a + bx$ where b is unity. It can be seen that the dispersion of the scatter about the regression line is constant, in accordance with the homoscedastic property of the normal surface. The stochastic relationship postulated between y and x is of the form $y = \alpha + \beta x + \eta$ where α is a constant and where η is an additive random variable with zero mean and variance σ_η^2. On taking antilogarithms this relationship takes the form

$$X_t = e^\alpha X_{t-1}^\beta \varepsilon \tag{9.10}$$

where e is the base of natural logarithms and ε is e^η. Clearly, if $b=1$ then on average the ratio of a firm's size at time t to its size at time $t-1$ is a constant. That is, $X_t/X_{t-1} = e^\alpha$. As can be seen in Figure 9.1, this result holds for small, medium and large firms at time $t-1$, so when $b=1$, it follows that the average proportionate growth is the same for firms of all sizes. This process of growth of firms is consistent with an increase in business concentration over time if the correlation between the logarithms of firms sizes at two dates is less than unity.

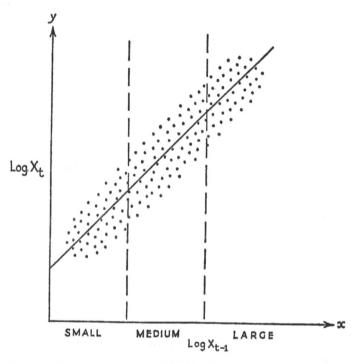

Fig. 9.1. Hypothetical scatter diagram of logarithms of companies' profits at times t and $t-1$.

The lognormal model of the growth of firms outlined above implies that the distributions of the proportionate growth of firms are the same for firms of all sizes: they are all lognormal with the same mean and variance of logarithms. There are also other important implications considered in [53], [51] but which are ignored here. Now while it is true that many observed size distributions of firms are approximately lognormal, it is also true that some size distributions of firms do not fit this theoretical distribution. Indeed, Simon and Bonini [85] argue that the lognormal curve is a special case of the Yule distribution, which is generated jointly by the law of proportionate effect and an assumed birth process, such as constant rate of birth of new firms in the smallest size-class. In this respect, the Yule distribution is superior to the lognormal distribution because it covers the birth and death of firms, implying zero size at one point of time, which cannot readily be included in a model based on a logarithmic curve.

Little is known about the relationship between the birth, death and size of firms in the United Kingdom. However, as noted in [53], [65] the chances of the death of companies quoted on the Stock Exchange seem to decrease with increases in size. This not very surprising conclusion also modifies the original statement that the growth rates are independent of absolute size. A similar modification has to be made to allow for birth of firms. But since it is most unlikely that new Stock Exchange quotations will be representative of births into the manufacturing sector as a whole, it is impossible to outline the form of the modification to the law of proportionate effect which is required. One suspects that the chances of birth, like the chances of death, decrease as the larger-size groups are reached, with the difference that, while a large firm is unlikely to die, it is not unusual for a new firm to be born large, especially when it is a subsidiary of a foreign enterprise.

Granted that there are changes in the business population which are necessarily beyond the explanatory scope of the law of proportionate effect, to what extent is the simple law of growth true for surviving companies? Some evidence which may help to answer this question is provided by calculations of the mean and variance of the proportionate changes in the profits of three sets of firms in the United Kingdom. Profits are measured gross of tax and net of depreciation, as explained in Chapter 2. It is true that profits are highly correlated with other measures of size, but their volatility is such that most economists would prefer assets, output, value-added or even employment as a measure of absolute size. In the present case, however, this volatility may be an advantage because it probably weights the tests against the hypothesis of equi-proportionate growth. For example, we should expect the profits of small firms to fluctuate more than those of large firms through the trade cycle. A large firm tends to be more diversified and to sell to a wider area than does a small or medium firm. There is more scope in a large firm for offsetting losses made in one part of the firm by the profits earned in another part. But this would still be consistent with similar proportionate changes in the profits of large, medium and small firms *on the average*, because each part of a medium or large firm with varying fortunes may be regarded as equivalent to a

154

small firm, and a cancelling-out process may work just as well between separate small firms as between separate parts of one large firm. However, if this happened it would follow that the *dispersion* of proportionate profit changes would tend to *decrease* with increases in firm size. Indeed Prais[78] has shown that over the period 1948–53 the dispersion of growth among the fifty largest firms was significantly lower than that among those ranked 51–100. Consequently it is necessary to test the law of proportionate effect directly, rather than to deduce it from the general shape of the size distribution of companies by profit.

The tests are first carried out using the profits data collected for the present study. These relate to small samples of firms in brewing, the industry chosen for pilot investigations, to all quoted companies in the drink industry 1950–54 (from data supplied by the National Institute of Economic and Social Research) and to the profits of small corporate and non-corporate firms in the Oxford Institute of Statistics Small Business Survey, described in Chapter 10.

It is convenient to denote the mean and variance of proportionate changes in profit by $\varkappa$ and γ^2 and estimates of them are denoted by k and c^2. The mean and variance of the logarithms of such changes are denoted by μ and σ^2 with estimators m and s^2 respectively. Table 9.1 gives values of k for thirty-three brewing companies 1931–37 with eleven firms in each of three size classes. Size classes are based on issued capital in 1930: Class 1 contains firms with under £0·5 million, Class 2 contains those with £0·5 to £1 million and Class 3 contains those with £1 to £2 million. The values of k for the ten largest breweries are not given here because their profits were enumerated in the compilation of Table 4.2, otherwise this sample of thirty-three is the largest obtainable from our data. From the first row it can be seen that between 1931 and 1932 profits fell very sharply. On average the profits of small companies in 1932 were only 79 per cent of those in 1931, and the corresponding figures for medium companies in Classes

TABLE 9.1. *Mean Annual Proportionate Change in Profits of Brewing Companies 1931–37*

YEAR			SIZE CLASS 1	SIZE CLASS 2	SIZE CLASS 3
1931–32	..	..	0·79	0·77	0·77
1932–33	..	..	1·10	0·99	1·01
1933–34	..	..	1·21	1·19	1·26
1934–35	..	..	1·11	1·13	1·08
1935–36	..	..	1·18	1·06	1·05
1936–37	..	..	1·04	1·08	1·07

2 and 3 were 77 per cent. In fact, the average proportionate changes in profits through the downswing and subsequent recovery were generally similar for each size of firm.

If an index of profits were constructed from the pooled data of Classes 2 and 3, its movements would not diverge from those of profits in Class 1 in periods 1931–32, 1933–34 and 1934–35. In 1932–33, when it is known from other sources that total brewing profits were in a trough and did not change much, and in 1935–36, when total profits were rising steadily, the average profits of small companies showed extraordinary increases—plus 10 per cent in 1932–33 and plus 18 per cent in 1935–36. An inspection of the original data shows that this was due to one or two extreme observations—that is, the dispersion of profit changes was very high among small companies in these years. But there was not always a higher dispersion among small companies, as can be seen in Table 9.2, which gives values of c^2 for the same data for 1931–32 and 1936–37, the years of downswing and upswing of the trade cycle being chosen to provide the most stringent test of the hypothesis of equal variance of growth of firms of different size.

TABLE 9.2. *Variance of Proportionate Change in Profits in Brewing Firms 1931–32 and 1936–37*

YEAR		CLASS 1	CLASS 2	CLASS 3	χ^2	df
1931–32	..	0·1419	0·0121	0·0177	12·13	2
1936–37	..	0·0394	0·0286	0·0167	1·21	2

Bartlett's test of the homogeneity of several estimates of the population variance was used to determine whether the variances in Table 9.2 are equal. An explanation of this test is given by Weatherburn[95], page 183. The calculated values of χ^2 are also given in Table 9.2. The conclusion to be drawn is that at the 5 per cent level of probability, the variances are significantly different, or heterogeneous, in the downswing 1931–32, but are homogeneous in the upswing 1936–37. It can be seen that in the downswing the variance of the proportionate change in profits of the small companies in Class 1 is higher than the variances of the larger companies in Classes 2 and 3. This finding is consistent with the expectation based on diversification of large firms, but is inconsistent with the law of proportionate effect.

Because the variances in each size class for 1931–32 are significantly different, Student's t-test cannot be used to test the significance of the differences between the mean proportionate changes in profit in each size class 1931–32. However, a test proposed by Welch,[96] for which tables have been prepared by Aspin,[26] shows no significant differences between the mean proportionate growth in each size class. For the period 1936–37 it is possible to use the t-test, and in fact this test also reveals no significant differences between mean proportionate growths in each size classes. That is, whether or not there are significant differences between the variances of changes in profit, the mean proportionate change in profit is similar for each size class of firm. This result is consistent with part of the law of proportionate effect and supports the sampling scheme described in Chapter 2. However, with only eleven companies in each size class, the samples are too small to support a strong conclusion. With such small samples, it is always possible for extreme changes of one or two firms, such as those observed for 1932–33 and 1935–36, to overwhelm the general tendency. The fact that this did not happen to the mean proportionate change in the downswing and upswing is interesting, but by itself is not convincing evidence in favour of the law of proportionate effect. Further evidence is required, preferably relating to larger samples.

Table 9.3 gives values of k and c^2 for 124 quoted business units in the drink industry (brewing, distilling, soft drinks) over the period 1950–54. These values have been calculated from standardized company accounts prepared by the National Institute which are more reliable than the pre-1948 Act accounts used in previous tables. It appears that the dispersion of proportionate profit changes tends to decrease with increases in firm size. Bartlett's test shows that the variances are heterogeneous ($\chi^2 = 23\cdot89$). However, Welch-Aspin tests show that the mean proportionate change in profits does not differ significantly between size classes of companies. This conclusion, based on superior data, confirms previous findings, and also supports the sampling scheme formulated in Chapter 2.

TABLE 9.3. *Means and Variances of Proportionate Changes in Profits of Medium and Small Business Units in the Drink Industry, 1950–54*

SIZE CLASS	UPPER LIMIT OF SIZE CLASS £'000	n	k	c^2
1	250	17	1·06	0·207
2	500	22	1·13	0·116
3	750	18	1·15	0·245
4	1,000	16	1·06	0·080
5	2,500	32	1·21	0·084
6	5,000	19	1·17	0·048

$\chi^2 = 23\cdot89$ degrees of freedom = 5

Table 9.4 gives values of k and c^2 for 229 unquoted firms 1953–54. Size is measured by total net assets and the size classes are equal on a logarithmic scale. It can be seen that the distribution approximates to the lognormal. In measuring profits, directors' remuneration was included, and all firms making a loss were excluded. In the editing stage, fourteen companies which increased their profits by more than threefold in one year were excluded as freak observations: there were seven below £12,500 assets and seven above.

In this case there is no tendency for c^2 to decrease with increases in size of firm. Bartlett's test showed that the estimates of the variance of changes in profit are homogeneous ($\chi^2 = 8\cdot13$, with 6 degrees of freedom) and Student's t-tests revealed no significant differences between the means of the proportionate changes in profit. These results are consistent with both parts of the law of proportionate effect and, once again, the sampling scheme developed in Chapter 2 seems justified.

TABLE 9.4. *Mean and Variance of Proportionate Changes in Profits of Unquoted Firms*

SIZE CLASS	UPPER LIMIT OF NET ASSETS	n	k	c^2
1	781	8	0·842	
2	1,563	7	1·076	0·2806
3	3,125	27	1·258	
4	6,250	31	1·241	0·2563
5	12,500	43	1·276	0·4110
6	25,000	43	1·087	0·2547
7	50,000	28	1·127	0·2535
8	100,000	20	1·214	0·4065
9	200,000	15	1·123	
10	400,000	4	1·542	0·4508
11	800,000	3	1·193	

$$\chi^2 = 8\cdot13 \qquad \text{degrees of freedom} = 6$$

Thus, two tests support the hypothesis that the dispersion of profit changes would be the same for firms of all sizes, and the other two tests contradict it. A possible economic explanation of this difference is that a firm has to be fairly large before it is diversified enough to offset profit variations among its constituent parts. Above this size c^2 tends to fall, below it c^2 tends to be the same for firms of all sizes. Table 9.4 provides the most reliable evidence of homogeneity of variance of proportionate changes in profit of firms of all sizes, but even the largest firms in this sample are under £800,000 net assets and are small compared with the firms in Table 9.3.

The tests used have been based on the assumption that the samples are derived from normal populations. However, the distribution of proportionate change in profits, being the ratio of two distributions of profits which are approximately lognormal, will itself be lognormal, because, after logarithmic transformation, it is a linear combination of two normal distributions. This suggests that the tests should have been applied to the *logarithms* of the proportionate changes in profit, for the logarithms will satisfy the conditions necessary for normal test theory.

On the other hand, the two marginal distributions of the bivariate lognormal distribution of firms by profit at years t and $t-1$ will be highly correlated. Since there will be little change over such a short period, it may be assumed that they have a common logarithmic variance, say σ^2, in which case, as noted by Aitchison and Brown[25], the logarithmic variance of the ratio of these distributions will be small, namely $2\sigma^2 (1-\rho)$, where the coefficient of correlation ρ is near unity. Though the distribution of proportionate changes in profit is lognormal, its logarithmic variance may be low enough to justify the use of normal test statistics, because in a lognormal distribution low σ^2 implies low degrees of skewness and kurtosis, which in turn imply small departures from the normal curve.

If this argument is rejected, it becomes necessary to test the significance of observed differences between the means and variances of the logarithms of the proportionate changes in profit of small and medium firms. The relationship between $\varkappa$, γ^2, μ and σ^2 are examined in detail by Aitchison and Brown.[25] Briefly, the *jth* moment about the origin of $\Lambda (x)$ denoted by λ'_j, is given by:

$$\lambda'_j = \exp\left(j\mu + \tfrac{1}{2}j^2\sigma^2\right) \tag{9.11}$$

The mean is given by:

$$\varkappa = \exp\left(\mu + \tfrac{1}{2}\sigma^2\right) \tag{9.12}$$

The variance is given by:

$$\gamma^2 = e^{2\mu + \sigma^2}\left(e^{\sigma^2} - 1\right) \tag{9.13}$$

$$= \varkappa^2 \xi^2 \tag{9.14}$$

where

$$\xi^2 = e^{\sigma^2} - 1 \tag{9.15}$$

The coefficient of variation is ξ and depends solely on σ^2. The coefficients of skewness and kurtosis are also governed by σ^2:

$$\lambda_3/\gamma^3 = \xi^3 + 3\xi \tag{9.16}$$

$$\frac{\lambda_4}{\gamma^4} - 3 = \xi^8 + 6\xi^6 + 15\xi^4 + 16\xi^2 \tag{9.17}$$

From (9.12) it can be seen that two distributions could have different μ and σ^2 and still have the same $\varkappa$, so that it is not always possible to draw conclusions about $\varkappa$ from tests on μ and σ^2. Similarly, equation (9.13) shows we cannot conclude that the γ^2 of distributions are different if their μ and σ^2 are different.

TABLE 9.5. *Mean and Variance of Logarithms of Percentage Changes in Profits of Sample of Companies in Table 9.3*

SIZE CLASS	m	s^2
1	1·9831	0·0415
2	2·0316	0·0199
3	1·9760	0·0240
4	2·0113	0·0132
5	2·0719	0·0087
6	2·0647	0·0038

$\chi^2=28\cdot85$ degrees of freedom$=5$

TABLE 9.6. *Welch-Aspin Tests of Significance of Differences between Estimates of μ for Each Size Class in Table 9.3*

SIZE CLASS	1	2	3	4	5
2	Yes	—	—	—	—
3	No	No	—	—	—
4	No	No	No	—	—
5	Yes	No	Yes	No	—
6	No	No	Yes	No	No

No = No significant difference at 5 per cent level.
Yes = Significant difference.

It seems worthwhile estimating μ and σ^2 for each size class, at least for the more reliable data in Tables 9.3 and 9.4, to see whether there is any association between size of firm and m or s^2. Table 9.5 gives estimates of the mean and variance of the logarithms of the percentage changes in profit of the companies sampled in Table 9.3, namely the proportionate changes in profits, multiplied by 100 for convenience, of companies in the drink industry quoted on the Stock Exchange, 1950–54. It can be seen that s^2 decreases with increases in size of firm and, in fact, Bartlett's test for the homogeneity of the variances reveals significant differences between the s^2. But there does not seem to be any association between m and size class of firm, as can be seen from Table 9.6, which gives the results of Welch-Aspin tests on the difference between each pair of means. The conclusion that m is the same for each size class but that s^2 is lower for large firms suggests that k, the estimate of the mean of the proportionate changes in profit, given by $k=\exp{(m+\frac{1}{2}s^2)}$, is also lower for the larger companies. However, the sampling scheme adopted in Chapter 2 used the *median* of the proportionate changes in profit and, in a lognormal distribution, the median is e^μ and does not depend on σ^2. The conclusion that m is independent of size of firm implies that e^m is also independent of size of firm.

TABLE 9.7. *Mean and Variance of Logarithms of Percentage Changes in Profits of Sample of Companies in Table 9.4*

SIZE CLASS	m	s^2
1, 2, 3	1·8815	0·1327
4	2·0520	0·0353
5	2·0606	0·0441
6	1·9938	0·0378
7	2·0077	0·0368
8	2·0399	0·0418
9, 10, 11	2·0141	0·0778

TABLE 9.8. *Welch-Aspin Tests of Significance of Differences Between Estimates of μ for Size Classes in Table 9.4*

SIZE CLASS	(1, 2, 3)	4	5	6	7	8
4	Yes	—	—	—	—	—
5	Yes	No	—	—	—	—
6	Yes	No	No	—	—	—
7	Yes	No	No	No	—	—
8	Yes	No	No	No	No	—
(9, 10, 11)	No	No	No	No	No	No

No = No significant difference at 5 per cent level.
Yes = Significant difference.

Table 9.7 gives estimates of μ and σ^2 for each size class of firm in Table 9.4. Bartlett's test reveals that the s^2 are heterogeneous, but there is no tendency for s^2 to decrease with increases in size of firm. Two qualifications must be made to this general conclusion: first, the sample consists of firms which may be too small to obtain the advantage of diversification, and, secondly, it is interesting to note that s^2 is much larger in the smallest size class than in any other class. Welch-Aspin tests on the differences between m in each size class show that in general there is no tendency for m to vary with size of firm. The results of the tests between each pair of means are given in Table 9.8. It is worth mentioning that Bartlett's test of homogeneity of c^2 in Table 9.4 revealed no significant differences between the estimates of γ^2 in spite of the fact that the s^2 are heterogeneous, the m are the same and the theoretical relationship between them is given by $c^2 = e^{2m+s^2}(e^{s^2}-1)$. But the distribution in Table 9.4 is certainly not sampled from a normal population, so one of the conditions necessary for the application of Bartlett's test on c^2 is not fulfilled.

This example illustrates the need for caution in reaching conclusions on the mean and variance of changes in profit, or on any other variate with a skew distribution. So far, the general conclusion is that in most cases there are significant differences between the variances of proportionate growth of firms of different sizes, but that the mean proportionate growth, measured by k or by m, is generally independent of firms' sizes. However, this conclusion must be subjected to more tests before it can be regarded as reliable. The American studies of proportionate growth of firms considered in the next section are particularly helpful in this respect.

9.3. GROWTH AND SIZE OF FIRM IN THE UNITED STATES

In recent years in the United States there have been several studies made of the relationship between the size of firms and their growth rates. The American studies considered here are those by Simon and Bonini,[85] by Ferguson,[40] by Hymer and Pashigian[57] and by Mansfield.[68]

Simon and Bonini[85] constructed transition matrices for the 500 largest US industrial corporations 1954 to 1955, and 1954 to 1956. From these matrices they were able to plot scatter diagrams of the logarithms of firms' sizes at the beginning and end of each time interval. They found that the regression of the logarithms of firm size at time t on the corresponding logarithm at time $t-1$ was linear and homoscedastic, and that the regression coefficient was approximately unity. The linearity and constant variance of the bivariate distribution of the logarithms of firms' sizes are consistent with the hypothesis of lognormality and the law of proportionate effect. The unit slope is consistent with the simple model of the law of proportionate effect in equation (5) in Hart and Prais,[53] where there is no regression towards the mean size in Galton's sense. However, it was also found that between 1954 and 1956 21.2 per cent of the net growth of assets of all firms with over \$200 million assets was due to new firms entering the giant class, which is inconsistent with the simplest lognormal model of growth.

In fact, Simon and Bonini[85] prefer the Yule distribution to the lognormal curve as a summary of the observed size distribution of firms. The Yule distribution gave good fits not only to the size distributions studied by Hart and Prais,[53] but also to the largest 500 American industrial corporations and to the ingot capacities of the ten leading steels producers in the United States in 1954. The conclusion to draw from this study of American data is that the law of proportionate effect appears to apply to American firms, but it is essential to qualify the simple lognormal model to allow for the entry of new firms into the business population and such a qualification leads to the generation of a Yule distribution instead of the lognormal.

However, it may be that the measurement of the contribution to total asset growth of new firms among the ranks of the top 500 exaggerates the influence of new firms, because it is likely that most of these newcomers to the giant class were not new entrants to the business population as a whole but simply fast growing medium-sized firms, so that the empirical findings of Simon and Bonini are not inconsistent with the hypothesis that newly-born firms do not contribute much to the total asset growth of all firms. The earlier study by Hart and Prais[53] found that the birth and death of firms in the population of companies quoted on the London Stock Exchange had little effect on the variance of the logarithms of the size distribution, compared with the tendency for surviving firms to increase their dispersion over time. For this reason a lognormal model of growth was used which excluded births and deaths in spite of the fact that it was known that the composition of the business population was continually changing. The weakness of this approach is that births and deaths of companies quoted on the stock market may not reflect the birth and death rates of firms in the business population as a whole, and the latter may exert a considerable influence on the dispersion of the size distribution of all firms and on average growth rates of firms. But the importance of their influence is not yet known in the United Kingdom.

But even if the neglect of births and deaths is justified on pragmatic grounds in the context of business concentration, there may be other contexts in which it is unjustified. For example, in Chapter 4 of the present study it was found that in some industries the frequency of losses made it very dangerous to ignore zero or negative observations, and the lognormal sampling scheme had to be abandoned in such cases.

In the second American study, Ferguson[40] estimated the rank correlation between asset size and growth of twelve firms in each of fifteen industries over the period 1947–56. In eleven of the industries the rank correlations were very low and not significantly different from zero. In three industries (aircraft, cement, food retailing) there was significant negative rank correlation between size and growth, and in the remaining industry, tobacco, there was significant positive correlation. Ferguson concluded that business size has no general and systematic effect upon the rate of growth, and his results were consistent with that part of Gibrat's law of proportionate effect which stipulates that proportionate growth is independent of absolute size, and support the sampling scheme adopted in Chapter 2.

Ferguson then estimated the rank correlation between size and coefficient of variation of his assets series over the period. All the coefficients were small and none was significantly different from zero at the 5 per cent level of probability. If his measure of variability is accepted as reflecting variations of proportionate growth between firms of different size, then his findings are consistent with the second part of Gibrat's law which states that variations in growth are independent of size.

The third American study considered here is that by Hymer and Pashigian[57] who analysed the thousand largest manufacturing firms in the USA in 1946, and compared the growth rates of different size classes of firms within this sample over the period 1946 to 1955. They performed several tests on their data and concluded that their sample of firms was not distributed lognormally. This conclusion raises some points of general interest which are worth a brief comment.

The graphic test of the size distribution of profits in Chapter 2 related to a lognormal distribution with two parameters, a mean and a variance of logarithms of profit, denoted by Λ (μ, σ^2) where μ is the mean and σ^2 is the variance of the logarithms of profit. But Aitchison and Brown[25] show that the two-parameter lognormal is merely one member of a class of lognormal distributions and they describe the properties of a three-parameter and of a four-parameter lognormal distribution. In addition to their theoretical analysis, they give examples of the use of the various types of lognormal distribution in economics, biology and other social and natural sciences. Sometimes the shape of these lognormal distributions is surprising: for example, the three- and four-parameter lognormal distributions can be *negatively* skew, and the four-parameter lognormal can be symmetric but highly leptokurtic. In view of the great flexibility of the lognormal distribution, it is very dangerous to rule out this distribution merely because the two-parameter lognormal curve does not give a good fit to the data; in such cases it is always possible that another type of lognormal curve would give a satisfactory fit, especially if the data suggest that there is some threshold value which can be used as a third parameter in addition to μ and σ^2. Aitchison and Brown cite the case of size distributions of income based on income tax data which exclude observations of income below the minimum level liable to income tax, and show that for such truncated size distributions, the relevant curve is a three-parameter lognormal distribution, denoted by $\Lambda\ (\tau, \mu, \sigma^2)$ where τ represents the minimum level of income. A similar modification to the two-parameter lognormal distribution seems necessary in the case of the sample of American firms drawn by Hymer and Pashigian. It is not a random sample, but consists of the largest 1,000 manufacturing firms in the USA in 1946 and is clearly a truncated distribution with many thousands of firms below the rank of 1,000, presumably constituting the larger part of the size distribution of all firms, excluded from the analysis. Such an exclusion may be permissible in the study of size and growth, but it is unreasonable to test such a sample for the properties of a two-parameter lognormal curve.

The samples of companies quoted on the London Stock Exchange studied by Hart and Prais[53] were not random and excluded numerous unquoted companies and firms. But there was no definite truncation as in the sample drawn by Hymer and Pashigian because many of the quoted companies were smaller than some of the unquoted companies. Even so, it could still be argued that the introduction of a third parameter would have improved the fits of the lognormal curve to the size distribution observed in [53], and it is certainly true that for some of the years studied there were statistically significant departures from the zero skewness and mesokurtosis of the logarithms of size required by the two-parameter lognormal distribution, as can be seen in Table 2 in [53]. But there were at least three reasons for not attempting to improve the fit: first, for some of the years the deviations from the two-parameter lognormal were not significant at the 1 per cent level of significance, secondly for those years where the deviations were statistically significant it remained true that the deviations were not very large, and thirdly the two-parameter lognormal distribution has many desirable reproductive properties which are not shared by its three-parameter counterpart. In particular, in the two-parameter case the ratio of two lognormal size distributions, giving the distribution of proportionate growth, is another lognormal distribution, whereas the distribution of the ratio of the two three-parameter lognormal distributions is not known, so that the theoretical distribution of growth could not have been formulated if Λ (τ, μ, σ^2) had been used. (Cf. Aitchison and Brown,[25] p. 15.)

The sample drawn by Hymer and Pashigian may be regarded as the top slice of the bivariate distribution of American manufacturing firms in 1946 and 1955, as illustrated in Figure 9.1. The univariate distribution of the largest 1,000 firms in 1946 cannot be expected to be a two-parameter lognormal, but the distribution of their sizes in 1955 may well be lognormal: after logarithmic transformation, the slice of the bivariate size distribution studied by Hymer and Pashigian is equivalent to cross-section of a supposedly normal surface, taken perpendicular to the x axis, and, as noted in section 9.2, an array taken from a normal surface is itself normally distributed. Moreover, from the homoscedastic property of the normal surface, each of these conditional distributions—or each of the quartiles into which the 1,000 firms are divided—should have the same variance. Again, as seen in section 9.2, the regression of y on x should be strictly linear. Finally, if the regression coefficient is unity, then on the average the ratio of Y to X, measuring the proportionate rate of growth, will also be the same for each quartile.

Hymer and Pashigian tested these properties directly by comparing the mean and standard deviation of proportionate growth rates for each quartile within the nine separate industries into which the 1,000 firms had been classified. Their first finding was that there is no relationship between size of firm and proportionate growth. Admittedly this conclusion was based on a casual inspection of their tables and no formal tests were used. However, they submitted their data to a regression analysis with a firm's proportionate growth as a dependent variable and its size as one of the determining variables, and concluded that the size variable had an insignificant effect on growth. This result is consistent with the law of proportionate effect, confirms the findings in [40], and provides further justification for the sampling scheme used in the present study and outlined in Chapter 2.

Their second conclusion, however, was that the standard deviation of proportionate growth rates decreases with increases in firm size: large firms may have the same average proportionate growth rates as small firms, but the dispersion of their growth rates is lower than that of small firms. The result is inconsistent with the law of proportionate effect, but similar results have been reported by Prais,[78] and in section 9.2. If the dispersion of proportionate changes in profits of firms sampled in the present study is lower than that of small firms, which had to be excluded for reasons given in Chapter 2, then the standard errors of changes in profits given in Tables 4.2, 6.3, and 6.4 are biased downwards, because they were computed solely from observations of the profit of large companies. This does not imply that the index numbers of profits are biased, but it does imply that their accuracy is lower than is indicated by the standard errors, though in view of the sources of error other than sampling, this deficiency should not be given too much weight and is unlikely to alter the broad conclusions on the reliability of the estimates in each chapter.

Hymer and Pashigian made it clear that their conclusions were tentative and that further testing was required. Two possible limitations of their analysis so far may be mentioned here. First, they did not report the results of normal statistical tests of significance on the difference between means and standard deviations of growth, and it is unsafe to rely on casual inspection of tables of results when testing economic theories. Secondly, their analysis is in terms of the mean and dispersion of proportionate growth, whereas the theoretical distribution of proportionate growth is lognormal and the analysis should have included tests of the difference between the mean and dispersion of the logarithms of proportionate growth. It is true that they may have had in mind the type of argument used in section 9.2 to show that the skewness and kurtosis of the distribution of proportionate growth is likely to be low, but this argument depends on the assumption that the variance of the logarithms of size at the two dates is the same and that the correlation between size and the two dates is high: both assumptions may be reasonable, when the two dates are close together, as in the year to year change in profits, but may be unreasonable when the time interval being studied is as long as the nine years considered by Hymer and Pashigian.

The fourth American study considered here is one section of a paper by Mansfield[68] concerned with Gibrat's law of proportionate effect and the growth of firms. He constructed transition matrices of firms' sizes in the steel, petroleum and rubber tyre industries in the United States for periods, generally decades, between 1916 and 1954. The basic data were available in sufficient detail to permit the construction of complete size distributions of firms in these industries, instead of the truncated distributions considered by Hymer and Pashigian, so that it was possible to study the growth of the smallest firms in an industry in addition to that of the larger firms which had been measured in previous work.

The transition matrices revealed information on the birth and death of firms, and Mansfield concluded that the chance of death decreased with increases in size of firm. This result has been noted

167

in previous studies in the United Kingdom [53], [65], seems plausible from an economic point of view, and may be regarded as generally accepted. However, it is certainly inconsistent with Gibrat's law of proportionate effect. But it must be remembered that even if the chance of death were the same for firms of all sizes, Gibrat's law still would not hold, because if a variate changes its size through time only by randomly distributed multiplicative shocks it is impossible for zero size to be reached and both births and deaths are excluded. Since it is known that firms do enter and leave the business population, Gibrat's law cannot hold unless some modification is introduced, such as the birth process in the Yule distribution, to take into account changes in the population of firms.

Mansfield then studied the growth of firms excluding births and deaths. For surviving firms he computed the distribution of Y/X for each size class of X and then used a χ^2 test to determine whether these distributions were the same in each class, as they should be if Gibrat's law operates for surviving firms. Of the ten transition matrices, six yielded distributions of proportionate growth which were consistent with Gibrat's law, but in the remaining four cases the values of χ^2 were high enough to reject the hypothesis. This is typical of the conclusions reached after testing the law of proportionate effect: the law appears to operate most of the time and yet the exceptions, though in a minority, are frequent enough to make it very risky to accept Gibrat's law as a general rule, even for surviving firms. The next step was to determine whether the distributions of proportionate growth varied between size classes because of differences between mean and dispersion of growth. The estimation of β, the coefficient of regression of y on x, in effect tests for the difference between mean proportionate growth of firms of different sizes, for, as shown in section 9.2, β should be unity if the mean proportionate growth is the same for firms of all sizes. Column (1) of Table 9.9 gives Mansfield's estimates of β for each of his transition matrices, together with their standard errors in Column (2). It can be seen that in most samples the observed b is slightly less than unity, though seven out of the ten estimates of β are not different from unity at the 1 per cent level of significance. It is difficult to be certain that the coefficient of 0·92 for steel 1935–45 is significantly different from unity at the 1 per cent level because the standard errors have been rounded to two decimal places. In fact, the only cases when it is reasonably certain that the regression coefficients are below unity relate to the samples drawn from the steel industry 1916–26 and from the petroleum industry for 1927–37. Thus it seems fair to con-

168

clude from Mansfield's data on surviving firms that part of Gibrat's law holds, namely that firms of all sizes have the same mean proportionate growth. This is consistent with previous findings in [85], [40], [57] and supports the sampling scheme adopted in Chapter 2 of the present study.

TABLE 9.9. *Mansfield's Estimates of β for the Steel, Petroleum and Rubber Tyre Industries, United States of America, 1916–54*

	b	S_b	t	df	SIGNIFICANCE
Steel:					
1916–26 ..	0·88	0·05	2·4	70	* *
1926–35 ..	0·99	0·04	0·2	64	n.s.
1935–45 ..	0·92	0·03	2·7	62	* *
1945–54 ..	1·00	0·04	—	67	n.s.
Petroleum:					
1921–27 ..	0·94	0·05	1·2	126	n.s.
1927–37 ..	0·88	0·04	3·0	114	* *
1937–47 ..	0·99	0·03	0·3	154	n.s.
1947–57 ..	0·94	0·04	1·5	104	n.s.
Tyres:					
1937–45 ..	0·97	0·05	0·6	32	n.s.
1945–52 ..	0·97	0·04	0·7	29	n.s.

Mansfield then estimated the variances of the proportionate growth of firms in each size class, grouped his results into two classes, 'small' and 'large' and used *F*-tests to determine whether there were any significant differences between the variances of proportionate growth in the two classes. In eight out of the ten samples available, the variance of the proportionate growth of 'small' firms was significantly larger than the corresponding variance for the 'large' firms. This finding is inconsistent with the law of proportionate effect, and confirms the results obtained by Hymer and Pashigian.[57] It is true that Mansfield grouped his variances into two classes, instead testing for the homogeneity of variances of growth between all the size classes available: it is also true that the tests were not performed on the variance of the logarithms of proportionate growth; but the conclusion that the variance of growth decreases with increases in size is so plausible from an economic point of view that it is doubtful whether additional tests would alter the result. However, it is still possible that different results will emerge and it is to be hoped further tests on Mansfield's original data will be carried out. Meanwhile, it still seems safe to conclude that the part of Gibrat's law which predicts equal variation of growth rates between firms of different sizes is unlikely to be true.

9.4. GROWTH AND SIZE OF FIRM IN THE UNITED KINGDOM, 1958–60

The Board of Trade[6] has recently published a bivariate distribution of 2,515 companies by their net assets in 1958 and by the ratio of their net assets in 1960 to their net assets in 1958. This sample of companies quoted on the Stock Exchange is analysed by five broad industry groups, but in the first instance the law of proportionate effect will be tested by the estimates for all industries combined, as shown in Table 9.10. The change in net assets was measured by deducting from the value of a company's assets at the end of 1960 the changes which occurred in the three preceding years. That is, no correction was made for the *revaluation* of assets which existed in 1958, so for the purpose of this test it must be assumed that there was no tendency for large companies to revalue their assets which was not shared by companies of all sizes.

Table 9.10 contains two open class intervals, under 90 and over 200, making it difficult to estimate the mean and variance of proportionate growth. This difficulty was overcome by fitting a theoretical curve to the distribution of proportionate growth in the bottom row of Table 9.10 and using it to estimate the limits of the distribution. The two-parameter lognormal curve gave a poor fit to the data, but the Pareto distribution gave an excellent fit to the observations above 110, which enabled the upper limit of the distribution to be estimated as 250, as can be seen in Figure 9.2. The lower limit was estimated as 80.

An inspection of the raw data on the growth rates of the largest 1,908 companies in [6] provided a check on these assumed limits. It was found that six companies, or about 0·3 per cent of the sample, had proportionate growths of less than 80 per cent. At the other extreme, the fitted Pareto curve in Figure 9.2 suggests that 1 per cent of companies had growth rates exceeding 250 per cent (antilog 2·4=251), whereas the raw data in [6] show that twenty-six of the 1,908 largest companies had growth rates exceeding 250 per cent. Thus the fitted Pareto curve seems justified, but the exclusion of just over 1 per cent of the extreme observations produces a downwards bias in the estimates of the variance based on the assumed limits of 80 and 250 per cent. It follows that tests of the significance of the difference between mean proportionate growths of firms of different sizes are weighted in favour of a significant difference and impose a stringent test on the law of proportionate effect.

170

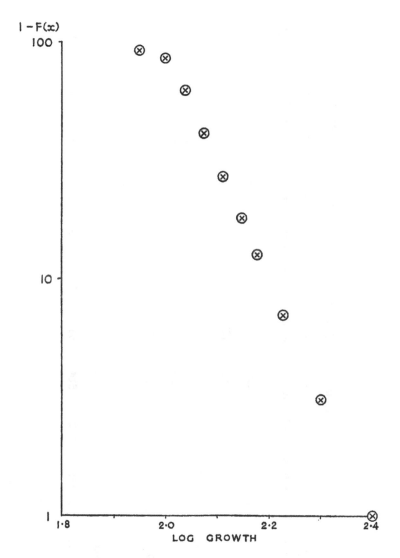

Fig. 9.2. Cumulative distribution of companies by proportionate growth illustrating fit of Pareto curve to data of Table 9.10.

171

TABLE 9.10. *Distribution of Companies by Size and Growth, 1958–60*

VALUE OF NET ASSETS AT BEGINNING—1958 £'000	INDEX OF VALUE OF NET ASSETS AT END—1960 (BEGINNING 1958=100)										TOTAL
	UNDER 90	90—99	100—109	110—119	120—129	130—139	140—149	150—169	170—199	200 AND OVER	
Under £500 ..	72	81	196	171	91	57	34	37	21	34	794
£500—£999 ..	19	46	110	129	75	50	34	32	22	13	530
£1,000—£2,499 ..	16	39	112	165	97	49	32	28	30	14	582
£2,500—£4,999 ..	5	15	50	68	49	28	20	16	12	11	274
£5,000—£9,999 ..	1	8	23	35	27	20	8	12	7	6	147
£10,000—£24,999 ..	3	3	13	22	28	16	9	15	5	2	116
£25,000 and over ..	—	—	10	13	21	9	9	6	4	—	72
Total ..	116	192	514	603	388	229	146	146	101	80	2,515

Using the assumed upper and lower limits, the mean and variance of proportionate growth were estimated for each size class, as shown in Table 9.11. The estimates of the variances are heterogeneous according to Bartlett's test and it can be seen that c^2 for the smallest class is much larger than that for the largest class. The estimates of γ^2 for classes 4 and 5 disturb the tendency for c^2 to fall systematically with increases in the size of firm, but the evidence is strong enough to support the conclusion that the variance of proportionate growth of large firms is generally lower than that for smaller firms. This result is inconsistent with the law of proportionate effect developed in section 9.2, but it agrees with many previous findings described in sections 9.2 and 9.3.

TABLE 9.11. *Mean and Variance of Proportionate Growth of Companies in Table 9.10, 1958–60*

CLASS	ASSET SIZE £'000	n	k	c^2
1	Under 500	794	120·3	10·0
2	500–999	530	124·6	8·1
3	1,000–2,499	582	124·3	7·3
4	2,500–4,999	274	127·7	8·4
5	5,000–9,999	147	131·2	8·0
6	10,000–24,999	116	130·8	6·3
7	25,000 and over	72	130·4	4·1

TABLE 9.12. *Welch-Aspin Tests of Significance of Differences between Estimates of $\varkappa$ for Each Size Class in Table 9.10*

SIZE CLASS	1	2	3	4	5	6	7
1	—	—	—	—	—	—	—
2	Yes	—	—	—	—	—	—
3	Yes	No	—	—	—	—	—
4	Yes	No	No	—	—	—	—
5	Yes	Yes	Yes	No	—	—	—
6	Yes	Yes	Yes	No	No	—	—
7	Yes	Yes	Yes	No	No	No	—

No =No significant difference at 5 per cent level.
Yes=Significant difference.

The results of applying Welch-Aspin tests to the means are shown in Table 9.12. It is clear that firms in size class 1, with under £500,000 net assets in 1958, had a lower mean proportionate growth than firms in any other size class, because there are significant differences reported in each cell of Column (1) of Table 9.12. There remain fifteen other differences between pairs of means and of these six are significantly different. But nine are not significantly different and are consistent with the law of proportionate effect and with the previous findings in sections 9.2 and 9.3. However, it is clear that the mean proportionate growths of firms in the classes 1, 2 and 3 were significantly lower than those in the larger classes and this result is inconsistent with the law of proportionate effect.

TABLE 9.13. *Distribution of Manufacturing Companies by Size in 1958 and 1960*

	SIZE IN 1958													
SIZE IN 1960	A	B	C	D	E	F	G	H	I	J	K	L	M	Totals
A 250	—	—	—	—	—	—	—	—	—	—	—	—	—	—
B 500	—	—	—	—	—	—	—	—	—	—	—	—	—	—
C 1000	3	81	279	6	—	—	—	—	—	—	—	—	—	**369**
D 2000	—	3	98	251	3	1	—	—	—	—	—	—	—	**356**
E 4000	—	—	1	90	169	—	—	—	—	—	—	—	—	**260**
F 8000	—	—	—	1	59	116	—	—	—	—	—	—	—	**176**
G 16000	—	—	—	—	3	44	57	—	—	—	—	—	—	**104**
H 32000	—	—	—	—	—	2	30	42	—	—	—	—	—	**74**
I 64000	—	—	—	—	—	1	1	10	15	—	—	—	—	**27**
J 128000	—	—	—	—	—	1	0	2	7	10	—	—	—	**20**
K 256000	—	—	—	—	—	—	—	—	3	5	3	—	—	**11**
L 512000	—	—	—	—	—	—	—	—	—	—	—	1	—	**1**
M 1024000	—	—	—	—	—	—	—	—	—	—	—	—	1	**1**
Total	**3**	**84**	**378**	**348**	**234**	**165**	**88**	**54**	**25**	**15**	**3**	**1**	**1**	**1399**

The tests were then repeated on the logarithms of proportionate growth. Bartlett's test revealed that the estimates of σ^2 were heterogeneous and a series of Welch-Aspin tests on the differences between the estimates of μ for each size class gave the same results as those in Table 9.12. Clearly, the differences in growth rates of firms of different size observed in Table 9.11 cannot be explained by the fact that the tests were performed on k instead of m. But because these results are inconsistent with those found in the previous studies reviewed in sections 9.2 and 9.3, some explanation is required. Unfortunately, the tables published in [6] do not facilitate statistical analysis, so it was necessary to compile new bivariate frequency distributions of size and growth of the largest 1,908 companies in the Board of Trade's sample.

Section I in [6] contains estimates of the net assets of each company in the Board of Trade's sample which had net assets of £500,000 and over at the end of 1960. In addition, the ratio of net assets at the end of 1960 to their value at the beginning of 1958 is given for 1,844 of these companies. It was therefore possible to compile the bivariate distribution in Table 9.13 showing the distribution of 1,399 manufacturing companies by their net assets at the end of 1960 and at the beginning of 1958. The size classes are equal on a logarithmic scale, the upper limit of each class being twice the lower limit. The analysis was confined to manufacturing companies in the first instance, in an attempt to obtain a reasonably homogeneous sample for the statistical analysis of the growth of firms described in section 9.2.

The regression of the logarithm of firm size in 1960 on the logarithm of firm size in 1958 is given by $b=0.97$, with standard error $S_b=0.0079$ and correlation coefficient $r=0.96$. It can be seen that $b^2 > r^2$ and that business concentration increased by 2 per cent over the three years, even though the regression coefficient was less than unity, which by itself would indicate that large firms did not grow more quickly than small firms. This result must be modified to allow for the fact that the Board of Trade data relate to firms with £500,000 or more net assets in 1960, and exclude companies which were larger than this size in 1958 but which declined below this threshold value by 1960. The effect of this is to introduce a downward bias in the estimate of β. The mean of each column of Table 9.13 is plotted against the size in 1958 in Figure 9.3. It can be seen that the means are collinear for values of X_{t-1} above £500,000, but there is a sharp curvature for values of X_{t-1} below this size. If the regression analysis is confined to those companies above this threshold size in 1958, then $b=1.02$, $S_b=0.0082$ and $r=0.95$, and business concentration increased by 17 per cent, much more sharply than the previous regression suggested. Moreover, the fact that $b>1$ suggests that in manufacturing, large firms grew more quickly than small firms over the period. It should also be noted that the linearity of the regression is consistent with lognormal theory.

However, to reach a reliable conclusion on the growth rates of small firms compared with large firms over the period 1958–60, it is essential to have more information on the sizes of the firms below £500,000 assets in 1960 and 1958. The Board of Trade[6] did not publish the raw data required for the closer study of the growth of small firms, but it was possible to estimate the frequencies of the small firms in the bivariate distribution of size in 1958 and 1960 from an extension of Table 9.13 to cover non-manufacturing industries, com-

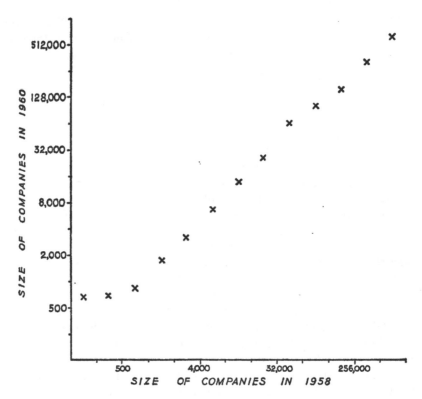

Fig. 9.3. Regression of company size in 1960 on size in 1958, using data of Table 9.13.

bined with the marginal distributions of size in 1958 and 1960 given in Tables 4 and 5 respectively in [6]. That is, the sizes of individual companies in the construction, distributive and service trades are given in Section I of [6], providing that their assets exceeded £500,000 in 1960. The ratio of their size in 1960 to their size in 1958 is also given, so it was possible to estimate their individual sizes in 1958. The extension of Table 9.13 to include non-manufacturing increased the heterogeneity of the sample, and imposed more severe conditions

176

for the test of the law of proportionate effect. The next step was to compare the marginal distributions of this new bivariate distribution with those for 1958 and 1960 published in [6]. For example, in the bivariate distribution compiled from the raw data, 129 companies (123+5+1) were found to be above £500,000 assets in 1960 but to be below this size in 1958. But the marginal distribution published in

TABLE 9.14. *Distribution of Companies by Size in 1958 and 1960*

SIZE IN 1960	SIZE IN 1958												
	AB	C	D	E	F	G	H	I	J	K	L	M	Total
AB 500	665	6	—	—	—	—	—	—	—	—	—	—	**671**
C 1000	123	390	7	—	—	—	—	—	—	—	—	—	**520**
D 2000	5	132	328	5	1	—	—	—	—	—	—	—	**471**
E 4000	—	2	131	214	—	—	—	—	—	—	—	—	**347**
F 8000	1	—	1	77	146	—	—	—	—	—	—	—	**225**
G 16000	—	—	—	6	51	66	1	—	—	—	—	—	**124**
H 32000	—	—	—	—	2	35	48	—	—	—	—	—	**85**
I 64000	—	—	—	—	1	1	15	20	—	—	—	—	**37**
J 128000	—	—	—	—	1	—	2	8	11	—	—	—	**22**
K 256000	—	—	—	—	—	—	—	3	5	3	—	—	**11**
L 512000	—	—	—	—	—	—	—	—	—	—	1	—	**1**
M 1024000	—	—	—	—	—	—	—	—	—	—	—	1	**1**
Total	**794**	**530**	**467**	**302**	**202**	**102**	**66**	**31**	**16**	**3**	**1**	**1**	**2515**

Table 4 of [6] shows that a total of 794 companies were below £500,000 in 1958 so that 665 companies must have been less than this size at both dates, which gives the entry in the cell in the first row and first column of Table 9.14. It follows that there must have been six companies above this size in 1958 but below it in 1960, because Table 5 in [6] shows that there were 671 companies below £500,000 in 1960. These six companies were assumed to be in the cell AB, C. Similar reasoning was applied to the second and third rows because the Board of Trade's size class £500,000–£1 million coincided with the logarithmic interval used here. Even so, it was still impossible to obtain frequencies for classes A and B separately, and is certainly desirable to have such information when measuring the relationship between growth and size of firm.

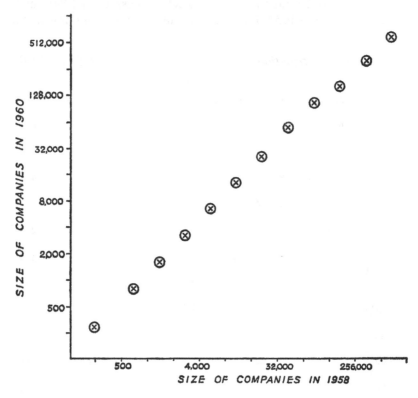

Fig. 9.4. Regression of company size in 1960 on size in 1958, using data of Table 9.14.

The means of the columns of Table 9.14 are plotted in Figure 9.4. It can be seen that they are collinear and are consistent with the law of proportionate effect. The linear regression of size in 1960 on size in 1958 is given by $b=1\cdot03$, with standard error $S_b=0\cdot0052$ and correlation coefficient $r=0\cdot97$. Once again, $b>r$ and business concentration increased by nearly 12 per cent over the three years between the beginning of 1958 and the end of 1960. In logarithms to the base 2, the estimate of σ^2 for 1960 is $3\cdot7$ compared with $3\cdot3$ for 1958. But the large increase in business concentration cannot be attributed solely to the growth of large firms relatively to small firms;

178

though b is significantly greater than unity according to the usual tests of significance, the fact remains that it is still too near unity to argue that the increase in concentration occurred primarily because the proportionate growth of large firms was slightly above that of small firms. This can be shown by rewriting equation (9.9) in the form in which it appeared in [53], where the relationship between the variance of the logarithms of size at two dates was given by

$$\text{Var } (y) = b^2 \text{ Var } (x) + \sigma^2_\varepsilon \qquad (9.18)$$

which may be evaluated in the present case as,

$$3 \cdot 7 = (1 \cdot 06 \times 3 \cdot 3) + 0 \cdot 2 \qquad (9.19)$$

where σ^2_ε is the residual variance. It can be seen that the regression coefficient, measuring the growth of large firms relative to small firms, explains only half (six of the observed twelve percentage points increase) of the increase in business concentration. The remaining half is explained by the residual variance ($0 \cdot 2 / 3 \cdot 3 = 6$ per cent).

The conclusion that the proportionate rate of growth of large companies was slightly above that of small companies during the period 1958–60 depends partly on the assumption made at the beginning of this section that there was no tendency for large companies to *revalue* their assets more quickly than small companies. It is also heavily dependent on the estimated growth of small companies below £500,000 in 1958. More information is needed about the sizes of small companies at the two dates before thoroughly reliable conclusions can be reached, but it is at least possible to draw some conclusions from this analysis which are fairly reliable. First, the various estimates of β are all in the neighbourhood of unity, though two are slightly above and one slightly below, depending on the size classes included. This is in broad agreement with the law of proportionate effect. Secondly, business concentration increased between 1958 and 1960 because each of these estimates of β exceeded the corresponding estimates of ρ. This is also consistent with the law of proportionate effect. Thirdly, the regression of y on x is linear, which is again consistent with the law of proportionate effect and with the assumption that the bivariate size distribution is lognormal.

However, the third conclusion must be qualified. The marginal distributions in 1958 and 1960 are not two-parameter lognormal curves. Formally, their degrees of skewness after logarithmic transformation, as measured by Fisher's g_1 statistic, are $1 \cdot 13$ ($0 \cdot 05$) for 1958 and $1 \cdot 20$ ($0 \cdot 05$) for 1960. Their degrees of kurtosis, as measured by Fisher's g_2 statistic, are $1 \cdot 10$ ($0 \cdot 10$) for 1958 and $0 \cdot 71$ ($0 \cdot 10$) for 1960. These results are not surprising since it is known that the size distributions are truncated, so that only part of the assumed log-normal bivariate distribution is observed. It is worth noting that the estimates of g_1 and g_2 for similar samples of companies given in [53] are much lower than those derived from Table 9.14. The explanation is that the measure of size used in [53] was the stock market valuation of each company's shares, and it is possible for this measure to become much lower than the company's own estimate of the value of its assets, especially in the case of unsuccessful firms. Thus the measure of size used also affects the skewness and kurtosis of the marginal distributions, and in the present case the use of net tangible assets to measure size imposes relatively strict threshold values, suggesting that the appropriate test should relate to a three-parameter rather than a two-parameter lognormal curve. Consequently, the third conclusion should be that the linearity of the regression of y on x is consistent with a *truncated* lognormal bivariate distribution of companies by size in 1958 and 1960.

9.5. CONCLUSION

This review of the relationship between the growth and size of firms in the United States and in the United Kingdom suggests the following general conclusions. Lognormal theory and Gibrat's law of proportionate effect are exceedingly useful tools in the analysis of the growth of firms, especially as a first approximation. Indeed, considering the complicated network of economic and political forces which influence a firm's growth, it is surprising how frequently the observed relationship between size and growth approximates to the simple lognormal model. There is a general agreement, however, that not all of the properties of this simple model apply to firms' growth, if only because it cannot readily cover the birth and death of firms.

There is no general agreement about the variation of proportionate growth and size of firm, but the evidence reviewed in sections 9.3 and 9.4 suggests that the variance of proportionate growth decreases with increases in size. This is inconsistent with the law of proportionate effect. Nor is there general agreement on the relationship between average proportionate rate of growth and size of firms, but the evidence reviewed here suggests that in most cases the mean proportionate rate of growth is the same for firms of all sizes. This is consistent with the law of proportionate effect and with the sampling scheme described in Chapter 2.

CHAPTER 10

THE PROFITS OF SMALL
MANUFACTURING FIRMS

BY JAMES BATES

10.1. INTRODUCTION

ONE of the difficulties of research based on published balance sheets and profit and loss accounts is that a large number of businesses do not publish their accounts. Information about aggregates is available from such sources as the Annual Reports of the Commissioners of Inland Revenue[1] and from publications of the Board of Trade,[6, 7, 8] but it is not possible to find out anything from such information about differences between firms. It is frequently desirable when discussing the economic characteristics of businesses to be able to analyse differences between individual firms, between firms in different industries, and between firms of different sizes. Information about many individual firms is fairly readily available from the published accounts of public companies, but the vast majority of companies and other businesses* do not have to publish any information of any kind, and it is not easy to find out anything about their activities.

In order to study the financial and other problems of small firms, a Survey was carried out at the Oxford University Institute of Statistics in 1956.† One product of this Survey was the collection and analysis of the balance sheets and profit and loss accounts of 335 small manufacturing businesses (49 unincorporated businesses and 286 private companies) for the years 1953 to 1956. A

* In Britain in 1958 there were 329,733 companies with share capital; only 10,933 of these were public, and subject to the need to publish financial information (see [5]). Unincorporated businesses (sole owners and partnerships) need to be added to private companies in order to get an estimate of the number of firms which do not publish information. These unincorporated businesses probably account for something like half of all business concerns in Britain (see [110]).

† The Small Business Survey was financed by a grant made under the Conditional Aid Scheme for the use of counterpart funds derived from United States Economic Aid.

181   DOI: 10.4324/9781003183266-12

TABLE 10.1. *Size Distribution of Firms in Small Business Survey*

SIZE MEASURE				NUMBER OF FIRMS IN SURVEY	TOTAL NUMBER OF ESTABLISHMENTS IN GREAT BRITAIN*
Employment					(*thousands*)
(number of employees)					
10 and under	..	..	..	20	†
11 – 19 ..	..	..	..	55	11·3
20 – 29 ..	..	..	..	62	8·3
30 – 39 ..	..	..	..	39	6·3
40 – 49 ..	..	..	..	41	4·5
50 – 74 ..	..	..	..	46	7·0
75 – 99 ..	..	..	..	17	4·0
100 –199 ..	..	..	..	34	7·1
200 –499 ..	..	..	..	20	5·1
Not ascertained	..	..	..	1	—
Total	..	..	..	**335**	**53·5**
Turnover (£'000)					
Under 10 ..	..	..	..	11	
10 – 19 ..	..	..	..	25	
20 – 29 ..	..	..	..	47	
30 – 39 ..	..	..	..	30	
40 – 49 ..	..	..	..	60	
50 – 74 ..	..	..	..	21	not available
75 – 99 ..	..	..	..	35	
100 –249 ..	..	..	..	31	
250 –499 ..	..	..	..	28	
500 –999 ..	..	..	..	7	
1,000 and over	..	..	..	27	
Not ascertained	..	..	..	13	
Total	..	..	..	**335**	
Net Assets (£'000)					
Under 5 ..	..	..	..	94	
5 – 9 ..	..	..	..	56	
10 – 24 ..	..	..	..	69	
25 – 49 ..	..	..	..	44	
50 – 74 ..	..	..	..	19	not available
75 – 99 ..	..	..	..	10	
100 –249 ..	..	..	..	25	
250 and over	..	..	..	12	
Not ascertained	..	..	..	6	
Total	..	..	..	**335**	

* Calculated from Census of Production data, which refers to manufacturing industry only.
† Not ascertained.

description of the Survey and sample available for analysis will be found in [29] and [30], and in other sources mentioned there, and it is not necessary to reproduce them in detail here; some indication of the coverage and characteristics of the sample may, however, be obtained from Tables 10.1 and 10.2. All of the firms in the Survey employed fewer than 500 people; 83 per cent employed fewer than 100 people. By this and other size measures all of the firms in the sample were small: fewer than 5 per cent of firms had net assets of more than a quarter of a million pounds; fewer than 10 per cent had turnover of over a million pounds. The Survey was also concentrated in four main industries, shown in Table 10.2: this was partly an accident of sample design, due to concentration on a few main areas, and partly a reflection of the fact that in these industries there is a large proportion of small firms. The main emphasis of the Survey, therefore, was on private companies employing between 10 and 100 people in the industries specified in Table 10.2: these facts should be borne in mind when interpreting the results of this chapter.

TABLE 10.2. *Small Business Survey: Principal Industries Represented in Sample*

INDUSTRY			NUMBER OF FIRMS	RESPONSE RATE (%)
Engineering	(6) ..	..	58	21
Metal manufacture	(8) ..	..	41	17
Clothing	(12) ..	..	50	18
Paper and printing	(15) ..	..	36	23
Other industries	..	..	150	—
Total	..	..	335	18

The information available does not permit the construction of a time-series of the profits of small manufacturing firms, but some cross-section analysis is possible. This chapter describes (by simple enumeration in the first instance) the principal characteristics of the trading and profit and loss accounts of firms in the Survey and, where possible, briefly compares small with large firms. More elaborate analysis will be presented in Volume II.

10.2. THE TRADING ACCOUNTS OF SMALL FIRMS

Neither public nor private companies are required to publish details from their trading and profit and loss accounts (that is, they do not have to divulge information about transactions undertaken *before* a balance of profit is arrived at); but respondents to the Small Business

Survey were frequently prepared to allow their trading accounts to be inspected. These permit some investigation of the cost structure of small firms.

TABLE 10.3. *Profit and Loss Account of Sub-Sample of 144 Small Manufacturing Businesses*

Year ended March 31, 1956

ITEM	TOTAL £	AVERAGE £ (I)	PER CENT OF TOTAL SALES (II)	(III)
1. Materials, etc.	4,705,928	32,680	48·6	48·6
2. Wages	2,359,071	16,382	24·4	24·5 (143)
3. Salaries	346,065	2,403	3·6	5·8 (88)
4. Directors' remuneration ..	343,209	2,383	3·5	4·5 (114)
5. Advertising	67,622	470	0·7	1·7 (59)
6. Rent and rates	66,098	459	0·7	0·8 (121)
7. Depreciation	198,312	1,377	2·0	2·2 (137)
8. Repairs and maintenance..	172,966	1,201	1·8	1·9 (137)
9. Other costs	797,461	5,538	8·2	8·2
10. Total costs	9,056,732	62,894	93·5	93·5
11. Net sales	9,693,720	67,318	100·0	100·0
12. Operating profit .. .. (11 *less* 10)	636,988	4,424	6·6	6·6
13. Other income	156,772	1,089	1·6	3·2 (72)
14. Total profit .. .. (12 *plus* 13)	793,760	5,512	8·2	8·2
15. Current tax	350,963	2,437	3·6	5·1 (103)
16. Net profit .. .. .. (14 *less* 15)	442,797	3,075	4·6	4·6
17. Dividends (ordinary) ..	104,803	728	1·1	4·0 (39)
18. Dividends (preference) ..	15,115	105	0·2	1·0 (21)
19. Minority interests ..	0	0	—	— —
20. Retained profit .. .. (16 *less* 17 *less* 18)	322,879	2,242	3·3	3·3
21. Total transfers to reserves (IV)	546,207	3,793	5·6	5·6
22. Value added (11 *less* 1) ..	4,987,792	34,638	51·4	
23. Direct costs (1 *plus* 2) ..	7,064,999	49,062	73·0	
24. Overhead costs (11 *less* 23)	2,628,721	18,256	27·0	

Notes: (I) Arithmetic Mean. (I) and (II) All firms did not incur all of these costs. (I) refers to the arithmetic mean of all firms, (III) refers to arithmetic mean of non-zero observations (figures in parenthesis indicate numbers of observations). (IV) Including depreciation, Prior year adjustments, etc.

TABLE 10.3—*continued*
The Appropriation of Income of 144 Small Manufacturing Businesses

Year ended March 31, 1956

ITEM	AVERAGE (£)	PER CENT OF GROSS EARNINGS	PER CENT OF TOTAL PROFIT
25. Gross earnings	9,272	100·0	169·0
(14 *plus* 7 *plus* 4)			
less Depreciation	1,377	14·9	25·0
less 21 Directors' remuneration	2,383	25·7	44·0
14. Total profit ..	5,512	59·4	100·0
15. Current tax ..	2,437	26·2	44·2
17. *plus* 18 Dividends ..	833	8·9	15·1
20. Retained profit	2,242	24·3	40·7
plus 7 Depreciation	1,377	14·9	25·0
plus Prior year adjustments, etc.	174	1·8	3·2
21. Transfers to reserves	3,793	41·0	68·9
SUMMARY			
Tax ..	2,437	26·2	
Total income distributed	3,216	34·6	
Total income retained ..	3,619	39·2	
(excluding adjustments)			

Methods of presentation of accounting information differ a great deal from firm to firm, and one of the major 'editing' tasks at the Institute of Statistics was the standardization of accounts. A standard form was evolved, which is illustrated in Table 10.3: this shows the main items of interest calculated on the same basis for all firms, without significant loss of detail.

Table 10.3 is illustrative only: the arithmetic mean of a skewed distribution may give a misleading impression of the importance of individual items, because it may be swamped by a few large observations; but it has the virtue, for illustrative purposes, that the components add up to the total. In order to portray the typical experience of firms however, a different approach is desirable, since it is necessary to discount the influence of a few large observations. Logarithms or geometric means could be employed, and would serve this purpose, but they are inappropriate to this particular sample, which contains many zero and negative observations.

Grouped frequency distributions present the data in a way which enables the observer to note typical experience; alternatively the mode or the median may be calculated. For present purposes frequency distributions have been prepared, but are not presented here;

medians have, however, been calculated (in the majority of cases they are not very different from the modes). Variances too have been calculated; these provide a measure of the dispersion of the distributions. Arithmetic means have also been calculated from the grouped data: these do not provide the same answers as the arithmetic means in Table 10.3, for the following reasons. Denoting the absolute amount of any component of costs of the *ith* firm as X_i, and the total sales of the firm as Y_i, the percentages of total sales presented in Table 10.3, Column (II), is:

$$\frac{\Sigma X_i}{\Sigma Y_i} \times 100$$

(for example, materials as a percentage of total sales are $\frac{4,705,928}{9,693,720}$ $\times 100 = 48 \cdot 6$ per cent). In Tables 10·4 and 10·5, however, the calculations of percentages of total sales are carried out individually for each firm, and the mean from grouped data is therefore of the form $\frac{1}{n}\Sigma\left(\frac{X_i}{Y_i} \times 100\right)$, which is not equal to $\frac{\Sigma X_i}{\Sigma Y_i} \times 100$. This mean from a grouped distribution has a similar advantage to the median, the mode and other measures discussed above, since it avoids the snag of the ordinary arithmetic mean: that is to say, it gives the percentage for each individual firm a weight of 1 (as distinct from a weight equivalent to the numerical value of the items being measured), and very large observations are to some extent discounted.

If we call $\frac{\Sigma X_i}{\Sigma Y_i} \times 100$ the weighted mean (this is available for 1956 only); and $\frac{1}{n}\Sigma\left(\frac{X_i}{Y_i} \times 100\right)$ the grouped mean, it is possible to compare both of these with the median for the main items of the profit and loss account.

For most items there were no significant differences between years (see Table 10.4), and it is not difficult to depict the typical cost structure of small firms. The experience of the four industries in the Survey is shown in Table 10.5, in which inter-industry differences between major cost items are presented.

The trading account of a firm is drawn up in order to show the composition of the costs of the firm. The economic significance of the main elements of costs is fairly simply described: a firm buys materials and components and adds value to them by the application of factors of production, whose costs (profit, wages, rent, depreciation, advertising, etc.) are a measure of the net output of the firm, or

TABLE 10.4. *Small Business Survey: Median, Arithmetic Mean and Variance of Major Items of Profit and Loss Account, Years Ending 31.3.1953, 31.3.1954, 31.3.1955, 31.3.1956**

PERCENTAGES OF TOTAL SALES

NUMBER OF FIRMS	1953 (20)			1954 (117)			1955 (244)			1956 (149)		
	MEDIAN	MEAN	VARIANCE	MEDIAN	MEAN	VARIANCE	MEDIAN	MEAN	VARIANCE	MEDIAN	MEAN	VARIANCE
Materials, etc...	45·0	44·1	439·70	44·6	45·0	358·86	44·0	43·5	306·27	44·8	44·8	286·29
Wages	28·6	34·1	385·55	27·4	29·5	225·24	28·8	30·7	198·47	28·2	29·4	218·88
Salaries	1·0	1·7	3·38	1·6	2·8	11·76	1·4	3·3	33·53	1·3	2·8	15·57
Directors' remuneration	5·0	4·8	22·28	4·0	6·4	62·84	4·4	6·4	45·14	4·4	5·4	27·45
Depreciation	1·6	2·0	3·02	1·3	1·8	2·62	1·4	1·8	3·14	1·3	1·8	3·29
Other costs	6·9	7·6	23·18	7·8	8·6	24·17	7·8	9·1	64·9	7·5	8·5	32·12
Total costs	94·5	92·6	446·0	95·4	94·2	105·29	95·1	93·2	97·28	94·7	92·5	227·20
Operating profit	7·2	8·0	38·50	3·0	5·6	40·97	3·8	6·2	57·18	3·6	7·0	101·76
Total profit	7·2	8·0	38·50	4·1	6·0	48·46	4·0	6·4	54·45	3·8	7·3	102·08
Gross income	12·9	13·8	100·81	12·3	13·3	85·17	12·3	13·3	84·64	13·0	13·9	114·39
Retained profit	0	2·0	14·13	0·9	1·8	5·09	2·0	2·7	14·30	2·5	3·4	20·74
Value added	56·0	54·1	643·35	56·6	56·1	344·84	56·1	56·1	311·56	55·5	55·6	292·10
Direct costs	73·8	73·9	570·25	74·9	72·3	339·83	74·5	72·8	241·18	74·0	73·4	224·96

* Calculated from grouped frequency distributions.

TABLE 10.5. *Major Cost Items by Industry*

COST ITEM AND INDUSTRY*	31.3.1954 MEDIAN	31.3.1954 MEAN	31.3.1954 VARIANCE	31.3.1955 MEDIAN	31.3.1955 MEAN	31.3.1955 VARIANCE	31.3.1956 MEDIAN	31.3.1956 MEAN	31.3.1956 VARIANCE
Materials									
6	43·0	37·9	189	39·4	37·0	157	38·3	38·3	214
8	35·8	33·5	545	38·0	38·4	301	41·6	38·9	201
12	61·3	48·0	639	56·7	50·2	398	50·0	48·4	431
15	34·0	33·8	221	33·3	34·6	303	33·3	34·5	274
Other	45·8	47·6	325	47·8	46·8	243	49·1	49·3	211
All	44·6	45·0	359	44·0	43·5	306	44·8	44·8	286
Wages									
6	32·5	36·3	227	33·2	33·6	134	32·2	31·6	159
8	33·0	32·6	139	34·6	33·2	174	30·0	29·1	218
12	23·8	31·8	456	27·8	32·5	300	20·0	35·0	360
15	35·0	32·5	211	35·8	34·0	155	36·3	36·9	101
Other	25·0	26·8	143	26·0	27·1	184	23·8	24·9	207
All	27·4	29·5	225	28·8	30·7	198	28·2	29·4	219
Salaries									
6	1·9	2·5	5·0	3·0	3·6	12·2	2·1	2·3	16·4
8	3·4	3·8	8·4	3·3	4·4	25·6	4·3	5·8	40·9
12	0	2·8	19·2	0	1·6	5·1	0	1·5	3·4
15		6·9	290·6	0	5·0	129·4	0	3·0	17·2
Other	1·6	2·7	11·8	1·1	3·3	34·1	0·5	2·3	11·0
All	1·6	2·8	11·8	1·4	3·3	33·5	1·3	2·8	15·6

TABLE 10.5—continued

COST ITEM AND INDUSTRY*	YEAR ENDING	31.3.1954 MEDIAN	31.3.1954 MEAN	31.3.1954 VARIANCE	31.3.1955 MEDIAN	31.3.1955 MEAN	31.3.1955 VARIANCE	31.3.1956 MEDIAN	31.3.1956 MEAN	31.3.1956 VARIANCE
Directors' Remuneration										
6	::	5·9	5·2	7·3	8·4	8·9	25·3	6·2	6·8	18·1
8	::	7·9	8·5	28·5	6·4	6·7	27·5	6·0	6·0	29·0
12	::	1·5	2·8	9·2	3·3	4·5	28·9	3·1	3·9	11·3
15	::	5·0	8·0	72·2	7·5	8·7	49·8	6·4	6·4	26·6
Other	::	3·5	6·9	106·0	3·0	5·5	62·0	3·1	5·1	37·2
All	::	**4·0**	**6·4**	**62·8**	**4·4**	**6·4**	**45·1**	**4·4**	**5·4**	**27·5**
Depreciation										
6	::	2·3	2·1	2·9	2·2	1·9	3·8	2·2	1·6	4·5
8	::	2·2	1·9	2·3	2·0	1·6	2·4	1·6	1·1	1·4
12	::	0·9	0·7	0·4	1·3	0·9	2·6	1·7	1·3	4·1
15	::	2·3	2·0	2·6	2·4	2·0	5·4	1·7	1·7	12·3
Other	::	1·7	1·1	3·6	1·6	1·1	2·6	1·3	0·9	1·8
All	::	**1·3**	**1·8**	**2·6**	**1·4**	**1·8**	**3·1**	**1·3**	**1·8**	**3·3**
Other Costs										
6	::	10·6	10·8	22·9	8·6	11·4	209·3	7·5	8·0	16·0
8	::	5·9	6·3	15·8	7·8	8·8	27·8	8·1	8·9	20·4
12	::	6·9	7·2	13·6	5·9	6·2	13·3	5·0	6·5	22·7
15	::	8·3	9·3	15·4	8·2	10·3	68·1	8·3	10·5	54·9
Other	::	8·2	9·4	26·4	8·1	9·1	32·2	7·9	8·9	38·7
All	::	**7·8**	**8·6**	**24·2**	**7·8**	**9·1**	**64·9**	**7·5**	**8·5**	**32·1**

189

TABLE 10.5—continued

YEAR ENDING COST ITEM AND INDUSTRY*	31.3.1954 MEDIAN	31.3.1954 MEAN	31.3.1954 VARIANCE	31.3.1955 MEDIAN	31.3.1955 MEAN	31.3.1955 VARIANCE	31.3.1956 MEDIAN	31.3.1956 MEAN	31.3.1956 VARIANCE
Total Costs									
6	85·0	92·9	33·9	94·3	93·1	37·6	94·2	92·8	24·4
8	95·0	94·4	16·6	94·7	93·4	40·5	94·5	92·7	30·0
12	94·0	96·3	7·9	93·2	96·1	7·8	99·1	97·3	3·5
15	97·5	95·0	30·0	94·7	93·3	40·9	94·4	93·4	34·3
Other	95·7	94·1	43·8	95·0	92·2	82·8	93·6	90·4	112·4
All	95·4	94·2	105·3	95·1	93·2	97·3	94·7	92·5	227·2
Total Profit									
6	6·8	7·9	48·3	6·5	7·3	34·8	5·0	7·2	46·4
8	4·6	5·4	19·7	4·6	6·7	36·0	3·5	9·7	32·1
12	4·1	4·8	14·0	2·4	2·7	6·6	1·7	2·6	7·3
15	2·5	5·0	32·5	5·0	6·7	37·4	4·3	6·7	35·2
Other	3·4	6·2	72·9	3·6	7·2	85·9	4·2	8·9	117·6
All	4·1	6·0	48·4	4·0	6·4	54·4	3·8	7·3	102·1
Gross Earnings									
6	15·5	15·0	29·5	16·4	16·1	52·4	13·6	13·6	63·8
8	14·5	15·3	54·2	13·8	14·0	54·4	12·9	17·0	358·5
12	6·8	7·3	20·0	6·1	7·7	43·5	6·0	7·3	30·4
15	15·0	15·3	55·3	16·7	16·3	52·2	16·0	15·6	77·7
Other	13·1	14·7	132·4	13·0	12·9	116·7	15·2	15·5	91·8
All	12·3	13·3	85·2	12·3	13·3	84·6	13·0	13·9	114·4

TABLE 10.5—continued

YEAR ENDING	31.3.1954			31.3.1955			31.3.1956		
COST ITEM AND INDUSTRY*	MEDIAN	MEAN	VARIANCE	MEDIAN	MEAN	VARIANCE	MEDIAN	MEAN	VARIANCE
Direct Costs									
6	69·2	65·7	166	70·8	69·3	103	70·8	69·7	74
8	70·7	70·9	92	70·9	71·5	93	72·9	71·7	97
12	81·9	77·7	241	84·4	83·1	82	84·4	83·0	96
15	75·0	66·9	547	73·8	70·1	319	72·9	72·5	106
Other	75·5	72·9	191	74·5	72·3	196	73·9	72·6	157
All	74·9	72·3	340	74·5	72·8	241	74·0	73·4	225
Value Added									
6	59·0	62·1	197	63·9	64·0	172	60·0	60·7	227
8	64·2	62·6	271	62·0	61·6	293	58·3	61·3	205
12	43·8	53·0	563	43·3	49·7	386	50·0	51·5	423
15	66·0	66·0	209	66·7	65·4	306	66·7	65·6	284
Other	54·6	53·3	290	52·3	53·3	265	52·2	51·0	208
All	56·6	56·1	345	56·1	56·1	312	55·5	55·6	292

* Industry numbers correspond to the Standard Industrial Classification.
Number of observations for each year are:

	1954	1955	1956
6 (Engineering)	15	43	30
8 (Metal Goods)	17	32	16
12 (Clothing)	15	32	20
15 (Paper and Printing)	10	24	16
Other	60	113	67
All	117	244	149

191

the value added by the processes of production. The difference between the costs of the final output and the receipts from sale of the output is one measure of the profit of the firm.

The main item of expenditure in most firms is the purchase of materials: this may be calculated for accounting purposes by taking the stock of materials at the beginning of an accounting period, adding the cost of new purchases during the period, and deducting the stocks at the end of the period. The weighted mean for material costs calculated in this way was 48·6 per cent for 1956, the grouped mean was between 43 and 45 per cent for the period, the median was between 44 and 45 per cent. Among industries represented in the sample, material costs appear to be relatively high in the clothing industry, and relatively low in engineering and paper and printing.

The major component of net output is the reward of labour. It was not always possible to distinguish wages and salaries from one another in the accounts of Survey firms; but the distinction was drawn whenever possible. The weighted arithmetic mean of wages was 24·4 per cent of total sales, the grouped mean was between 29 and 30 per cent for the three years 1954–56, the median between 27 and 29 per cent. The fact that the weighted mean was lower than the grouped mean and the median may mean that wages tend to fall as a proportion of sales as the size of firm increases; a proposition which is examined later. Weighted mean salaries were 3·6 per cent of total sales, the grouped mean was around 3 per cent, the median between 1·3 and 1·6 per cent. There may be two reasons for the relatively low level of salaries in small firms: first is that small firms rarely carry a large salaried clerical staff; second is that much of the work for which salaries are paid in bigger firms is done in smaller firms by the directors themselves. These directors receive part of their remuneration at least (the proportion is a matter for the discretion of the Board of Directors) in the form of directors' fees, or possibly in the form of dividends. Directors' remuneration is high in Survey firms, accounting for 3·5 per cent of total sales (weighted mean), approximately 6 per cent in terms of the grouped mean, and a median value of around 4 per cent. The lowest level of directors' fees in Table 10.5 was in the clothing industry. The practice of paying directors in this way has further implications, which are considered later.

Inter-industry differences in wages are not considerable: median wages are lowest in the clothing trade and highest in paper and printing; but the differences are probably not significant.

Depreciation is notionally the sum which a business should put by

THE PROFITS OF SMALL MANUFACTURING FIRMS

from a year's trading in order to maintain its fixed assets, but there are so many complications in practice that this ideal is rarely achieved. Before a realistic figure for depreciation allowances can be reached it is necessary for the firm to value its assets in some manner which reflects either earnings capacity or replacement cost (see the discussion in Chapter 8); but many firms simply write off the historical cost of their fixed assets over a period of years. There is a number of ways in which this may be done* (for example, by writing off 10 per cent of the historical cost every year for ten years—the straight line method—or by writing off a fixed percentage of a diminishing balance): attempts were made in a pilot survey (see [32]) to find out how small firms did account for depreciation, but the results of the inquiry were not useful and no further attempts were made to find this out. Many firms simply write off the amount which the Inland Revenue authorities are prepared to allow as a cost against tax; others attempt to add something to account for the rising costs of replacement; but there is such a wide variety of practices that, in the absence of a special survey, it is not possible to say very much about depreciation practices. In Survey firms depreciation accounted typically for about 2 per cent of total sales, and, despite the varied practices, there were not many differences between firms in the amounts charged. The clothing industry, which is not very capital-intensive, has slightly lower depreciation than other industries in the sample.

Another way of looking at depreciation allowances is to relate them to the assets to which they may be supposed to refer. Table 10.6

TABLE 10.6. *Depreciation as Percentage of Tangible Fixed Assets*

PERCENTAGE				NUMBER OF FIRMS
0–2·4	..	..	..	18
2·5–4·9	..	..	..	26
5–7·4	..	..	..	39
7·5–9·9	..	..	..	44
10–19·9	..	..	..	111
20 and over	..	..	..	30
Not ascertained		..	..	67
Total	..	..	..	335

shows depreciation as a proportion of tangible fixed assets for the last balance sheet date available for Survey firms: the weighted arithmetic mean was 8·8 per cent, the grouped mean was 12·4 per

* An admirable account of the various methods of depreciation employed by the accountancy profession may be found in [76].

cent, the median was 10·63 per cent of the value of their tangible assets each year.

Advertising is perhaps one of the more interesting (if not numerically the most important) of other costs. The weighted arithmetic mean was only 0·7 per cent of total sales, the grouped mean was 0·54 per cent, the median was between 0·10 and 0·16 per cent. Most of the advertising of small manufacturing firms consists of advertisements in the trade press and the classified columns of newspapers; there are significant economies of scale in advertising (which is to a large extent indivisible, see [31]) and few small firms can afford to incur the heavy overhead costs of such expenditure. Nor would it do them much good to incur heavy advertising expenditure, since success could be embarrassing if it did not go hand in hand with other expansion plans. A comparison of the advertising expenditures of large and small firms would be illuminating, but adequate information is not available about the advertising costs of large firms.

It is not necessary to break down other costs into individual items, since in few cases were any of the items important in themselves. The typical firm might incur expenditure on a host of items—rent, repairs, carriage, packing, insurance, stationery, travel, cleaning, telephone, postage, legal expenses and so on*— but no one of these items accounted for as much as 1 per cent of total sales on average, and it is convenient to lump them all together as 'other costs'. The weighted arithmetic mean of other costs was 8·2 per cent, the grouped mean was between 8 and 9 per cent, the median was between 7·5 and 8 per cent. In total these costs were important, individually they were small.

All of the foregoing items add up to total costs; the weighted mean of which was 93·5 per cent; the grouped mean varied from 92·5 per cent to 94·2 per cent in 1954; the median was fairly constant around 95 per cent. The difference between total costs and total sales represents the operating profit of the firm (the profit from its normal manufacturing and trading operations): the weighted mean of this item was 6·6 per cent of total sales; the grouped mean varied from 5·6 per cent in 1954 to 8·0 per cent in 1953 (this was a year in which there were so few observations, however, that the figure may not be very meaningful); the median was much lower, between 3 and 4 per cent.

Any other income of the firm, such as rents received, interest on marketable securities etc., needs to be added to operating profit of the

* For a detailed breakdown of costs of one of the firms in the Survey see [31], p. 177.

firm in order to provide a figure of total profit (or income) of the firm. In most small firms such extra income is small, and was not big enough in Survey firms to affect earnings significantly.

The item 'gross income' in Table 10.4 consists of total profit plus depreciation allowances, plus directors' remuneration: it is an attempt to calculate the grossest possible measure of the earning capacity of a firm; the reasons underlying this classification are discussed later in this chapter. The lowest rates of profit by either measure were in the clothing industry.

Three other features of economic significance may be distinguished from the cost accounts of firms. Net output is a measure of the value added to purchased materials by the productive processes of the firm; it also describes the incomes which arise from these productive processes; and is measured by the difference between total sales and cost of materials purchased. The weighted mean for value added was 51.4 per cent, the grouped mean was around 56 per cent, as was the median. Net output was lowest in the clothing industry; an industry with fairly low overhead costs and high material costs.

Direct costs consist of the cost of materials and wages and salaries (strictly the wages and salaries should include only those which the firm itself would classify as paid to 'direct labour', or labour whose contribution to output was measurable; but it is not possible to ascertain this from the accounts). Effectively this measures the cost of labour and materials; these account for about 73 per cent of total costs on average (both measures), the median is slightly higher at between 74 and 75 per cent. Direct costs were highest in the clothing industry. The difference between direct costs and total sales represents the overhead costs (plus profit) of the firm: this is what the businessman usually calls his 'gross margin', and the accountant calls 'gross profit'. The weighted mean was 27 per cent, the grouped mean 26 per cent, and the median 25 per cent. Description of the typical experience of small firms does not tell us much about one of the more interesting aspects of this gross margin—the implications for pricing theory—some analysis of this is in progress. In order to say anything useful about profit margins it is necessary to examine differences between firms and between years (and ideally between products over shorter time periods); such analysis will be presented in Volume II.

Simple description of the salient features of the accounts of small firms brings to light information not previously available, but it does not go far enough. The next stage is to try to compare small firms

TABLE 10.7. *Structure of Costs of Larger Establishments in Manufacturing Industry, 1954**

PERCENTAGE OF TOTAL SALES

COST ITEM	ALL MANUFAC-TURING INDUSTRY	ENGINEERING	METAL MANUFACTURES	CLOTHING	PAPER AND PRINTING
(1) Gross output (Sales)†	100·0	100·0	100·0	100·0	100·0
(2) Purchases of materials and fuel ..	56·1	44·7	54·7	56·1	45·0
(3) Wages and salaries	19·6	31·5	23·9	25·9	24·8
(4) Net output (value added)‡	43·9	55·3	45·3	40·3	55·0
(5) Direct costs ((2)+(3))	75·7	75·2	78·6	82·0	79·8
(6) Overhead costs ((1)—(5))	24·3	24·8	21·4	18·0	20·2

* Calculated from data in [4].
† Includes payments for transport and any duty paid.
‡ Gross output *minus* cost of materials, payment for work given out and transport charges; duty paid was also deducted.

with the population of all firms, and here one immediately runs into difficulties. Such information as is published from the trading accounts of firms is usually in the form either of arithmetic means (weighted) or aggregates of all firms. This is a major shortcoming of much published information, and it is not inappropriate to make a plea here for more imaginative presentation of official statistics: merely to present medians would be a significant advance on current practice; measures of dispersion, or grouped frequency distributions would be even better, and would certainly permit much more intelligent appreciation and analysis of data.

There are two main sources from which such comparisons may be made: the *Census of Production*,[4] and *the Reports of the Commissioner of Inland Revenue*.[1] Nevin[73] has recently re-classified manufacturing costs, and further rough comparisons are possible there. The main data from these sources are tabulated in Tables 10.7 and 10.8 (Census data—[4]), Table 10.9 (derived from data in Nevin[73]) and Table 10.10 (calculated from Inland Revenue data[1]).

It is also possible to make a few comparisons between industries: Table 10.5 shows the main items of cost of Survey firms for the four main industries represented in the sample; Tables 10.7, 10.8 and 10.10 present data referring to the same industry groups.

Calculations in these tables are frequently on a different basis from Survey data, and a few explanations of items are required.

Table 10.7 contains calculations, based on Census data, of purchases of materials, wages and salaries, and value added as percentages of total sales; direct costs and overhead costs have been derived from this data. Gross output is the approximate equivalent of sales in Survey firms, but there are some qualifications. Inter-firm purchases within an industry have not been excluded, and there is therefore some double counting in the Census figure; the sum also includes changes in stocks of finished goods and work in progress during the year (in Survey firms this particular change in stocks was included along with changes in stocks of materials in purchases of materials); the Census figure also includes transport outwards, included in 'other costs' in Survey firms. Net output in the Census is defined as gross output minus cost of materials and transport payments; in the Survey it is simply sales minus material costs. In the Survey, therefore, material costs plus value added (or net output) equal 100 per cent of sales; in the Census they do not, for the reasons given in the preceding sentence. Wages and salaries are on a similar basis in both the Census and the Small Business Survey (payments to working proprietors were excluded from Census data; as far as

TABLE 10.8. Net Output and Wages and Salaries in Selected Industries in United Kingdom, 1954*

PERCENTAGE OF TOTAL SALES

INDUSTRY (S.I.C. ORDER)†

SIZE GROUP (NUMBER OF EMPLOYEES)	NET OUTPUT					WAGES AND SALARIES				
	VI	VIII	XII	XV	ALL	VI	VIII	XII	XV	ALL
11 – 24	59·5	45·6	46·5	53·8	36·8	36·2	26·6	29·0	32·7	21·4
25 – 49	55·0	36·6	42·3	52·3	35·2	33·9	23·8	27·5	30·0	20·6
50 – 99	{ 53·5	42·0	40·0	51·5	51·5	{ 31·4	24·7	26·2	29·2	19·8
100 – 299		{ 43·4	39·4	47·5	35·0		{ 24·9	25·3	24·6	19·3
300 – 399	52·0		38·6	45·3	33·6	30·5		25·3	23·1	17·8
400 – 499	49·8		{ 39·3	{ 43·7	34·8	29·3		{ 24·5	{ 24·9	18·6
500 – 749	49·5	{ 41·2			36·5	29·4	{ 22·2			19·4
750 – 999	47·2		40·0		34·4	28·4		26·8		18·2
1,000 – 1,499	{ 46·6		{ 40·8	45·8	36·0	{ 28·4		{ 27·6	24·4	18·0
1,500 – 1,999				50·0	33·3				28·6	18·0
2,000 and over	51·7			42·7	36·0	34·8			21·6	20·8
Total	51·0	41·9	40·3	46·8	35·1	31·5	23·9	25·9	24·8	19·6

* Calculated from data in *Census of Production for 1954*, Summary Tables, Part II, Table 10, pp. 4–7 (H.M.S.O., 1958).

† Standard Industrial Classification Orders are:
  VI   Engineering, Shipbuilding and Electrical Goods.
  VIII Metal Goods not elsewhere specified.
  XII Clothing.
  XV   Paper and Printing.

possible they were also excluded from Survey data). Table 10.7 employs the same concepts as Table 10.8.

In Tables 10.7 and 10.8 turnover is defined as total receipts from sales of goods and services, net of discounts (also excluded in Survey data), and including payments made on account of work in progress (this was also included in Survey data, and is to be distinguished from the firm's own valuation of such stocks, which was excluded from Survey turnover figures). Cost of materials is also net of discounts (as in the Survey), it also includes cost of fuel (as in the Survey), transport repairs, (both excluded from Survey data), and tax and excise duty (as in the Survey). Wages and salaries are on a similar basis to the Survey, except that in Inland Revenue data directors' fees are included (an adjustment can easily be made for this item), as are travelling and expenses; both of these are excluded from Survey data. Depreciation and other costs are on similar bases in both cases, save that other costs in Survey firms include directors' and other expenses.

TABLE 10.9 *The Structure of Manufacturing Costs, 1954-56*

PERCENTAGE OF TOTAL SALES

COST ITEM				1954	1955	1956
Materials	..	..	..	45·8	46·0	45·6
Wages and salaries	..	..	..	35·4	35·8	36·7
Self-employed income		..	..	0·7	0·7	0·7
Capital consumption		..	..	3·2	3·4	3·9
Total costs	..	..	..	85·1	85·9	86·9
Total profit	..	..	..	14·9	14·1	13·1
Total sales	..	..	..	100·0	100·0	100·0

Source: Nevin[73].

Table 10.9 is different again. Nevin attempted a reconstruction of cost data, based on macro-economic data (national income accounts, etc.). Wages and salaries were taken from national income accounts, and adjusted to exclude the incomes of working proprietors. Material costs exclude purchases within manufacturing industry. Capital consumption is an attempt to estimate depreciation on a replacement cost basis. Nevin's figures are therefore constructed on a completely different basis from those in the Census, Inland Revenue Reports, and the Small Business Survey; but his direct costs, as a proportion of total sales, are not so very different from the other estimates.

In view of all the differences in methods of calculation between the several sets of data, it would be unreasonable to expect to draw many conclusions about similarities or differences between components of total costs between Survey firms and the economy as a whole. A few general comments may be made however.

Nevin's material costs are similar to those of Survey firms; material costs in Census and Inland Revenue data are higher than in Survey firms. Part of these differences may be due to Nevin's exclusion of inter-firm purchases. There are also differences between industries in Census and Inland Revenue data, which are broadly similar to inter-industry differences in the Small Business Survey. Since material costs in Survey data are calculated on a basis nearer to that of the Census than Nevin, this may well mean that material costs are relatively low in small firms; but the data are not really adequate to permit a firm judgment on this point. Value added is correspondingly lowest in Census and Inland Revenue data, and highest in Survey firms and Nevin's data.

Wages and salaries are lowest in Census data (as a proportion of total costs, although in total they are in fact similar to Nevin's). The crude size analysis of Census data in Table 10.8 provides some indication that, up to a point, wages and salaries decline with size of firm; this may be part of the explanation of the fact that wages and salaries in Survey firms appear to be proportionately higher than in all manufacturing firms, according to Census and Inland Revenue data. Direct costs are similar in Census and Survey data, and in both cases the clothing industry has the highest direct costs. Inland Revenue data and Nevin's calculations yield rather higher direct costs.

TABLE 10.10 *Companies' Costs and Appropriation of Income in Selected Industries, 1951-52*

PERCENTAGE OF TURNOVER

	ENGINEERING	METAL GOODS	CLOTHING	PAPER AND PRINTING
Turnover	100·0	100·0	100·0	100·0
Cost of materials	52·4	57·5	68·1	54·2
Increase in stocks	0·3	0·9	3·3	1·4
Wages and salaries	29·1	25·9	23·6	26·5
Depreciation	1·9	2·4	0·9	2·5
Other costs	4·1	4·2	3·6	5·4
Income	12·8	11·4	7·4	13·7
Tax	5·7	4·8	3·2	5·7
Dividends	2·9	3·5	1·9	4·2
Balance	4·3	3·2	2·3	3·7

Source: See [1].

Nevin's total profit as a proportion of total sales is not very dissimilar from that shown in Inland Revenue data, and it is much higher than in Survey firms. In whatever way profit is calculated (subject to the reservations implied by the payment of director's fees) it seems that the profit on sales of small firms is lower than that of all businesses in the economy. However, calculations of profitability involve rather more sophisticated considerations than have been possible in the present analysis; further evidence on this topic will be presented in Volume II.

10.3. THE APPROPRIATION OF INCOME

Companies in the Small Business Survey also provided details of their appropriation accounts, from which it is possible to describe the allocation and distribution of income of the firms in the sample. The second part of Table 10.3 shows a specimen account, with a weighted arithmetic mean calculated for 1956, showing allocations as proportions of gross earnings and total profits. Table 10.11 shows the main items of the appropriation account of Survey firms, expressed as a proportion of total profit: grouped means, medians and variances are shown, as in Table 10.4.

The item gross earnings in Table 10.3 represents an attempt to measure the earning capacity of the firm: this is rather difficult to ascertain in the small business. In order to make the measure as gross as possible, depreciation has been added back; strictly this item should be excluded, since it should represent the sum necessary to maintain earning capacity intact, and thus be treated as a cost; it has been included, however, for the rather illogical reason that it is frequently treated as an allocation of income and as a source of funds from which capital expenditure may be financed, and as such is transferred to the balance sheet of the firm as part of transfers to reserves.

But the main reason for the difficulty in estimating earning capacity lies in the attribution of director's remuneration: this is an important cost item in most small firms, typically accounting for about 4 per cent of total sales. In the standardized accounts prepared for the Small Business Survey, this item was treated as a cost for two reasons: first, it is arguable that, since in most small firms the directors are also the managers of the firm, the item contains a large element of management salary; second, the Inland Revenue authorities are prepared to allow directors' remuneration up to a point as a cost of the firm, and therefore allowable against tax, although there is

TABLE 10.11. *Major Items of Appropriation Accounts*

PERCENTAGES OF TOTAL PROFIT*

	1953			1954			1955			1956			1954†		
	MEDIAN	MEAN	VARIANCE	MEDIAN	MEAN	VARIANCE	MEDIAN	MEAN	VARIANCE	MEDIAN	MEAN	VARIANCE	MEDIAN	MEAN	VARIANCE
Tax .. .. ::	0	20·8	796	17·4	27·5	865	29·1	27·9	743	33·7	28·2	620	56·1	56·5	142
Dividends .. ::	0	26·1	1,435	0	14·0	562	0	19·7	1,004	0	15·9	767	17·8	18·8	76
Retained profit ::	46·8	56·8	1,283	55·7	57·7	1,136	55·5	58·5	1,177	54·8	59·6	1,038	44·5	46·7	369
Depreciation ::	—	—	—	—	—	—	—	—	—	—	—	—	20·0	24·2	409
Transfers to reserves‡	70·0	64·5	1,039	75·9	69·4	1,059	76·2	69·3	987	76·8	71·1	849	47·7	50·5	417

* Calculated from grouped distributions.
† Sample of seventy-eight largest quoted public companies.
‡ Retained profit *plus* depreciation *plus* prior year adjustments.

a definite upper limit beyond which payment of directors is treated as a distribution of income and not as a cost. This procedure has advantages for the individual since directors' fees, being earned income, attract allowances against personal tax, whereas if payment were made in the form of dividends it would not attract such allowances.

Thus it is possible to treat directors' fees either as a distribution of income or as a salary item: in the former case, they should strictly be added to total profit in order to produce an accurate measure of the earnings of the firm from which distributions are paid; in the second case they should be omitted from the sum and earnings should be expressed net of directors' fees (this latter is the measure which has been used for total profit in Table 10.11). In most small firms the truth probably lies somewhere between these two positions, and part of directors' fees should be treated as a salary, and part as a distribution; the only distinction between a directors' fee and a salary in the cost sense being that directors' fees are declared after the accounts have been drawn up and the profit position ascertained (they are thus frequently non-contractual and dependent on the size of profits); salaries are paid in advance and are contractual.

The extent to which directors may pay themselves in this way is determined partly by the extent to which directors control the firm: in the Oxford Survey 94 per cent of the firms taking part were director-controlled in the sense that they owned a majority of the shares; in 43 per cent of the firms the directors were all members of one family; and in two-thirds of the firms there were fewer than six shareholders. The net result is that the majority of firms used this form of payment in preference to dividend distributions.

Strictly, it should be possible to allocate part of directors' fees as salaries and part as earnings of the firm from which distributions are made. In the sense implied by Inland Revenue regulations, all of the directors' fees could be called salaries, since they were in fact allowed against tax; but it is by no means certain that in the economic sense this was so, since some at least of this income could be thought of as distributed profit. An arbitrary allocation could be made, using some crude opportunity cost concept (for example, what it would cost to employ a manager to do the job performed by the director): this has not been done for the present exercise.

The best that can be done at present is to show the effect of attributing directors' remuneration in both ways, showing profit expressed both net and gross of directors' fees. The results of such calculations (for all accounts for all years added together) are shown in Table 10.12: in 11.5 per cent of cases, what appear to be losses become profits if earnings are expressed gross of directors' fees; and the general effect is an upward revaluation of profits. Profit net of directors' remuneration was less than 5 per cent of sales in 57.5 per cent of firms; gross of directors' remuneration the corresponding proportion was 26 per cent. As is to be expected, the discrepancy was smallest in firms whose profit on turnover was greater than 20 per cent.

The median for total profit was 4.1 per cent, for profit gross of directors' remuneration it was 9.8 per cent. The median profit *net* of directors' remuneration for a group of 116 large quoted public companies [6] was 10.8 per cent. The ratio of directors' remuneration to total profit (net of directors' fees) is shown for all firms, with no distinction between years, in Table 10.13. In 43 per cent of cases directors' remuneration exceeded total profit; and in 103 cases a loss could be converted into a profit if income were declared gross of directors' remuneration; in only 19 cases was income negative regardless of the measure employed. This needs to be borne in mind

TABLE 10.12. *The Effect of Directors' Remuneration on Profits*

PERCENTAGE OF TURNOVER				TOTAL PROFIT	TOTAL PROFIT PLUS DIRECTORS' REMUNERATION number of firms
Loss	..	..	..	84	25
0 – 4·9	..	..	..	221	113
5 – 9·9	..	..	..	119	131
10 – 14·9	..	..	..	52	112
15 – 19·9	..	..	..	26	82
20 – 24·9	..	..	..	12	35
25 and over	..	..	..	15	31
Total	..	..	..	**529**	**529**

TABLE 10.13. *Directors' Remuneration as a Percentage of Total Profit*

PERCENTAGE				NUMBER OF FIRMS
Nil	..	..	..	34
Positive income				
0·1 – 9·9	..	..	..	22
10 – 24·9	..	..	..	40
25 – 49·9	..	..	..	46
50 – 99·9	..	..	..	78
100 and over		..	..	255
Negative income		..	..	103
Income zero	..	..	..	8
Total	..	..	..	**586**

in the discussion of the importance of dividends in small businesses: if directors' remuneration is treated similarly to dividends, as a distribution of profit, total distribution is much higher than it appears from dividends alone.

It might also be argued that from some points of view the expenses of directors should be treated as part of their income and taken into account in discussion of business incomes. This is a controversial issue, which has been avoided in the present discussion; and no attempt has been made to take account of such expenses.

From the point of view of the sum available for distribution, however, total profit net of directors' fees is the conventionally calculated sum (although the Companies Act requires that directors' remuneration be shown separately); and it is on this basis that, for present purposes, the accounts of Small Business Survey firms have been drawn up. Total profits net of directors fees, and net of depreciation, is the sum from which distributions and allocations of profit are made in the appropriation account. These allocations, for Small Business Survey firms, and for a group of the largest quoted public companies, are shown in Table 10.11.

In discussion of the appropriation account, comparisons may be made with two main sets of data. The first is a group of seventy-six very large quoted public companies, whose accounts have been loaned by the National Institute of Economic and Social Research: there is only one year for which direct comparisons are possible (the year ending March 31, 1954), and these giant companies are probably not typical of quoted companies as a whole, but for quick comparisons the data are quite useful. The second source is the Report of Her Majesty's Commissioners for Inland Revenue;[1] this presents aggregates only, for large samples of companies, and is therefore of limited use, but some crude comparisons may be made. An appropriation account drawn up from Inland Revenue data is shown in Table 10.14; the data for quoted public companies is incorporated in Table 10.11.

The structure of company taxation is rather complex and the effects on business behaviour are a matter of some dispute.* The incidence of taxation has important implications for company policy in respect of savings and dividends; a fuller analysis of these matters will be presented in Volume II. Profits are normally assessed on a 'preceding year' basis, so that deductions in fact do not refer to the year which the profit was made. Two taxes are imposed on companies: income tax is charged on assessed profits at standard rate; profits tax

* For a discussion see [67].

TABLE 10.14. The Profits of Companies*

PERCENTAGES

	1953–54		1954–55		1955–56	
	OF TURNOVER	OF INCOME	OF TURNOVER	OF INCOME	OF TURNOVER	OF INCOME
Turnover ..	100	—	100	—	100	—
Trading profit ..	10·29	—	10·34	—	10·28	—
Capital allowances†	1·76	—	1·93	—	1·99	—
Net trading profit ..	8·54	—	8·41	—	8·29	—
Losses ..	0·18	—	0·16	—	0·26	—
Other income ..	0·89	—	0·76	—	0·93	—
Total income ..	9·25	100	9·01	100	8·96	100
Distributions (gross)						
(a) Dividends ..	2·65	28·7	2·49	27·6	2·39	26·6
(b) Interest, etc.	0·22	2·4	0·20	2·2	0·21	2·3
Profits tax ..	0·72	7·7	0·69	7·7	0·67	7·5
Income tax ..	2·70	29·2	2·65	29·4	2·70	30·2
Balance ..	2·96	32·0	2·98	33·1	2·99	33·4

* Source: See [1].

† The statutory investment initial and annual allowances in respect of plant and industrial buildings, including balancing allowances, and allowances for scientific research and patents.

is an additional charge, which was at a different rate on distributed profits (27½ per cent) and undistributed profits (2½ per cent) during the period of the Survey. The standard rate of income tax worked out at about 45 per cent on assessed profits during the period. A special concession was allowed during the period in the form of investment allowances (which replaced initial allowances in 1954); these are given in respect of expenditure on certain types of fixed assets, the rate on plant and machinery being 20 per cent; the net effect of initial allowances is to reduce tax payable on profits during the year in which capital expenditure was undertaken.

Since profit and loss experience may fluctuate considerably from year to year, it is to be expected that there should be considerable variations in the proportions of income paid as tax. The weighted arithmetic mean for Survey firms was 44.2 per cent of total profit, the grouped mean was around 28 per cent, the median varied from 17 per cent to 34 per cent; in the large quoted public companies in 1954 both the grouped mean and the median were about 56 per cent; for Inland Revenue companies the weighted mean was between 36 per cent and 37 per cent over the period. It is not easy to explain these differences: the relatively low level of taxation on private companies is due partly to the allowance of directors' fees as a cost, which reduces taxable profits; in consequence distributed profits, which attracted higher tax were low (dividends are discussed shortly), and taxable income therefore attracted only income tax and profits tax at the lower level. In addition there were more losses in private companies (17 per cent made losses in 1954, 21 per cent in 1955, and 17 per cent in 1956). The fairly high weighted mean for Survey companies is due to the effect of a few large companies, whose behaviour was similar to that of the public companies, and whose tax payments were correspondingly higher. The explanation of the relatively low figure for taxation in Table 10.14, using Inland Revenue data, is partly that dividends are declared gross of tax. Some of the companies concerned also made losses (although the total level of losses was not high); the total would also be pulled down by private companies; nothing can be said about unquoted public companies, about which information is not available, but it must be supposed that their taxation was not so high as that of quoted public companies.

It seems therefore that the tax burden of small firms may be less severe than that of larger firms, since they pay a smaller proportion of their income in tax. But lest this should be thought to represent greater financial ease in smaller firms, it is important to enter two reservations. There is probably a scale effect to be borne in mind: the absolute levels of both income and savings in small firms are low, and may not be adequate for self-financing, and the effects of taxation may therefore be proportionately more important than they appear from simple consideration of percentages of profits lost in this way. Secondly, since small firms can avoid the penalty of higher tax rates on distributed profits, *via* directors' remuneration, there may be a tendency to distribute profits rather than to keep them in the firm for expansion. (For a further discussion of these and other points, see [30], Chapter 3.)

Dividends are low in private companies: the median is fact zero (that is to say, over half of the firms paid no dividends at all); both the weighted and the grouped arithmetic mean are typically over 15 per cent of total profits, reflecting the higher dividends paid by the larger companies in the sample.

In small private companies in the Survey, 47 per cent paid dividends in 1954, 47 per cent in 1955, 45 per cent in 1956. In 1954, 32 per cent of the Survey firms paid dividends of over 20 per cent of total profit, in 1955 the proportion was 30 per cent, in 1956 it was 26 per cent. There is not much difference between the median and the grouped mean of the large quoted public companies, which typically paid about 18 per cent of their profits out in the form of dividends. There is a considerable difference between this figure and the level of approximately 27 per cent in the Inland Revenue Table: part of the explanation lies in the fact that dividends are gross of tax, but it is also possible that a large number of fairly big companies paid fairly high dividends in the period.

The dividend policy of large companies is complex* and is affected partly by taxation and partly by the desire of companies to pay dividends in order to facilitate the later raising of capital through the New Issue Market (see [79]). The latter consideration only affects small private companies at certain stages of their career (most notably when they are contemplating becoming public companies and undertaking share issues†). The whole question is also tied up with that of retained profit, since the company has only the two alternatives when deciding what to do with profits after tax has been paid.

As a proportion of income, retained profit is much higher in Survey firms than in the large quoted public companies in Table

* For an analysis of the determinants of company dividends and savings in the USA, see [38].

† Private companies rarely make new share issues. For a discussion of this and other aspects of the finance of small firms, see [30].

10.11: typically private companies retained about 55 per cent of their total profit, compared with about 46 per cent in the large companies. Inland Revenue figures show about one third of total profit being retained. Again, this does not necessarily mean that small companies are more thrifty than large: they are retaining a larger share of a proportionally smaller income. A further rather crude calculation* can be made for another group of large companies (the group considered earlier) for 1960: their retained profit was about 2 per cent of total sales, which is not very different from that of Survey firms, shown in Table 10.4.

For present purposes it is only possible to look very briefly at the further implications of the differences between the savings of large and small companies: these are topics which will be considered in more detail in Volume II; but some discussion may also be found in [30] and [92].

One of the interesting questions is: to what extent are large and small firms self-financing? There are several possible measures of the degree of self-financing, of which two may be briefly considered here: the first, the savings/investment ratio relates gross company savings (retained profits plus depreciation plus prior year adjustments) to material investment in fixed assets and stocks (this investment figure is also gross of depreciation); the second, the savings/expenditure ratio, relates company savings to expenditure on operating assets (material investment plus changes in net trade credit granted or received, which may be thought of as expenditure on fixed assets and working capital). Both of these ratios are shown for Survey firms and seventy-eight large quoted public companies in Table 10.15. Investment expenditure tends to be undertaken in fairly large discrete quantities, and comparison on a year-to-year basis may not therefore reflect typical experience; but the table may be regarded as illustrative of this type of calculation, and it does give a general idea of the experience of the two groups. The typical ratio of savings to investment in private companies was between 55 per cent and 65 per cent, with fairly wide fluctuations from year to year; in the large public companies it was 136 per cent (median and grouped mean are similar). This means that, for this particular year

---

* Calculated as follows. The median of transfers to reserves as a proportion of sales in 1960 was 2·3 per cent, the grouped mean was 3·1 per cent. A crude allowance for depreciation and prior year adjustments—both of which are added to retained profit in order to reach a figure for retained in reserves—based on information in Table 10.11 and other information, brings these down to approximately 2·0 and 3·8 per cent respectively.

the very large public companies saved a third more than they spent on fixed assets and stocks; but this may not be typical of all quoted public companies, for which Tew[92] found that on average for the period 1949–53 the self-financing ratio was 86 per cent. It is arguable that, since stocks are to some extent financed from short-term credit in the form of bank borrowing and trade creditors, savings should be related to the acquisition of longer-term assets. Looked at in this way, quoted public companies [92] had an average self-financing ratio of 130 per cent, compared with 86 per cent if stocks are included; the median for Survey firms is approximately 150 per cent (details of these calculations may be found in [30]).

There are slight differences between the two groups in their ratios of savings to expenditure: large public companies financed just over half of their expenditure on operating assets from their own savings;

TABLE 10.15. *The Ratio of Savings to Investment and Expenditure*

YEAR ENDING 31ST MARCH			1953	1954	1955	1956	1954*
Savings/Investment							
Median	..	..	0	55·0	63·8	57·9	135·7
Mean ..	..	..	100·0	204·7	154·8	139·0	133·9
Variance	..	..	30,992	148,426	75,842	62,634	3,594
Savings/Expenditure							
Median	..	..	0	39·2	50·8	59·0	53·1
Mean ..	..	..	22·9	123·1	125·3	107·4	54·1
Variance	..	..	2,334	82,520	66,571	43,389	1,496

* Sample of seventy-eight large quoted public companies.

private companies financed between 40 per cent and 60 per cent in this way in the three years for which adequate information is available. The proportion for all quoted public companies (calculated from data in [92], page 10) was approximately 57 per cent; this is not very different from the largest companies.

For the private companies the grouped mean is very different from the median, and the variances of the distributions are large. This reflects the fact that experience of individual firms is very varied: in a quarter of all companies in each year savings were greater than expenditure, and in some of the companies savings were more than ten times expenditure; in over a third of all companies savings were greater than investment, and in this instance too there were several cases where companies saved more than ten times as much as they invested during the year. There are two possible reasons for this: the lumpiness of investment expenditure means that in certain years investment expenditure of the firm will be very low whilst at the same time the firm's savings may be maintained at relatively high levels; it is also possible that, among small firms, there may be some which are particularly thrifty and which habitually save a great deal more than they spend on capital equipment and stocks (though it is not easy to see why they should continue to do this).

This very brief survey suggests that the very largest and the smallest companies tend to finance a large part of their capital expenditure from their own savings; other public companies and unquoted companies possibly finance a rather smaller proportion in this way. But this can only be a tentative suggestion, and more analysis is required.

10.4. CONCLUDING COMMENTS

The salient features of the profit and loss accounts of small manufacturing firms may be summed up briefly, subject to the reservations made in the course of the chapter. Materials account for approximately 45 per cent of total sales, and the evidence suggests that they may be rather lower in small firms than in large; similarly value added appears to be rather high in Survey firms. This may be due to slightly higher wage and salary payments in small firms than in manufacturing industry as a whole; the relatively high level of proprietors' income (reflected in this Survey by directors' fees) may be added to this, and on the whole this suggests that labour costs are relatively high in small firms. This may be due in part to the lower efficiency of labour in small firms, which may be partly due to lower capital intensity.

Profitability on sales of small firms appears to be rather lower in small businesses than in the economy as a whole; but there are so many complications involved in the measurement of earnings and in the comparison of small and big firms that this conclusion may only be advanced with reservations. Further analysis is required.

Small firms pay a smaller proportion of their income in tax than do large firms: this is partly due to their more variable profit experience, and partly to the fact that the payment of directors' remuneration does not attract company taxation. Such directors' fees constitute a large part of the total gross earnings of small manufacturing firms; these fees are an alternative to the payment of dividends, which are much lower in small manufacturing firms than in quoted public companies and the company sector as a whole.

Retained profits, expressed as a proportion of income after the payment of directors' fees, are rather higher in Survey firms than in the company sector as a whole; but as a proportion of total sales retained profits in the two groups are similar. This simply means that small firms tend to retain a larger share of a proportionately smaller income than do large firms. Small firms tend to finance a large part of their expenditure from their own savings; but this does not necessarily mean that they are in a position of relative financial ease. Their difficulties in raising outside capital may simply mean that small firms are forced to trim their capital expenditure closely to the availability of internal funds.

Finally, this chapter illustrates the need for a comprehensive study of the profits of small firms: it is not possible to say very much about profits in the economy as a whole from aggregate information. The data presented in this chapter suggests that there may be considerable differences between the behaviour of small firms and large firms, and any analysis of profits in the economy as a whole needs to take account of this fact. It has been estimated [110] and [20], that between a quarter and a third of all profits in the economy are earned outside the quoted public company sector: if different factors affect different sectors of the economy it is not sufficient to look at aggregates. It is perhaps appropriate to conclude with a plea for the improvement of published statistics, and the allocation of more resources to their analysis.

LIST OF WORKS CITED

1. OFFICIAL PUBLICATIONS

1 BOARD OF INLAND REVENUE (annual), *Report of the Commissioners of H.M. Inland Revenue*, London: HMSO.
2 BOARD OF TRADE (MINES DEPARTMENT) (annual), *Annual Report of the Secretary for Mines*, Statistical tables on costs of production, proceeds and profits of the coal-mining industry, and on average quarterly earnings of coal-miners, London: HMSO.
3 BOARD OF TRADE (annual), *Returns relating to all Authorized Gas Undertakings in Great Britain*, London: HMSO.
4 BOARD OF TRADE, 1924, 1930, 1935, 1954, 1958, *Census of Production of the United Kingdom*, London: HMSO.
5 BOARD OF TRADE (1959), *Companies: General Annual Report of the Board of Trade for the Year Ended December 31, 1958*, London: HMSO.
6 BOARD OF TRADE (1962), *Company Assets, Income and Finance in 1960*, London: HMSO.
7 BOARD OF TRADE (quarterly in Board of Trade Journal from 1963), *Income and Finance of Public Quoted Companies*, London: HMSO.
8 CENTRAL STATISTICAL OFFICE (annually each February, in Economic Trends before 1963), *Income and Finance of Public Quoted Companies*, London: HMSO.
9 CENTRAL STATISTICAL OFFICE (annual), *National Income and Expenditure of the United Kingdom*, London: HMSO.
10 CENTRAL STATISTICAL OFFICE (1956), *National Income Statistics: Sources and Methods*, London: HMSO.
11 ELECTRICITY COMMISSION (annual), *Returns of Engineering and Financial Statistics relating to Authorized Undertakings in Great Britain*, London: HMSO.
12 MINISTRY OF HEALTH, *Annual Report*, Statistical Appendix, Command Paper.
13 MINISTRY OF HEALTH, *Local Government Financial Statistics* (before 1934–35, issued under title 'Annual Local Taxation Returns'), London: HMSO.
14 MINISTRY OF TRANSPORT (annual), *Railway Returns: Returns of the Capital, Traffic, Receipts and Working Expenditure, etc., of the Railways of Great Britain*, London: HMSO.
15 NORTHERN IRELAND GOVERNMENT, *Local Taxation Returns*, N.I. Command Paper.
16 *Parliamentary Debates (Hansard), House of Commons Official Report*, London: HMSO.
17 *Report of the Chief Registrar of Friendly Societies* (annual), Part 3, Industrial and Provident Societies, London: HMSO.
18 *Report of the Committee on National Debt and Taxation* (1927), The Colwyn Report, Command Paper 2800.
19 *Report of the Committee on National Debt and Taxation: Appendices* (1927), Pages 65–114 in Appendix XI of the Colwyn Report. The incidence of income tax by W. H. Coates, Appendices to Command Paper 2800.
20 *Report of the Committee on the Working of the Monetary System* (1959), The Radcliffe Report, Command Paper 827.

21 *Royal Commission on Food Prices* (1925), First Report, Vol. I, Command Paper 2390.

22 SCOTTISH HOME DEPARTMENT (two-yearly), *Local Taxation Returns* (up to 1933-34 Scottish Office publication).

23 *Statistical Abstract for the United Kingdom,* Command Paper, annual up to 83rd number, published 1940.

2. BOOKS AND ARTICLES

24 ADELMAN, M. A. (1951), The measurement of industrial concentration: *Review of Economics and Statistics,* 33, 269–96.

25 AITCHISON, J., and BROWN, J. A. C. (1957), *The Lognormal Distribution,* Cambridge: Cambridge University Press.

26 ASPIN, A. A. (1949), Tables for use in comparisons whose accuracy involves two variances, separately estimated, *Biometrika,* 36, 290–6.

27 BARNA, T. (1957), The replacement cost of fixed assets in British manufacturing industry in 1955, *Journal of the Royal Statistical Society,* 120, 1–36.

28 BARNA, T. (1962), *Investment and Growth Policies in British Industrial Firms,* National Institute of Economic and Social Research, Occasional Paper XX, Cambridge: Cambridge University Press.

29 BATES, J. A. (1958), The finance of small business, *Bulletin of the Oxford University Institute of Statistics,* 20, 153–8.

30 BATES, J. A. (1964), *The Financing of Small Business,* London: Sweet and Maxwell.

31 BATES, J. A., and PARKINSON, J. R. (1963), *Business Economics,* Oxford, Blackwell.

32 BATES, J. A., and STEWART, H. (1956), Small manufacturing businesses: accounting information from a pilot survey, *Bulletin of the Oxford University Institute of Statistics,* 18, 141–78.

33 BELLERBY, J. R. (1955), Agricultural income, *Journal of the Royal Statistical Society,* A, 118, 336–44.

34 BOWEN, I., and ELLIS, A. W. T. (1945) The building and contracting industry, *Oxford Economic Papers,* 7, 111–24.

35 CARRUTHERS, A. S. (1939), The trend of net profits of commercial and industrial enterprises, 1928–37, *Journal of the Royal Statistical Society,* A, 102, 63–80.

36 CHAPMAN, A. L., assisted by KNIGHT, R. (1953), *Wages and Salaries in the United Kingdom 1920–1938,* Cambridge: Cambridge University Press.

37 CLARK, C. (1937), *National Income and Outlay,* London: Macmillan.

38 DOBROVOLSKY, S. P. (1951), *Corporate Income Retention 1915–43,* New York: National Bureau of Economic Research.

39 EVELY, R. S., and LITTLE, I. M. D. (1960), *Concentration in British Industry,* National Institute of Social and Economic Research, Cambridge: Cambridge University Press.

40 FERGUSON, C. (1960), The relationship of business size to stability: an empirical approach, *Journal of Industrial Economics,* 9, 43–62.

41 FISHER, G. R. (1961), Some factors influencing share prices, *Economic Journal,* 71, 120–41.

42 FISHER, R. A., and YATES, F. (1948), *Statistical Tables for Biological, Agricultural and Medical Research,* 3rd edition, revised and enlarged, London and Edinburgh: Oliver and Boyd.

214

43 FLORENCE, P. S. (1953), *Logic of British and American Industry*, London: Routledge and Kegan Paul.

44 FLORENCE, P. S. (1957), New measures of the growth of firms, *Economic Journal*, **67**, 244–8.

45 FLORENCE, P. S. (1959), Size of company and other factors in dividend policy, *Journal of the Royal Statistical Society*, A, **122**, 77–98.

46 FLORENCE, P. S. (1961), *Ownership, Control and Success of Large Companies*, London: Sweet and Maxwell.

47 FOLDES, L. P., and WILSON, S. S. (1961), Fifty-five iron and steel companies, 1948–59, *London and Cambridge Economic Bulletin*, N.S., **37**, vi–vii.

48 GIBRAT, R. (1931), *Les Inégalités Économiques*, Paris: Sirey.

49 HART, P. E. (1957), On measuring business concentration, *Bulletin of the Oxford University Institute of Statistics*, **19**, 225–48.

50 HART, P. E. (1962), The estimation of time-series of profits in British industries 1920–38, *Bulletin of the Oxford University Institute of Statistics*, **24**, 257–67.

51 HART, P. E. (1962), The size and growth of firms, *Economica*, N.S., **29**, 29–39.

52 HART, P. E. (1963), Profits in non-manufacturing industries in the United Kingdom 1920–38, *Scottish Journal of Political Economy*, **10**, 167–97.

53 HART, P. E., and PRAIS, S. J. (1956), The analysis of business concentration: a statistical approach, *Journal of the Royal Statistical Society*, A, **119**, 150–81.

54 HAZLEWOOD, A. (1957), Telecommunications Statistics, in Kendall's *Sources and Nature of the Statistics of the United Kingdom, Part II*, London and Edinburgh: Oliver and Boyd.

55 HOEL, P. G. (1962), *Introduction to Mathematical Statistics*, 3rd edition, New York: Wiley.

56 HOPE, R. (1949), Profits in British industry from 1925–35, *Oxford Economic Papers*, N.S., **1**, 159–81.

57 HYMER, S., and PASHIGIAN, P. (1962), Firm size and rate of growth, *Journal of Political Economy*, **70**, No. 6, 556–69.

58 ISSERLIS, L. (1938), Tramp shipping, cargoes and freights, *Journal of the Royal Statistical Society*, A, **101**, 53–134.

59 KEYNES, J. M. (1927), The Colwyn report on national debt and taxation, *Economic Journal*, **37**, 198–212.

60 KLEIN, L. R. (1953), *A Textbook of Econometrics*, Evanston, Illinois: Row.

61 LEAK, H., and MAIZELS, A. (1945), The structure of British industry, *Journal of the Royal Statistical Society*, **108**, 142–207.

62 LIPSEY, R. G., and STEUER, M. D. (1961), The relation between profits and wage rates, *Economica*, N.S., **28**, 137–55.

63 LOMAX, K. S. (1959), Production and productivity movements in the United Kingdom since 1900, *Journal of the Royal Statistical Society*, A, **122**, 183–210.

64 LYDALL, H. F. (1959), The growth of manufacturing firms, *Bulletin of the Oxford University Institute of Statistics*, **21**, 85–111.

65 MA, R. (1960), Births and deaths in the quoted public company sector in the United Kingdom 1949–53, *Yorkshire Bulletin*, **12**, No. 2, 90–6.

66 MACGREGOR, J. J. (1957), Timber Statistics, in Kendall's *Sources and Nature of the Statistics of the United Kingdom, Part II*, London and Edinburgh: Oliver and Boyd.

67 MACKINTOSH, A. S. (1963), *The Development of Firms*, London: Cambridge University Press.
68 MANSFIELD, E. (1962), Entry, innovation and the growth of firms, *American Economic Review*, **52**, 1023–51.
69 MAXCY, G. E., and SILBERSTON, A. (1959), *The Motor Industry*, London: Allen and Unwin.
70 MAYWALD, K. (1954), An index of building costs in the United Kingdom 1845–1938, *Economic History Review*, **7**, 187–203.
71 MAYWALD, K. (1960), Domestic capital formation in the United Kingdom, *London and Cambridge Economic Bulletin*, N.S., No. **34**, vi–viii.
72 MORGENSTERN, O. (1950), *On the Accuracy of Economic Observations*, Princeton: Princeton University Press.
73 NEVIN, E. T. (1963), The cost structure of British manufacturing, *Economic Journal*, **123**, 642–64.
74 PARKINSON, H. (1938), British industrial profits—a survey of three decades, *Economist*, **133**, 597–603.
75 PENROSE, E. T. (1959), *Theory of the Growth of the Firm*, Oxford: Blackwell.
76 PICKLES, W., and DUNKERLEY, G. W. (1955), *Accountancy*, London: Pitman.
77 PRAIS, S. J. (1955), The measure of income for shareholders and for taxation, *Accounting Research*, **6**, 187–201.
78 PRAIS, S. J. (1957), The financial experience of giant companies, *Economic Journal*, **67**, 249–64.
79 PRAIS, S. J. (1959), Dividend policy and income appropriation, *Studies in Company Finance*, 26–41, National Institute of Economic and Social Research, Cambridge: Cambridge University Press.
80 PREST, A. R. (1948), National income of the United Kingdom 1870–1946, *Economic Journal*, **58**, 31–62.
81 RADICE, E. A. (1939), *Savings in Great Britain 1922–35*, Oxford University Press, London: Humphrey Milford.
82 REDFERN, P. (1955), Net investment in fixed assets in the United Kingdom, 1938–53, *Journal of the Royal Statistical Society*, A, **118**, 141–82.
83 ROY, A. D. (1952), An exercise in errors, *Journal of the Royal Statistical Society*, A, **115**, 507–20.
84 SIMON, H. A. (1955), On a class of skew distribution functions, *Biometrika*, **42**, 425–40.
85 SIMON, H. A., and BONINI, C. P. (1958), The size distribution of business firms, *American Economic Review*, **48**, 607–17.
86 STAMP, J. C. (1916), *British Incomes and Property: The Application of Official Statistics to Economic Problems*, London: London School of Economics and Political Science, No. 47.
87 STAMP, J. C. (1937), *The National Capital*, London: King.
88 STEINDL, J. (1945), *Small and Big Business*, Oxford: Blackwell.
89 STONE, J. R. N. (1945), Analysis of market demand, *Journal of the Royal Statistical Society*, A, **108**, 286–382.
90 STONE, R., assisted by ROWE, D. A., and others (1954), *The Measurement of Consumers' Expenditure and Behaviour in the United Kingdom, 1920–1938, Volume I*, Cambridge: Cambridge University Press.
91 TEW, B. (1959), Self-financing, *Studies in Company Finance*, 42–53, National Institute of Social and Economic Research, Cambridge: Cambridge University Press.

92 TEW, B., and HENDERSON, R. F. (Eds.) (1959), *Studies in Company Finance*, National Institute of Social and Economic Research, Cambridge: Cambridge University Press.

93 TINBERGEN, J. (1939), Statistical testing of business cycle theories, *League of Nations Economic Intelligence Service*, 12, 115.

94 VALLANCE, A. (1955), *Very Private Enterprise: An Anatomy of Fraud and High Finance*, London: Thames.

95 WEATHERBURN, C. E. (1961), *A First Course in Mathematical Statistics*, Cambridge: Cambridge University Press paperback.

96 WELCH, B. L. (1947), The generalization of 'Student's' problem when several different population variances are involved, *Biometrika*, 34, 28–35.

3. PERIODICAL PUBLICATIONS, YEARBOOKS AND OTHER SOURCES

97 AL-ATRAQCHI, M. (1963), *A Statistical Analysis of the Iron and Steel Industry in the United Kingdom 1920–60, with special reference to the Production, Profitability and Size-Distribution of Firms*, M.A. Thesis, University of Bristol.

98 COASE, R. H.; EDWARDS, R. S., and FOWLER, R. F. (undated), *The Iron and Steel Industry 1926–35*, Cambridge: London and Cambridge Economic Service Special Memorandum, No. 49.

99 DEPARTMENT OF APPLIED ECONOMICS, UNIVERSITY OF CAMBRIDGE, *Capital Formation in the United Kingdom 1920–38*, Cambridge: Department of Applied Economics, mimeograph.

100 *Economist*, London: The Economist Newspaper Ltd.

101 FEDERAL RESERVE SYSTEM (1958), *Financing Small Business*, Report to the committees on banking and currency by the Federal Reserve System, Washington D.C.: United States Government Printing Office.

102 *Field's Analysis of the Accounts of the Principal Gas Undertakings in England, Scotland and Ireland*, compiled by the accountants to the Gas Light and Coke Company, London: Eden Fischer (annual).

103 *Fortune Directory*, Lists of the 500 largest United States' industrial corporations (July 1960) and the 100 largest foreign industrial corporations (August 1962). Address: Room 2063, Time and Life Building, New York 20, New York.

104 *Gascke's Manual of Electrical Undertakings*, London: Electrical Press (annual).

105 HARRIS, R., and SOLLY, H. (1959), *A Survey of Large Companies*, London: Institute of Economic Affairs.

106 HOPE, R. (1949), *Profits in British Industry from 1924–35*, unpublished Oxford D.Phil. Thesis.

107 *London and Cambridge Economic Bulletin*, London: Times Publishing Company.

108 Moody's Economist Services Ltd., A service for the information of their subscribers; issues extracts summarizing statistics from the reports of the main public companies on the Stock Exchange official list. Address: King William Street House, Arthur Street, London, E.C.4.

109 NATIONAL INSTITUTE OF SOCIAL AND ECONOMIC RESEARCH (1956), *A Classified List of Large Companies Engaged in British Industry*, Cambridge: Cambridge University Press.

110 NATIONAL INSTITUTE OF ECONOMIC AND SOCIAL RESEARCH (1956), *Company Income and Finance 1949–53*, Cambridge: Cambridge University Press.
111 OXFORD INSTITUTE OF STATISTICS, *Survey of Profits*, to be published.
112 Porter's Financial Statistics Ltd., An investors' statistics service. Address: 41 St. Vincent Place, Glasgow, C.1.
113 *Stock Exchange Official Year-Book*, London: Skinner (annual).
114 *Wheeler's Company Tables*, Leicester: Arthur Wheeler and Co.

LIST OF TABLES

page

1.1   Summary of the Time-Series of Gross Profit by Industrial Sector, United Kingdom, 1920–38 (£m.)   21

1.2   Review of Estimates of Total Profit, United Kingdom, 1927, 1932, 1936–38 (£m.)   29

1.3   Comparison of Inland Revenue Total Gross True Income with Estimates of Total Gross Profits, United Kingdom, 1920–38 (£m.)   30

1.4   Comparison of Estimates of Total Gross Profit with Index Numbers Compiled by Stamp and by *The Economist*, 1936=100   30

2.1   Comparison of Inland Revenue Measurements of Profit, United Kingdom, 1951 (£m.)   35

2.2   Standard Rates of Income Tax, United Kingdom, 1920–38, in Shillings Per Pound   43

2.3   Net Receipts by the Exchequer from the Excess Profits Duty and the Munitions Levy, United Kingdom, 1920–38 (£m.)   45

2.4   Size Distribution of Companies by Trading Profit Assessed under Schedule D, United Kingdom, 1949   49

2.5   Estimates of Profits in Brewing, United Kingdom, 1920–38   54

3.1   Gross Profits in the Extractive Industries, United Kingdom, 1920–38 (£m.)   60

3.2   Gross Profit in Fishing, United Kingdom, 1920–38 (£m.)   63

3.3   Profits in Mining and Quarrying, United Kingdom, 1920–38   64

3.4   Comparison of Net Profit with Gross True Income in Coal-mining, United Kingdom, 1936–38 (£m.)   64

4.1   Gross Profit in Manufacturing Industries, United Kingdom, 1920–38 (£m.)   70

4.2   Proportionate Changes in Gross Profit of Samples of Companies in Manufacturing Industries, United Kingdom, 1920–36   74 & 75

4.3   Losses in the Manufacture of Beet Sugar, United Kingdom, 1924–38 (£m.)   77

4.4   Published Profits of Domestic Tobacco Companies, United Kingdom, 1920–36 (£'000's)   79

4.5   Index Numbers of Gross Profit in the Metal and Vehicles Trades, United Kingdom, 1920–36, 1936=100   81

4.6   Index Numbers of Gross Profit in the Textile Trades, United Kingdom, 1920–36, 1936=100   83

4.7   Index Numbers of Net Profit in Motor and Cycles Trade, Iron, Coal and Steel Trades, Textile Trades, and in Shops and Stores, *The Economist* Linked Series, 1936=100   89

5.1   Gross Profit in Construction and Public Utilities, United Kingdom, 1920–38 (£m.)   93

5.2   Census of Production Data for Building and Contracting, 1924, 1930, 1935   95

5.3   Output, Employment and Gross Margin in the Building and Contracting Industry, United Kingdom, 1920–38   96

5.4   Gross Profit in the Electricity, Gas and Water Supply Industries, 1920–38 (£m.)   99 *page*

6.1 Gross Profit in Transport Industries, United Kingdom, 1920–38 (£m.) 105

6.2 Gross Profit in the Distributive Trades, United Kingdom, 1920–38 (£m.) 105

6.3 Gross Profit in Transport Industries, United Kingdom, 1920–36 (£m.) 109

6.4 Proportionate Changes in Gross Profit in the Distributive Trades, United Kingdom, 1920–36 114

7.1 The Appropriation of Company Profits in Manufacturing Industry, United Kingdom, 1920–38 (£m.) 118

7.2 Ratio of Dividends and Interest to Total Income of Companies in Manufacturing Industries, United Kingdom, 1920–38, per cent 121

7.3 Comparison of Estimates of Net Business Saving as a Percentage of Profit, United Kingdom, per cent 128

8.1 Balance Sheet Value of Physical Assets Expressed as Percentage of Insured Value 141

8.2 Correlations of Alternative Size Measures 147

9.1 Mean Annual Proportionate Change in Profits of Brewing Companies 1931–37 155

9.2 Variance of Proportionate Change in Profits in Brewing Firms, 1931–32 and 1936–37 156

9.3 Means and Variances of Proportionate Changes in Profits of Medium and Small Business Units in the Drink Industry, 1950–54 157

9.4 Mean and Variance of Proportionate Changes in Profits of Unquoted Firms 158

9.5 Mean and Variance of Logarithms of Percentage Changes in Profits of Sample of Companies in Table 9.3 160

9.6 Welch-Aspin Tests of Significance of Differences between Estimates of μ for Each Size Class in Table 9.3 160

9.7 Mean and Variance of Logarithms of Percentage Changes in Profits of Sample of Companies in Table 9.4 161

9.8 Welch-Aspin Tests of Significance of Differences between Estimates of μ for Size Classes in Table 9.4 161

9.9 Mansfield's Estimates of β for the Steel, Petroleum and Rubber Tyre Industries, United States of America, 1916–54 169

9.10 Distribution of Companies by Size and Growth, 1958–60 172

9.11 Mean and Variance of Proportionate Growth of Companies in Table 9.10, 1958–60 173

9.12 Welch-Aspin Tests of Significance of Differences between Estimates of $\varkappa$ for Each Size Class in Table 9.10 173

9.13 Distribution of Manufacturing Companies by Size in 1958 and 1960 174

9.14 Distribution of Companies by Size in 1958 and 1960 177

10.1 Size Distribution of Firms in Small Business Survey 182

10.2 Small Business Survey: Principal Industries Represented in Sample 183

10.3 Profit and Loss Account of Sub-Sample of 144 Small Manufacturing Businesses 184 & 185

10.4 Small Business Survey: Median, Arithmetic Mean and Variance of Major Items of Profit and Loss Account, Years Ending 31.3.1953, 31.3.1954, 31.3.1955, 31.3.1956 187

LIST OF TABLES

		page
10.5	Major Cost Items by Industry	188–91
10.6	Depreciation as Percentage of Tangible Fixed Assets	193
10.7	Structure of Costs of Larger Establishments in Manufacturing Industry, 1954	196
10.8	Net Output and Wages and Salaries in Selected Industries in United Kingdom, 1954	198
10.9	The Structure of Manufacturing Costs, 1954–56	199
10.10	Companies' Costs and Appropriation of Income in Selected Industries, 1951–52	200
10.11	Major Items of Appropriation Accounts	202
10.12	The Effect of Directors' Remuneration on Profits	204
10.13	Directors' Remuneration as a Percentage of Total Profit	204
10.14	The Profits of Companies	206
10.15	The Ratio of Savings to Investment and Expenditure	221

LIST OF FIGURES

		page
1.1	Time-series of gross profit by industrial sector	23
1.2	Comparison of Inland Revenue total gross true income (3) and total gross profit (4) in Table 1.3	31
1.3	Comparison of index numbers of total gross profit (1), with the Stamp index (2) and *The Economist* index (3) in Table 1.4	32
2.1	Logarithmic probability graph for the data of Table 2.4	50
4.1 (a)	Time series of gross profit in manufacturing industries in columns (1), (2), (7), (9), (10) and (12) of Table 4.1	72
4.1 (b)	Time series of gross profit of manufacturing industries in columns (3), (4), (5), (6), (8), (11), (13) and (14) of Table 4.1	73
9.1	Hypothetical scatter diagram of logarithms of companies' profits at times t and $t-1$	153
9.2	Cumulative distribution of companies by proportionate growth illustrating fit of Pareto curve to data of Table 9.10	171
9.3	Regression of company size in 1960 on size in 1958, using data of Table 9.13	176
9.4	Regression of company size in 1960 on size in 1958, using data of Table 9.14	178

INDEX

A

Accounts, 17
  appropriation, 116, 201, 205
  balance sheets, 16, 19, 42, 139, 143, 193, 201
  banks', 20
  company, 11–19, 25, 34–48, 52–9, 63–9, 71–92, 102, 106–15, 116, 120, 127, 128, 139, 157
  deposited with Registrar of Companies, 19, 20, 42, 109
  Inland Revenue, inspection of, 24, 37
  iron and steel companies, 19
  local authority, 106, 108
  profit and loss, 16, 19, 42, 181, 183, 184t, 186, 187t, 211
  published, 11, 14, 19, 25, 42, 76, 78, 85, 106, 107, 126, 139, 144, 146, 181, 183
  samples of, 19, 25, 34, 40, 47, 48–55, 59, 69, 74–5t, 76, 77, 82, 84, 85, 86, 87, 102, 109, 114, 116, 117, 120, 123, 128, 183
  social, 1, 20, 21, 24, 36, 43, 93, 199. See also Income, national
  standardization of, 185, 201
  trading, 16, 18, 20, 41, 42, 183, 184, 186, 197
  unpublished, 14, 42, 52, 55, 109, 144, 176, 181
Agriculture
  See Extractive industries, agriculture
Aircraft
  See Manufacturing, also Transport
Aitchison, J., and Brown, J. A. C., 151, 159 164 165, 166
Al-Atraqchi, M., 58, 81
Aspin, R. A., 157, see also Welch-Aspin
Assets, 139–44, 146, 150, 154, 158, 162, 163, 170, 173t, 176, 177, 180, 193, 210
  fixed, 139, 141–4, 193, 207, 209, 210
  insurance value of, 140, 141, 147t, see also valuation of
  market value of, 139
  net, 134, 135, 139, 143, 145, 147t, 148, 170, 172t, 173, 175, 182t, 183
  net tangible, 51, 149, 180, 193, 194
  operating, 209, 210
  stocks, 197, 199, 200t, 209, 210
  total, 139, 148, 158
  valuation of, 139–42, 143, 170, 180, 193

B

Barna, T., 19, 140n, 141, 142
Bartlett's test, 156, 157, 158, 160, 161, 162, 163, 164
Bates, J. A., 12, 133, 181
Bellerby, J. R., 61, 67
Board of Trade, 13, 19, 68, 146, 150, 170, 175, 176, 181
  Board of Trade (Mines Department), 15, 62, 65
  Board of Trade, returns relating to authorized gas undertakings, 100
Bonini, C. P., see Simon, H. A., and Bonini, C. P.
Bowen, I., and Ellis, A. W. T., 95
Brewing, see Manufacturing, drink
British Broadcasting Corporation, 21
Brown, J. A. C., see Aitchison, J., and Brown, J. A. C.
Business Saving, 43, 90, 116–29, 208–12, see also Profits, undistributed
  behaviour of, 13
  measurement of, 14
  of large companies, 12, 209–11
  of small firms, 208–12
  previous studies of, 16–20, 128
  relation with dividends and profits, 13, 90, 208–9
  taxation on, 32, 43, 90, 116, 118t, 119, 123

C

Capacity, 137, 143
Capital consumption, 24, 199t. See also Costs, depreciation and Wear and tear
Carruthers, A. S., 19, 26, 28, 86, 87–8
Census of Production, 182n
  amalgamation with other sources, 20

mistakes in returns, 25
size measures in, 139, 144
source of data for comparison of small and all firms, 197–200
source of data for construction, 94–8
source of data for mineral output excluding coal, 65–6
source of data for total sales and value added, 20
Central Electricity Generating Board, 21
Central Electricity Authority, 41
Central Statistical Office, 45
profit estimates, agriculture, 61
profit estimates, coverage, 39
profit estimates, reliability of, 24, 56, 67, 86, 114
profit estimates, sources and publication of, 34, 36
size measures, 146
Chamber of Shipping, 107
Chancellor of the Exchequer, 54, 55
Chapman, A. L., 11, 13, 25
Chapman's wages estimates
construction, 95–7
mining and quarrying other than coal, 65–7
fishing, 62
Chemicals. See Manufacturing, chemicals
Clark, C., 17, 19, 20, 128, 129
Clothing. See Manufacturing, leather, clothing and footwear
Coal mining. See Extractive industries, mining
Coase, R. H., Edwards, R. S., and Fowler, R. F., 19, 86
Coates, W. H., 17, 18
Colwyn Committee on National Debt and Taxation, 17, 126, 127
Companies Acts, 19, 42, 157, 205
Comparability of estimates. See Reliability and comparability of estimates
Construction, 20, 22, 24, 25, 33, 41, 93, 93t, 94–8, 102, 176
building and contracting, 51, 88, 93, 94, 95t, 96t, 97, 101, 102
cement, 102, 164
contracting, see building and contracting

Co-operative societies, see Distributive trades
Corporation duty, see Tax
Corporation profits tax, see Tax
Costs, 35, 36, 42, 62, 66, 76, 97, 184, 186, 187–91t, 194, 194n, 195, 197, 199t, 200t
advertising, 184t, 186, 194
delivery costs, 63, see also transport costs
depreciation, 11, 32, 34–8, 42–8, 61–6, 80, 81, 87, 90, 116, 120–9, 139, 140, 144, 154, 184t, et seq. See also Capital consumption and Wear and tear
direct costs, 184t, 187t, 191t, 195, 196t, 197, 199, 200
fuel, 66, 196t, 199
loan charges, 98, 100
maintenance, 62, 184, 194, 199
materials, 66, 97, 116, 136, 144, 184t, et seq.
personnel costs, 116, 211
rents and rates, 63, 184t, 186, 194
repairs, see maintenance
selling, 63, 95
stores, 63
transport, 95, 196n, 197, 199. See also delivery costs
wages and salaries, 61, 62, 63, 66, 90, 144, 146, 184t, et seq. See also Employee compensation
Coverage, see Industrial classification
Cotton, see Manufacturing, cotton

D

Debenture interest, 32, 38, 42, 43, 82, 87, 90, 93, 116, 119, 123, 124, 129, see also Interest
Definitions of profit, 34, 35–9. See also Profit
Department of Applied Economics (University of Cambridge), 11, 20, 41, 43, 87
Depreciation, see Costs, depreciation
Distributive trades, 21, 22, 25, 27, 33, 85, 88, 90, 103, 104, 105t, 112–14, 114t, 117, 176
catering, 21, 103
co-operative societies, 26, 28, 29t, 104, 105t, 113

hotels, 21, 103
laundries, 21, 103
retail, 48, 51, 103, 104, 105t, 107, 112–15
shops and stores, 89t, 90, 91, 103
wholesale, 48, 51, 103, 105t, 107, 112, 113, 114t, 144
Dividends, 34, 42–3, 116–27, 184t, *et seq.*
    determinants of, 13, 122, 208, 208n
    distribution of, 11, 12, 19, 119–24, 201, *et seq.*
    index of, 123–4
    measurement of, 14
    minority interests, 184t
    ordinary dividends, 42, 43, 90, 116, 119, 123, 128, 184t
    preference dividends, 42, 43, 116, 119, 123, 128, 184t
    relation with profits and saving, 13
Drink, *see* Manufacturing, drink

E

Economist
    profit appropriation, 117, 128, 129
    profit index, 26, 28, 30t, 32t, 86, 89t, 90
    profit samples, 11, 19
Edwards, R. S., *see* Coase, R. H.; Edwards, R. S., and Fowler, R. F.
Electricity Board for Northern Ireland, 21
Electricity, authorized undertakings, 106, 118
Ellis, A. W. T., *see* Bowen, I., and Ellis, A. W. T.
Employee compensation, 11, 13, 43, 65, 66, 67, 95t, 96, 97. *See also* Chapman and Costs, wages
Employment, 66, 94, 96t, 133–49, 150, 154, 182t, 183, 198t
Engineering, *see* Manufacturing, engineering
Errors, 14, 15, 16, 24–8, 32–3, 40, 56, 57, 58, 67, 85–6, 94, 101, 114–15, 126, 127–9, 165, 167, 175
Excess profits, 44–5, *see* Tax, excess profit duty
Extractive industries, 22, 33, 60–8
    agriculture, 22, 26, 28, 29t, 40, 41, 60–8

coal-mining, *see* mining
fishing, 22, 41, 60–8
forestry, 60, 61–2
mining, 20, 26, 27, 41, 60, 126
    coal mining, 15, 22, 24, 60t, 62–5, 67, 68, 87, 88, 144
    other mining and quarrying, 60t, 64t, 65–7, 68
    petroleum, 167, 169t

F

Federal Income Tax Authorities, 18
Federation of British Industries, 17
Feinstein, C. H., 20, 22, 43
Ferguson, C., 162, 163, 164
Finance, professions and other profits, 20, 21, 24, 26, 27, 41, 47, 60, 104, 116
    banking, 20
    entertainment, 21
    finance, 20, 21, 27, 28
    insurance, 20
    professions, 20, 21
Financial Risks Committee, 44
Fisher, R. A., 179
Fishing, *see* Extractive industries, fishing
Florence, P. Sargent, 122, 149
Foldes, L. P., and Wilson, S. S., 19
Food, *see* Manufacturing, food
Footwear, *see* Manufacturing, leather, clothing and footwear
Forestry, *see* Extractive industries, forestry
Fortune, 146
Fowler, R. F., *see* Coase, R. H., Edwards, R. S., and Fowler, R. F.
Friendly Societies, Chief Registrar of, 113

G

Galton, F., 162
Garton, G., 13
Gas undertakings, *see* Board of Trade and Public Utilities
Gibrat, R., 51, 151, 164, 167, 168, 169, 180
Growth of firms, 122, 150–80
    in United Kingdom, 168, 170–80
    in United States, 162–9

H

Hansard, 54, 55, 56
Harris, R., and Solly, H., 133, 145
Hart, P. E., and Prais, S. J., 142, 162, 163, 165
Hazlewood, A., 103n
Henderson, R. F., see Tew, B., and Henderson, R. F.
Hoel, P. G., 151
Hope, R., 19, 25, 68, 86, 90–2, 102, 111–15, 117, 128, 129
Hymer, S., and Pashigian, P., 162, 164–7, 169

I

Income
  actual, 35t, 37
  distribution of, 13, 116, 129, 201–11
  from overseas, 27, 28. See also Undertakings abroad
  gross, 26, 29t, 30t, 35t
  gross assessed, 26, 37
  gross true, 18, 26, 27, 29t, 30t, 31t, 34–58, 61–6, 78–90, 98–101, 104–13, 117–26
  incentive, 61, 62, 67
  net true, 18, 32, 35t, 37, 117–27
  national, 13, 24, 67, 87, 119, 144, 199. See Accounts, social. See also National Income Blue Book
  total, see Profit, total
Industrial classification, 34, **39–41**
Interest, 34, 116–27, 194, 206t. See also Debenture interest
Interpolation methods, 58–9
Investment, 13, 209, 210t, 211
  funds available for, 120, 201, 209
  large companies, 12
  self financing of, 209, 210
  small firms, 201
Iron and steel, see Manufacturing, iron and steel

K

Keynes, J. M., 15
Klein, L. R., 58
Kylsant case, 106

L

Law of proportionate effect, see Gibrat, R.

Leather, see Manufacturing, leather, clothing and footwear
Lipsey, R. G., and Steuer, M. D., 90
Local government financial statistics (England and Wales), 98, 100
Local taxation returns (Scotland and Northern Ireland), 98
Lomax, K. S., 94, 97, 98
London Passenger Transport Board, 21, 41

M

MacGregor, J. J., 62
Mansfield, E., 167–9
Manufacturing, 11, 20–33, 41, 48, **69–92**, 104, 116–29, 154, 165, 166, 181–212. See also Profit, appropriation of
  aircraft, 164, see also Transport
  brewing, 38, 48, 53–7, 74t, 78, 91, 150–7. See also drink
  chemicals (and allied trades), 70t, 74t, 79–80, 88, 91, 121t
  clothing, see leather, clothing and footwear
  cotton, 70t, 71, 76, 83–4, 87, 88, 120–2
  drink, 70t–8, 87, 91, 121t, 155, 157t, 160
  electrical goods, 198n
  engineering, 62t, 74t, 76, 81–2, 88, 121t, 183t, 188–91t, 192, 198n, 200t
  food, 70t, 74t, 76–7, 88, 90, 91, 121t, 164
  footwear, see leather
  iron and steel, 19, 58, 80, 81, 86, 88, 163, 167
  iron, coal, and steel, 89t, 90
  leather, clothing and footwear, 70t, 75t, 76, 88, 92, 121t, 183t, 188–91t, 192, 195, 198n, 200t
  locomotive and wagon trades, 82, 91
  metals, 70t, 71, 76, 80–1, 91, 121t, 183t, 188–91t, 200t
  metal goods (N.E.S.), 70t, 76, 82–3, 198
  motor and cycle, 89t, 90, and see also vehicles
  other manufacturing industry, 70t, 75t, 85, 121t, 183t, 188–91t

paper and printing, 40, 70t, 75t, 76, 85, 87, 91, 121t, 183t, 188–91t, 192, 198n, 200t
petroleum, 167, 169t
rubber tyres, 167, 169t
shipbuilding, 48, 81, 91, 198n
steel, 163, 167, 169t. *See* iron and steel
storage, 69, *see also* Transport
textiles, 51, 89t, 90, 91, *see* cotton and woollens
tobacco, 51, 70t, 78–9, 88, 91, 121t, 164
vehicles, 70t, 76, 81t, 82, 120, 121t
woollens, and other textiles (apart from cotton), 51, 70t, 76, 83t, 84, 88, 121t
Maywald, K., 25, 40, 97
Maxcy, G. E., and Silberston, A., 82
Metals, *see* Manufacturing, metals
Methods of estimation
    construction, 94–8
    distribution, 112–15
    extractive, 61–7
    manufacturing, 76–86
    profits appropriation, 122–9
    public utilities, 98–101
    transport, 107–12
Mines Department of Board of Trade, *see* Board of Trade
Mining, *see* Extractive industries, mining
Ministry of Health, annual reports of, 100
Ministry of Labour, 14, 138
Ministry of Transport, 107
Moody's Economist Services Ltd, 41, 43, 90
Morgenstern, O., 13

N
National Income Blue Book, 21, 24, 34, 36, 116
National Institute of Economic and Social Research, 13, 19, 155, 157, 205
Nevin, E. T., 197, 199, 200, 201

O
Overcharges, 35t, 37
Overseas, *see* Undertakings abroad, 27

Oxford Agricultural Economics Research Institute, 40
Oxford University Institute of Statistics
    Survey of Profits 1927, 1932, 1936–1938, 18, 34, 58–9
    Survey of Small Business, 12, 134–48, 155, 158t, 181, *et seq.*

P
Pareto curve, 170, 171t
Parkinson, H., 19, 90
Pashigian, P., *see* Hymer, S., and Pashigian, P.
Payroll, 139, 146, 147t, 149
Porter's Financial and Statistical Service, 41, 109, 110
Prais, S. J., 19, 155, 166. *See also* Hart, P. E., and Prais, S. J.
Profit, *see also* Income
    analysis of, 18–27, 34–8, 212
    appropriation of, 11, 33, 34, 42, 116–29, 118t, 185t, 200t, 201–11
    as size measure, 139, 145–6, 154
    assessed, 18–29t, 36–49t, 104, 205, 207
    average of (mean, median, etc.), 26, 33, 56, 58, 69, 80–5, 100, 142
    brewing, 54t, 54–7. *See also* Manufacturing, drink
    central government authorities, 41, 93
    construction, 21t–4, 93–8, 93t, 96t. *See also* Construction
    definition of, 19, 27, 34, 35–9, 46
    distributive trades, 21t–9t, 48, 76, 85, 88, 91, 103–7, 105t, 112–15. *See also* Distributive trades
    double counting of, 78, 91
    extractive, 21t, 22, 60–8. *See also* Extractive industries
    finance, professions and other, *see* Finance, professions and other profits
    gross trading profit, 11, 27, 29t, 35t, 37, 38, 41, 49t, 106, 116, 187t, 194, 206t
    growth of, 12, 48, 106. *See also* Growth of firm
    index numbers of, 15, 19, 26–30t, 38,

41, 57–9, 65, 68, 78–90, 94–102, 108–14, 145, 156, 167

Inland Revenue measures of, 35t, 37, *see also* Income

iron and steel, *see* Manufacturing

local government authorities, 27, 28, 41, 93, 101. *See also* Public utilities and transport

manufacturing, *see* Manufacturing

margins, 13, 62–7, 95–8, 195

non-corporate, 22, 126

large companies, 12, 38, 49–59, 124, 150, 154–5, 166

small firms, 12, 34, 38, 52n, 145, 150, 154–8, 166, 167, 181–212

undertakings abroad, *see* Undertakings abroad

previous studies of, 16–20, 168

public corporations, *see* Public corporations

public utilities, *see* Public utilities

railways, *see* Transport, railways

shipping, *see* Transport, shipping

size distribution by, 49–58, 71, 145

total, 28–33

transport, *see* transport

undistributed, 34, 116, 129, 184t, *et seq. See also* Transfers to reserves

Profitability, 12, 18, 20, 71, 109, 134, 201, 211

Public authorities

central government authorities, 41, 93

local authorities, 27, 28, 93, 98, 100, 101. *See also* Transport

Public corporations, 21, 22, 41, 116

Public utilities, 20, 21, 22, 25, 33, 41, 47, 93–101

electricity, 21, 93, 94, **98–102**, 110

gas, 93, **98–102**

water, 93, 98, **100–1**

Q

Quarrying, *see* Extractive industries, other mining and quarrying

R

Radice, E. A., 19, 128, 129

Redfern, P., 141

Reductions and discharges, 26, 29t, 30t. *See also* Overcharges

Registrar of Companies, 19, 20, 42, 109

Reliability and comparability of estimates, 24–33, 34, 67–8, 85–92, 101–2, 114–5, 127–9, 197–201

Reserves, 106, 122, 143, 184t, 185t, 201, 209. *See also* Transfers to reserves

Roy, A. D., 14

Royal Commission on Food Prices, 113

Royalties, 38, 63–5, 116–19, 126, 127

S

Sales, 20, 34–6, 41, 42, 63, 64t, 116, 139, 143, 144, 147t, 184t, 186, 193, *et seq. See also* Turnover

Sampling

sampling scheme, 48–54, 54–8, 157

stratified, 51

Savings, *see* Business savings

Scottish Special Housing Association, 21

Silbertson, A., *see* Maxcy and Silbertson

Simon, H. A., and Bonini, C. P., 51, 153, 162, 163

Size of firm, 49, 133–80, 182t

absolute, 135, 136, 146–8, 154

average, 134

effects on its financial performance, 3–4, 150–80

measures of, 4, 51, **133–49**, 150, 183

financial measures, 139–46

physical measures, 137–9

relative, 135, 136, 146

Small Business Administration (USA), 134, 139

Small firms, 134–5, 144, 165, 166, 169, 175–9, 181, 212

appropriation of income of, 201–11

definition of, 134–5, 139

finances of, 12, 134–5, 181, 209–11

investment by, *see* Investment

problems of, 134, 181

profits of, *see* Profit

savings of, *see* Business saving

trading accounts of, 183–201

Solly, H., *see* Harris, R., and Solly, H.

Stamp, J. C., 17, 19, 26–33

Statistical Abstract, 61, 62, 98, 99, 100, 107, 108

Steuer, M. D., *see* Lipsey, R. G., and Steuer, M. D.

Stock appreciation, 24, 34, 36, 107

Stock Exchange, 11, 12, 19, 38–42, 48–52, 77, 80, 109–13, 150, 154, 160–5, 170

Stone, R., 11, 12, 70, 78

T

Tax, 16, 18, 19, 32, 34, 37, 41–8, 76, 79, 90, 106, 108, 116, 119–29, 140, 145, 148, 193, 199–207, 211

  corporation duty, 43

  excess profits duty, 24, **43–6**, 45t, 55, 106

  excise duty, 196n, 199

  import duties, 20

  income, 18, 19, 28, 37, 38, 39, 42, 43, 46, 47, 64, 67, 100, 104, 115, 116, 119, 120, 127, 165, 202t, **205–7**, 206t

    schedule A, 38, 43, 47

    schedule B, 40, 43

    schedule C, 43

    schedule D, 37, 39, 41, 43, 49t, 50

    schedule E, 43

  munition levy, 45t

  national defence contribution, 27, 43, 46, 47, 55, 59, 98, 120

  overseas taxes, 44

  profits tax, 38, 43, 46, 116, 205–7

Tew, B., 210, *see also* Tew and Henderson

Tew, B., and Henderson, R. F., 19, 50

Trade credit, 209, 210

Transfers to reserves, 98, 184t, 185t, 201, 202t, 209n. *See also* Profit, undistributed

Transport, 22, 24, 27, 33, 41, **103–12**, 196n, 197, 199

  air transport, 103

  docks, harbours and canals, 103, 104, **105t**, 106, 109t, 110–11, 114

  local authorities, 106, 108, 109t, 110, 111, 114

railways, 28, 47, 103, 104, 105t, 107–8, 111, 114, 115, 117, 129

road transport, 39, 103, 104, **105t**, 106, **108–10**, 14

shipping, 103, 104, 105t, 106, 107, 109t, **111–12**, 114, 115, 117

storage, 103, *see also* Manufacturing

telephones, 103, 110

Textiles, *see* Manufacturing, cotton and woollens

Tobacco, *see* Manufacturing, tobacco

Turnover, 18, 116–26, 134–48, 182t–206. *See also* Sales

U

Undertakings abroad, 22, 29t, 39, 41, 119, 129

  mining, 39

  oil, 39

  plantations, 39

V

Vallance, A., 106n

Value added, 20, 66, 94–7, 114–15, 134–46, 154, 184t–211

Vehicles, *see* Manufacturing, vehicles

W

Wage estimates, *see* Chapman

Wages, *see* Costs

Wear and tear, 18, 26, 37, 47, 65, 117, 118t, 125, 126, 140. *See also* Costs, depreciation and Capital consumption

Weatherburn, C. E., 156

Welch, B. L., 157

Welch-Aspin test, 157, 160t, 161t, 173t, 174

Wheeler's company tables, 41, 42

Wilson, S. S., *see* Foldes, L. P., and Wilson, S. S.

Working capital, 139, 209

Y

Yule distribution, 51, 153, 154, 162, 163, 168